Making the Invis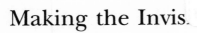

Making the Invisible Visible

A Multicultural Planning History

EDITED BY

Leonie Sandercock

UNIVERSITY OF CALIFORNIA PRESS

Berkeley   Los Angeles   London

University of California Press
Berkeley and Los Angeles, California

University of California Press, Ltd.
London, England

© 1998 by the Regents of the University of California

The essays by Leonie Sandercock, James Holston, Moira Rachel Kenney, Clyde Woods,
Gail Lee Dubrow, and Barbara Hooper were previously published in the journal
Planning Theory 13 (Summer 1995) and are reprinted here, with revisions, by permission.

Library of Congress Cataloging-in-Publication Data

Making the invisible visible : a multicultural planning history /
edited by Leonie Sandercock.
    p.   cm.—(California studies in critical human geography :
2)
    Includes bibliographical references and index.
    ISBN 978-0-520-20735-6 (pbk. : alk. paper)
    1. City planning—History—Cross-cultural studies.
I. Sandercock, Leonie, 1949- .   II. Series.
HT166.M2464   1998
307.1'2'09—dc21   97-16212
                                                                    CIP

Printed in the United States of America
12 11
9 8 7 6 5 4

To my UCLA students, 1986–1996

CONTENTS

ILLUSTRATIONS

FIGURES

TABLE

PREFACE

This book began as a much more modest project. In the fall of 1993 Luigi Mazza, editor of the journal *Planning Theory*, invited me to serve as guest editor of a special issue devoted to the relationship between planning history and planning theory. On the grounds that nobody could agree on what constituted planning theory, I proposed instead to look at the importance of theory to planning history. Luigi graciously accepted my proposal.

The resulting special issue of *Planning Theory* (no. 13, Summer 1995) contained essays by James Holston, Clyde Woods, Moira Kenney, Gail Dubrow, and Barbara Hooper, with a long introduction in which I outlined what I see as shortcomings in the field of planning history, particularly in terms of who and what has been excluded from the "official story" and why it is important for planning historians to pay more attention to theory. My contributors produced such interesting essays that I decided that I had tapped into a rich lode. I talked to more scholars, commissioned more essays, and the result is this volume.

I would like to thank Luigi Mazza, not only for being the catalyst for this project, but also for permission to reproduce the original essays. The essays by Holston and Kenney are reprinted here, unrevised. Those of Dubrow, Woods, and Hooper have been revised for this volume, as has my original introduction. All other chapters have been specially commissioned for this volume.

I would particularly like to thank my Ph.D. and master's students in the Department of Urban Planning at the University of California, Los Angeles, where I taught courses in planning theory and planning history from 1987 to 1996, for their enthusiastic responses and critical insights. Without them, this book would never have been conceived.

I am indebted to James Holston, whose concept of insurgent citizenship helped to crystallize my own thoughts about insurgent planning.

And to John Friedmann—who provides the music of my daily life *and* helpful in-house criticism—gracias por todo, siempre.

Leonie Sandercock
Los Angeles

INTRODUCTION

Framing Insurgent Historiographies for Planning

Leonie Sandercock

Subversive historiography connects oppositional practices from the past and forms of resistance in the present, thus creating spaces of possibility where the future can be imagined differently—imagined in such a way that we can witness ourselves dreaming, moving forward and beyond the limits of confines of fixed locations.
BELL HOOKS (1994)

THE POWER OF HISTORY

Professions (like nations) keep their shape by molding their members' (citizens') understanding of the past, causing them to forget those events that do not accord with a righteous image, while keeping alive those memories that do. The novelist Milan Kundera has said that the struggle of people against power is a struggle of memory against forgetting (quoted in Appleby, Hunt, and Jacob 1994: 270). For historians, the struggle of particular memories against particular omissions or suppressions also involves power. Stories about the past have power and bestow power. The impulse to tell new stories about the past shows that time itself is a perspective in the construction of histories. Successive generations of scholars do not so much rewrite history as revisit it and re-present it, investing it with contemporary meaning.

The contributors to this volume set out to revisit planning history and to re-present it, both as a story and interpretation of events and as a particular kind of textual and theoretical practice. In doing so, we are engaging with the power of history. In constructing its history, the planning profession is always engaged in molding its members' understanding of past struggles and triumphs and simultaneously creating a contemporary professional culture around those memories, those stories. In choosing to tell some stories rather than others, a professional identity is shaped, invested with meaning, and then defended. But what are the erasures and exclusions implicit in the process of forging a professional identity?

In revisiting planning history we discover an "official story," which keeps

I

being repeated—the story of the modernist planning project, the representation of planning as the voice of reason in modern society, the carrier of
the Enlightenment mission of material progress through scientific rationality. This must be the story that we desire to believe about ourselves, as
planners. It is a heroic story. But is it a true story? Or is it a myth, a legend?
Is there a noir side to this story? The official, or modernist, version of
planning history is the story of planning by and through the state, part of
a tradition of city and nation building. But alternative traditions of planning have always existed outside the state and sometimes in opposition to
it. These *insurgent planning histories*[1] challenge our very definition of what
constitutes planning. In uncovering or recovering them, we are challenging the accuracy of the official story and exploring its underlying dynamics—political-economic, social, psychological, and cultural—and the
power relations implicit therein. In presenting this collection of insurgent
planning histories we desire to go beyond the modernist planning paradigm, to present alternatives to it, as ways of both understanding the past
and imagining a different future for planning.

This introductory essay examines and critiques the official story, exposes
its noir side, and argues the importance of introducing broader historiographical and theoretical debates into the field of planning history. I see
this not as an esoteric intellectual project but rather as an emancipatory
one, leading to a broader and more inclusive view of planning and to a
practice with a strongly self-critical edge. We cannot imagine a different
future for planning unless we understand the shortcomings of the modernist planning project. The essays that follow take up this emancipatory project in two ways: firstly, by recovering or uncovering insurgent practices in
the past, and second, by providing critical readings of planning history's
texts, looking for hidden meanings and practices, and offering critical theoretical and methodological tools for reexamining the past. The geographic focus is primarily on planning history in the United States, but the
line of questioning is informed by and relevant to debates well beyond
these territorial boundaries.

THE OFFICIAL STORY

The subfield of planning history has emerged as part of the discipline of
planning (rather than as a subfield of history, like urban history) only in

---

1. Without James Holston's contribution to this volume (chapter 1), I would not have
arrived at this characterization. His essay helped to crystallize my own thoughts about this
project, for which I am most appreciative.

the past thirty years.[2] Since the first major works in American city planning history in the 1960s—J. W. Reps's *The Making of Urban America* (1965) and Mel Scott's *American City Planning Since 1890* (1969)—interest in the field has grown and its scope has broadened. There are now many volumes of essays on the subject, the best known and most widely used of which are those edited by Donald Krueckeberg, *The American Planner* (1983) and *Introduction to Planning History in the United States* (1983), and Daniel Schaffer, *Two Centuries of American Planning* (1988). There is a recent best-seller by Peter Hall, *Cities of Tomorrow* (1988), the scope of which includes but goes well beyond the United States. And there are a host of historical case studies of particular pieces of planning history, covering an era, or an agency, a city, or a theme. Almost without exception these studies come from within planning—Mel Scott's book was literally an official history, in that it was commissioned by the American Institute of Planners on the occasion of the fiftieth anniversary of the institute—and all are unabashedly modernist in their orientation. What does this mean? Why should it be a problem?

To answer this we need to begin with a very basic question. What is planning history? What constitutes its proper field of inquiry? The answer given by the historians identified above is a fairly simple one: to chronicle the rise of the profession, its institutionalization, and its achievements. There are various strands to these histories, from the emergence of the profession itself to accounts of the key ideas and/or people (always great men) shaping the emergence of planning to histories of specific policies within the field—housing, garden cities, transportation, the regional idea, and so on. All of these works adopt a descriptive approach in which the rise of planning is presented as a heroic, progressive narrative, part of the Western or Enlightenment project of modernization, part of the rise of liberal democracy with its belief in progress through science and technology and faith that "the rational planning of ideal social orders" can achieve equality, liberty, and justice (Harvey 1989: 11–13). The choice of individual hero or heroes in these narratives may seem to be eclectic, with some championing Ebenezer Howard, others Patrick Geddes or Le Corbusier, as

---

2. Planning histories differ from urban histories in at least two significant ways. While urban historians seek to make sense of the city, in all its vast multiplicity, historians of planning are trying to make sense of planning interventions in cities and regions. To do the latter presupposes a definition of planning, both as a set of ideas and as a body of practices. (Arriving at this definition is itself a political act, which then determines what boundaries we draw around our planning history.) A second distinction stems from the fact that planning is a field of practice, of *action*. Thus planning historians are usually politically interested and involved in outcomes—in what works and what doesn't, and why, in defending some sets of ideas and practices over others, and so on—in ways that urban historians may not be.

the founding fathers of the profession, and most also giving prominence to such "local heroes" as Daniel Burnham, Frederick Olmsted, and Robert Moses. But beyond these individuals, Planning itself is the real hero, battling foes from left and right, slaying the dragons of greed and irrationality and, if not always triumphing, at least always noble, always on the side of the angels.

In these modernist portraits of planning, the hero, Planning, has no fatal flaws. If battles are sometimes, or even often, lost, it is not the fault of the hero but of the evil world in which "he" must operate. Common to these mainstream histories are the following characteristics. The role of planning and of planners is unproblematic. It is assumed that we know and agree on what planning is and who is and is not a planner. It is assumed that planning is a "good thing"—a progressive practice—and that its opponents are reactionary, irrational, or just plain greedy. It is assumed that planners know or can divine "the public interest" and possess an expertise that ought to prevail (in a rational society) over politics. It is taken for granted that planners have agency—that what they do and think has autonomy and power. It is seen as natural and right that planning should be "solution-driven" rather than attentive to the social construction of what are defined as "urban problems" (Epstein, this volume). There is no application of theories of power/knowledge/control to the domain of planning. There is no scrutiny of the ideology, class, gender, or ethnic origins or biases of planners, or of the class, gender, or ethnic effects of their work. The rise of the profession is, simply, a cause for celebration rather than for critical scrutiny. There is little soul searching about planning's failures. In other words, we are squarely in the modernist tradition—a tradition that equates planning with progress—not just in terms of subject matter but also in terms of historical method. These histories are straightforward chronological accounts, with the authors' allegedly impersonal, objective voice being the sole point of view. Mostly, these accounts are written from inside the profession, and there is an obvious collective self-justificatory motive at work.

For example, Mel Scott's *American City Planning Since 1890* outlines what have become the familiar themes of U.S. planning historiography: beginning with the attempts to grapple with issues of urban sanitation, slum housing, and population congestion on the part of late-nineteenth-century reformers and settlement house workers, followed by transformations in the city's built environment according to the standards of the City Beautiful movement of the early twentieth century; the development of a "scientific" foundation for the profession under the crusade of the City Functional movement; the emergence of planning at regional and national scales by midcentury; and finally, a call for a renewed human-centered comprehensiveness. In this sweeping narrative, Scott offers the history of planning as an almost seamless evolutionary continuum in which ideas take root and mature into legislative proposals, which in turn give birth to planning agencies and institutions, which must then develop procedures of policy implementation. Along the way, there are many obstacles that the hero, with his "will to plan," must overcome.

Similarly, Peter Hall's *Cities of Tomorrow* chooses a dozen major themes, rounding up all the usual suspects—slum and sanitation reform, the garden city, the City Beautiful, the birth of regional planning, the Corbusian city of towers, the automobile city, and more—and devotes a descriptive chapter to each. His method is to trace these themes to the ideas of a few "visionaries," most of whom lived and wrote in the few decades straddling the turn of the twentieth century, and then to follow the fate of these grand ideas and visions as others (implicitly lesser mortals) seek to implement them. Hall's main theme, what he describes as "the real interest in history," is individual human agency. He wants to show, in the face of what he calls the economic reductionism of Marxist historians, that individuals can and do make a difference, "especially the most intelligent and most original among them" (Hall 1988: 4–5). Hall's heroes are Ebenezer Howard and Patrick Geddes—the "fathers of modern city planning. . . . [T]here were, alas, almost no founding mothers" (Hall 1988: 7)—and their interpreters in the new world like Lewis Mumford, Clarence Stein, Stuart Chase, Benton McKaye, Rexford Tugwell, and Frank Lloyd Wright. But there is an elegaic note in his lament over the gap between the visionary quality of the ideas and their diluted impacts on the ground, where sometimes these grand ideas are "almost unrecognisably distorted," and indeed, after a hundred years of planning, "after repeated attempts to put ideas into practice, we find we are almost back to where we started" (Hall 1988: 11). What begins as an evolutionary tale, then, ends in a kind of circular finale and lament: despite the progressive intentions and visions of planners, the "urban underclass" is still with us. Hall claims to be unable to offer any explanation for this gap between vision and reality except to say that implementation was in the hands of lesser mortals. But in fact, in his final chapter, Hall does make a very clear argument about the reason for the persistence of urban poverty. Bringing out some dusty stereotypes from his conservative closet, he characterizes poor people as dangerous, incompetent, and ignorant. For example, he attributes the cause of the dereliction of public housing not to inadequate planning policy or design or siting but rather to the fact that "very poor welfare families, with large numbers of children, with a deep fatalism about the power to influence their environment, could not cope with this kind of building, nor it with them" (Hall 1988: 239). He describes a typical public housing resident as "a welfare mother born in a Georgia shack and dumped in St. Louis or Detroit with a brood of uncontrollable children" and specifically blames poor women of color who are raising children in single-parent households. "The inevitable results [of single motherhood] were juvenile delinquency and illegitimacy" (Hall 1988: 240). He further describes such women as lacking a strong sense of family attachments or deep psychological concern for their children. Uncritically accepting the concept of an underclass and of the undeserving poor, Hall's work ultimately reinforces the conservative tradition of blaming the victim by stigmatizing her or him. In closing his hundred-year account he describes planning as now facing "a nightmarish return of the oldest of urban problems, the problem of the urban underclass, waiting as a sullen and disaffected mass outside the gates" (Hall 1988: 361). Such an "explanation" overlooks the patterns of structural inequality and discrimination and planning policies that have anchored poverty in inner-city neighborhoods. It also ignores the agency of poor people and their history of struggles for shelter and other urban services (Lingafelter 1996: 5). For example, the struggles of public housing tenants, led mostly by women of color such as the African American Bertha Gilkey, to reverse the decline of their projects and to establish tenant unions and self-management of public housing projects received wide and favorable publicity in the 1980s, at the very time when Hall was writing. A case could be made—but it certainly has not been made by Hall—that these poor women are the planning visionaries of the end of the twentieth century and that their struggles constitute one of a number of oppositional planning histories that have yet to be written.

WHAT IS MISSING?

At the most fundamental level there has been a failure to address two basic questions in these mainstream modernist histories. What is the object of planning history? And who are its subjects? The boundaries of planning history are not fixed, not a given. These boundaries shift in relation to the definition of planning and to the historian's purpose. If we define planning as the profession, and its objective as city building, we generate one set of histories. If we define planning as community building, we generate another. If we define planning as the regulation of the physicality, sociality, and spatiality of the city, then we produce planning histories that try to make sense of those regulatory practices over time and space. But if we emphasize planning as a regulatory or disciplinary practice, we may miss its transformative possibilities, which in turn may be connected to histories of resistances to certain planning practices and regulatory regimes. The point is that the writing of histories is not simply a matter of holding a mirror up to the past and reporting on what is reflected back. It is always a representation, a textual reconstruction of the past, rather than a direct reflection of it. What we see is shaped by the questions we ask, which in turn are shaped by the (sometimes implicit, sometimes explicit) theories that we bring to our subject. Modernist, mainstream planning historians have seen their subject as the profession and their object as describing and celebrating its emergence and achievements. This approach has at least two significant limitations. If the subject of planning is the profession, then only those who qualify as "professionals" are seen as relevant historical agents. The result is a narrative about the ideas and actions of white middle-class men, since women and people of color were, at least until recently, systematically excluded from the profession, through their exclusion from the institutions of higher education. And if the object of planning history is the emergence of the profession and its achievements, then there is the privileging of a heroic story (Planning as Progress) at the expense of any kind of critical insight into or scrutiny of the actual practices of planning, including its knowledge bases. And there is the presentation of planning as only that which is driven by and through the state, the project of state-driven futures, at the expense of that whole realm of community-driven and community-based planning (sometimes in opposition to the state) which arguably has a significantly longer history than that of the profession (see for example, Jojola, Woods, and Kenney, this volume). These sins of omission are the noir side of planning.

The Noir of Planning History

In his critical, dystopian history of Los Angeles, *City of Quartz* (1990), Mike Davis delineates a tradition of boosterism in the writing about this city that parallels what I have been describing as the "mythologizing" of the planning profession in modernist, mainstream planning histories. In the absence of a critical tradition of historical writing about the city from the forties to the seventies, Davis argues that L.A. came to understand its past, instead, through a robust fiction genre known as noir in which the image of the city is repainted as a deracinated urban hell. The noir novelists (James Cain, Horace McCoy, Nathaniel West, and Raymond Chandler are the best known), created a regional fiction concerned with puncturing the image of southern California as the golden land of opportunity and the fresh start (Davis 1990: 38). Particularly significant was the brief appearance of "black noir," exemplified in the fiction of writers like Langston Hughes and Chester Himes, who portrayed L.A. as a racial hell in which blacks are destroyed or driven to self-destruction by the capricious and psychotic dynamics of white racism (Davis 1990: 43).

My goal, in this introduction and in this collection, is a puncturing or demythologizing of the heroic image of planning history by means of injecting a series of critical themes, theories, and methodologies. Perhaps the most conspicuous omission from the saga of the "rise of planning" is

the absence of all but white professional males as the actors on the historical stage. Where are women? Where are Native Americans, African Americans, Mexican Americans, Japanese and Chinese Americans? Where are
gays and lesbians? Where are they, both as subjects—doing planning, contributing to city and community building, researching urban problems—
and as objects (victims, if you like) of planners' neglect or desire to have
control over these groups' particular concerns and needs in cities?

Let's take the absence of women. Peter Hall (1988) justifies their absence from his book by asserting that there were no "foremothers of city
planning." That is simply wrong, as the works of feminist scholars such as
Dolores Hayden (1981), Eugenie Birch (1983), Jacqueline Leavitt (1980),
Susan Wirka (1989, 1994), Barbara Hooper (1992), and Gail Lee Dubrow
(1991, 1992) have clearly shown. Feminist approaches to planning history
range from the chronicling of the "great women" (Jane Addams, Melusine
Fay Pierce, Charlotte Perkins Gilman, Catherine Bauer, Edith Elmer Wood,
Mary Simkhovitch) to the documenting of a whole tradition of feminist
home design and community planning (Hayden 1981; Wirka 1989, 1994)
to critiquing the ways in which women's contributions have been memori-
alized (Dubrow 1991, 1992, forthcoming). Some feminist historiographers
are challenging the traditional periodizations of city planning history
(Sandercock 1990); others are doing new textual readings of "old material" in order to explore new themes, like the social control elements of
planning practice (Wilson 1991, 1992; Hooper 1992; and several of the
contributors to this book). Susan Wirka (1989) and Peter Marcuse (1980)
have each argued persuasively for a redefinition of planning history so that
it includes the City Social as well as the City Practical, a move that would
both recenter the social and draw more attention to the contributions of
women social reformers and community builders.

In the absence of such a definition of planning, mainstream historians
have failed to appreciate the contributions of the many activist and articulate women working outside of a profession that either did not yet exist (in
the case of the late-nineteenth-century work of Addams and others) or
soon came to exclude them from its ranks. Mel Scott's official history has
two references each to Addams and Simkhovitch, none longer than half a
sentence. Addams is noted as the founder of Hull House, one of the first
settlement houses, and as someone who, along with Jacob Riis, had early
insight into the social needs of the community (Scott 1969: 72), but Scott
devotes a paragraph to Riis, attributing his special insight to his recent
immigrant status and his empathy for the plight of poor immigrants.
Meanwhile, Jane Addams at Hull House had been working with poor immigrants on the South Side of Chicago since 1889 and had pioneered social
survey research among them. And Mary Simkhovitch, whom Scott mentions only in passing—noting her as an outstanding settlement house

worker—was a member of the 1907 Committee on Congestion of Population and a lifelong housing activist who served as president of the National Public Housing Conference in 1931. Despite her obvious longevity in the planning and housing movements, her contributions are never evaluated in the way that those of her male contemporaries are. But, as Wirka's research has shown, Simkhovitch not only wrote extensively on housing and social planning issues, she also worked tirelessly as a public activist on these issues and was the first to outline a comprehensive vision of neighborhood planning and to locate such planning in its metropolitan context (Wirka 1989, 1994). The work of recovering the contributions of individual women to mainstream planning continues, as does the task of reconceptualizing women's work in urban and social reform issues and in community development as another kind of planning, albeit at the grassroots level rather than through state agencies.

And what of the absence of African Americans, and other ethnic minorities, from mainstream accounts? There is an unspoken assumption here that there are no African/Mexican/Asian American forefathers or foremothers of city planning. There is a further implicit assumption that planning has been race neutral in its practices, rather than supportive of the white power structure's policies of segregation and discrimination. Joan Fitzgerald and William Howard (1993) have addressed the first assumption, making a convincing case that there is indeed a black planning history and that blacks were involved in urban planning long before the civil rights era. They focus on the activist research of W. E. B. Du Bois, beginning with his monumental study *The Philadelphia Negro* in 1898 and continuing in his investigations reported in the Atlanta University Publications which provided a comprehensive portrait of urban African Americans. Through these publications, Du Bois "made a great contribution to urban research and community development planning, especially as such planning related to the black community" (Fitzgerald and Howard 1993: 10–11). Du Bois's conclusions and prescriptions almost one hundred years ago are remarkably similar to recent analyses of black urban poverty (see Goldsmith and Blakely 1992; Massey and Denton 1993). Along with the work of the Urban League, black churches, and black women, there is a body of research, political action, and urban social services that collectively represents a distinctive African American urban planning and community development tradition. Cheryl Gilkes (1988), Gail Dubrow (1992, forthcoming), and Dolores Hayden (1995) are among a growing group of scholars documenting the role of black women in community building.

If we redefine "planning" to include the community-building tradition—what we might call planning from below—then we create the possibility of a far more inclusive set of narratives, embracing not only the African American community but also the Latino and Asian American communities who have all, in response to their exclusion from mainstream planning, developed counterplanning traditions of self-help, community solidarity, and community organizing for social and economic development. There are at least three reasons why this community-building tradition has been ignored both by the emerging planning profession and by mainstream histories. First, the researches of Du Bois and of the Urban League drew attention to histories of racial tensions in American cities; however, in the world of urban planning, as it emerged in the early twentieth century, the issue of racism seems to have been an unmentionable subject, at least until the challenges of the civil rights era. Second, as Fitzgerald and Howard (1993: 19) argue, the planning tradition that came to dominate the emerging planning profession was based on shaping the physical environment—the city-building tradition—while the focus of the African American (and other ethnic groups') traditions was on employment and economic concerns, social work and urban service delivery, and collective political action. Third, the story of community building, although it is clearly about (economic development and social) planning, is not one that glorifies the roles of the planning profession. On the contrary, it is a story that demonstrates the capacities of ordinary people to plan on their own behalf, in spite or perhaps because of the forces of exclusion, discrimination, and marginalization that characterized professional planning practice and urban politics for most of this century.

The silence of mainstream planning historians on the issue of racism in planning has led to the systematic thematic avoidance of the ways in which planning practice has worked to reinforce racial segregation and discrimination. "Racial issues" are first mentioned on page 423 of Scott's *American City Planning Since 1890,* at which point he has reached the 1950s in his chronological narrative. It is another 160 pages before there is any further mention of racial issues, but still there is a refusal to implicate planners. "City planners," Scott writes, "began to be painfully aware that urbanization had placed on the political doorstep problems of race and poverty unlike any that had previously been brought to the attention of earnest social workers, elected officials and the general public" (Scott 1969: 590). Here Scott's very sentence construction evades the issue. He has planners being made aware rather than being in any way responsible. Instead, the abstraction called "urbanization" is responsible for problems of "race and poverty" (as opposed to racism and inequality), which in Scott's account only becomes a "problem" in the 1960s. One needs to go to the work of the legal scholar C. E. Vose (1967) for a systematic study of the ways in which whites used the planning tool of restrictive covenants to exclude blacks, Jews, Mexicans, Japanese, and Chinese from their neighborhoods for at least the first half of this century, until the NAACP and the ACLU took the matter to the courts. And we need to go to the new ethnic histories for glimpses of the multiple ways in which minorities have been excluded from large parts of American cities (see Camarillo 1979; Romo 1983; Chan 1991; Takaki 1993; Almaguer 1994; Kim 1996).[3]

The racist consequences of urban and regional planning schemes receives full engagement in a recent paper by June Manning Thomas (1994) and in a brilliant dissertation by Clyde Woods ([1993] 1997). Thomas argues for a more racially conscious perspective in planning history, one that is "more sensitive to the history of African American urbanization." She suggests a whole new (four-part) periodization of city planning history to bring it into some relationship with the black urban experience. This periodization begins with the era during and immediately after World War I, which saw the first great migration of southern blacks to northern cities and the first major race riots of the twentieth century and which created industrial, civic, housing, and religious issues for city officials. The planning response was the rise of residential controls: zoning for social segregation by race and restrictive covenants built into land titles (Thomas 1994: 2–3). The second stage is the era of public housing, after 1937, including World War II housing and postwar urban renewal—a period in which residential segregation was reinforced and ghetto boundaries consolidated as local politicians worked to keep black housing projects out of white neighborhoods. This was also the era of the second great migration of southern rural blacks to the north and west and the era of clearances of "black slums" for freeways (Thomas 1994: 3–4). The third stage is the era of civil rights and civil rebellions, in which the planning profession developed a consciousness of and a conscience about race and racism and in which social planning and advocacy planning were responses to this new awareness. In the fourth period, encompassing the 1970s and beyond, which Thomas describes as the "racially separate metropolis," the black community has experienced an increase in political power but also increasing economic disadvantage. Thomas describes how planning affects, and is affected by, race and racism and shows the historical linkages between urban development and racial oppression.

Similar studies are needed for other minorities, from the exclusionary zoning actions against nineteenth-century Chinese immigrants (Kayden and Harr 1989) to the restrictive covenants against Mexicans and Jews through the first half of the twentieth century (Fogelson 1967; Romo 1983)

3. This story is not unique to the United States. For an account of the role of planners in South African apartheid, see Beauregard, this volume; for a comparison of the United Kingdom and Sweden, see Khakee and Thomas 1995; on the United Kingdom, Thomas and Krishnarayan 1994; on Vancouver's Chinatown, see Anderson 1991. Kristin Ross's discussion of postwar French planning is also illuminating concerning the spatial and social reorganization of Paris, targeting black African immigrants (Ross 1995).

to the whole system of "planned reservations" for Native Americans and internment for Japanese Americans (Kim 1996; Yonemura 1996) as part of a broader reinterpretation of the work of planning as the restriction and control of certain bodies in space—those of women, racial minorities, the poor, and indigenous peoples, among others. This may be the noir side of planning history, something we would rather not face in our collective professional past, but unless we do discuss these effects of planning we are likely to continue to be blind to the racist and classist as well as sexist effects of contemporary planning practices.

Like any other oppressed group, gays and lesbians have stories to tell about the ways in which their lives in cities and neighborhoods have been and are impinged on by social and spatial policies and how they, in turn, respond to and contest certain policies. Making these stories an integral part of planning history requires us to address questions like the following. Have homosexuals, as individuals or as couples, been excluded from particular housing developments or certain neighborhoods? How have zoning and housing policies created or reinforced such barriers? How have policies regarding the design and use of public spaces affected the ability of gays to live openly and without harassment? What assumptions about the "normal" family or household are built into suburban zoning codes, and how do they effect discrimination against gay couples or households? How do public housing agencies and private landlords treat gays who are parents? How can planners help to create safer streets and neighborhoods for gays and lesbians? How have gays and lesbians acted to create and protect their urban places? How have they made parts of cities their own? How have they interacted with planners in this pursuit? Gay urban politics and social movements inevitably spill over into planning issues and into questions of who controls city councils and planning agencies. Gays and lesbians have become involved in electoral struggles precisely to influence the kinds of neighborhoods in which they live, to provide services specific to their economic, recreational, and health needs. There are parallels here with feminist planners' arguments that the needs of women in cities, and the ways in which women use cities, are different from those of men (and different for women of different classes and races) and require special policy considerations. In other words, just as we have established that planning policies are neither gender nor race neutral (see Sandercock and Forsyth 1992; Grigsby 1994), we can make the same argument with respect to gay and lesbian communities. They too have particular needs with respect to urban services and spatial policies. It is important to understand how planning policies historically have affected the quality of urban life of gays and lesbians, including how such policies may have reinforced their oppression. Young scholars like Moira Kenney (1994) and Eric Reyes (1993) are doing pioneering work in these areas, employing but transforming cognitive mapping and other techniques to make visible the histories of gays and lesbians in Los Angeles. Elizabeth Wilson's tantalizing historical studies (1991, 1992) of cities and planning have suggested that "the androgynous woman, the lesbian, the prostitute, the childless woman . . . all aroused fears and created anxieties concerning the eroticization of life in the metropolis" (1992: 106). She argues that the emerging planning profession was preoccupied with controlling menacing sexualities in the city, thereby posing planners as early enemies of homosexual lifestyles. While more speculative than substantiated in Wilson's work, these ideas demand further historical research and rereading of classic planning texts and documents.

HISTORY AND THEORY

There is a fundamental critique embedded in drawing attention to some of the glaring absences in mainstream accounts of planning history. These absences are not innocent. They are systematic exclusions. They emerge from prior ontological and epistemological positions—concerning the subject and object of planning, concerning the writing of history, concerning the relationship of planning to power and the power of systems of thought. To understand these systematic exclusions, we need theory. Historians have acknowledged the importance of theory for their profession at least since the inception of the journals *History and Theory* (1961), *Radical History Review* (1974), and *Marxist Perspectives* (1978). Over the past two decades there has been a proliferation of "new histories"—feminist, postcolonial, ethnic, queer, cultural, for example. The very titles of some of these works, *Remaking History* (Kruger and Mariani 1989), *The New Cultural History* (Hunt 1989), *Selected Subaltern Studies* (Guha and Spivak 1988), indicate the challenges across many fronts to traditional histories not only of "dates and greats" but also of masculinist, white, and Eurocentric accounts. Many of the new histories begin with the recovery of neglected, repressed, or forgotten cultures, the recuperation of names and faces erased from past accounts. This process of recovery, or what Joan Kelly (1987) has called "compensatory histories," is essential in disrupting mainstream accounts of planning history. But the process of recovery is not the end of the story. There are further levels of excavation and analysis. The awareness of new voices with new stories to tell has produced what Michel Foucault has described as "a new form of history that is trying to develop its own theory" (quoted in Kruger and Mariani 1989: x).

These new histories are crossdisciplinary, drawing on tools of analysis originating in feminist literary-critical studies and in their rereadings of psychoanalytic texts; in cultural studies, with its focus on race and representation; in poststructural and postcolonial examinations of the relationship between knowledge and power, discursive practices and regulatory regimes, ideology construction and its operation through political, cultural, and social spheres, and the interplay between hegemony and forces of resistance. Within urban history over the past two decades new approaches have been developed which take ethnic diversity as a starting point and recognize the disparate experiences of class and gender in a much more inclusive approach to cities, exploring the whole as seen from African American, Latino, and Chinese and Japanese American perspectives and emphasizing the sharpness of spatial as well as cultural divisions and distinctions (Hayden 1995: 40). These new urban histories not only draw attention to the contribution of different ethnic communities in the building of American cities. They also place women at the center rather than at the periphery of economic and social life in the city.

With a couple of notable exceptions (Boyer 1983; Foglesong 1986), planning historians have remained remarkably immune to any of these developments in critical social theory and historiography and have clung tenaciously to their modernist, liberal progressive framework.[4] In the mid-1990s this is finally changing as young scholars, influenced by a wide range of critical theories, begin to re-present planning histories. In my discussion of the noir of planning history, I have drawn attention to the absences of certain stories. Here I want to argue that simply adding new stories is not enough. There is a difference between rewriting history by adding the forgotten or repressed contributions of (for example) women and retheorizing history by using gender or race as categories of analysis (Lerner 1976; Kelly 1984). The recent evolution of feminist histories provides a good example of the difference that theory makes. There has been a general pattern of, first, detailed descriptive work, discovering the activities and contributions of women, followed by a discussion and exposé of patriarchal relationships and how the system of patriarchy has limited women's participation in the public domain. Feminist historiographers then argued that exposing patriarchy was not enough. A truly human, as opposed to male-centered history, would also explore those domains in which women have been most active: the family and personal life, the home, the neighborhood, and community work. Feminists working in planning history have traversed all of these terrains since the late 1970s (see Leavitt 1980; Hayden 1981; Birch 1983; Wirka 1989; Dubrow 1992, forthcoming).

---

4. Significantly, neither Boyer nor Foglesong have worked within planning. Boyer is an architectural historian and social critic; Foglesong, a political scientist influenced by the "new Marxism" coming out of France and Germany since 1960s.

While there is much more of this kind of work still to be done, feminist historiography suggest further challenges.

In a pathbreaking theoretical essay a decade ago, Joan Kelly (1984) argued that women's history has shaken the conceptual foundations of historical study by making problematic three of the basic concerns of historical thought: periodization, categories of social analysis, and theories of social change. One of the themes of feminist scholarship has been the issue of women's status—that is, the roles and positions women hold in society by comparison with those of men. In historical terms, this means we look at ages or movements of great social change with respect to their liberation or repression of women's potential. Once we do this, the period, or set of events, may take on a wholly different meaning from the normally accepted one. According to Kelly, "If we apply Fourier's famous dictum—that the emancipation of women is an index of the general emancipation of an age—our notions of so-called progressive developments, such as classical Athenian civilization, the Renaissance, and the French Revolution, undergo a startling re-evaluation" (1984: 5). Kelly's own work on the question Was there a renaissance for women? provides the substantive evidence for her theoretical argument. Keeping in mind the question of whether significant turning points in history have the same impact for women as they do for men, we can turn to planning histories and examine their periodizations from a very different point of view (see Sandercock 1990: 28–33). Instead of celebrating every milestone in the evolution of planning as a profession, we need to ask whether women were part of this emerging profession and what effect each "milestone" had on their lives in cities. Were women active in writing or propagating any of the early formative ideas? Were women organizing around urban issues at this time? How did the ideas of the "founding fathers" affect the lives of women in cities? What are the male-female relationships implied in ideas about "the good city" or good planning? Were women involved in formulating planning legislation and/or implementing it? And if so, what difference did they make? What were the consequences of particular pieces of planning legislation on women's lives? Has any planning legislation ever tried to broaden the opportunities for women to participate in public life? What assumptions about relations between the sexes are built into plans and planning legislation?

Similarly with Kelly's second challenge, the categories of social analysis. If gender becomes a category as fundamental to our analysis of the social order as other classifications such as class, and we regard the relation of the sexes, just as those of class, as socially rather than naturally constituted, this might lead a planning historian to ask, of any set of planning ideas or practices, What are the male-female relationships implied here? For example, what roles are being assigned to women when we design houses and neighborhoods and transportation systems?

Kelly's third challenge is based on the second. If the relation of the sexes is as necessary to an understanding of human history as the social relationship of classes, then a theory of social change that derives from a gender-neutral perspective must be abandoned. We can no longer assume that when "things" change for the better (for men), those "things" will be better for women too. A feminist planning history would demonstrate that this has rarely been the case, as Hayden (1984) and other feminists have argued with respect to postwar suburbia and women's isolation, for example. Planners who want to create a better world for both men and women need to construct a theory of social transformation that has at its heart a consideration of the relations between the sexes, how those relations are shaped by and in the built environment, and how that built environment is socially produced in accordance with preexisting notions of the appropriate relations between the sexes.

While Kelly's work presents major challenges to planning historians, these are not the only challenges that feminist historiography and theory have to offer. From a different direction entirely, the work of French feminists has focused on the body as a social construction. Linking that insight with the theories of Foucault, feminists have become interested in urban regimes of regulation and in discourses about regulatory regimes. The first scholar to apply this mode of theorizing to the history of planning was Christine Boyer, in *Dreaming the Rational City* (1983). Boyer opened her book with a summary of the work of Foucault and indicated that one of her concerns would be with "the disciplinary order of the planning mentality" (xii). Despite this declaration, the bulk of her study actually has little in common with Foucault's writings, standing rather more firmly in the tradition of Western Marxism (see Kramsch, this volume; Sandercock 1990).

A more successful application of Foucault's work to planning (although planning is not the center of his study) is Paul Rabinow's *French Modern* (1989), a study of "the construction of norms and the search for forms adequate to understand and regulate modern society" (9). Rabinow is interested in how, beginning in the nineteenth century, the "corrective sociology" of the positivist social and natural sciences began to define and valorize norms—along the binaries healthy/pathological, normal/abnormal, productive/nonproductive, and so on—and to provide these norms with architectural and urban forms. He explores the ways in which the rising professions and professional experts created disciplinary practices that served to control and regulate people in modern societies—essentially, to regulate bodies in space. But interestingly, neither Boyer nor Rabinow picks up on the gender-specific implications of applying Foucault's work to planning practices. Such an inquiry would ask how planning, as a profession, has functioned as a regulatory regime, specifically in its discourse on and rules concerning the "appropriate" (or "normal" or "natural") place of women, of gays, and of people of color in the city.

We find a tantalizing beginning of such a project in Elizabeth Wilson's *The Sphinx in the City* (1991) and in her essay in *New Left Review:* "With the intensification of the public-private divide in the industrial period, the presence of women on the streets and in public places of entertainment caused enormous anxiety, and was the occasion for any number of moral and regulatory discourses" (1992: 90). Wilson suggests that during the nineteenth century there was an increasing preoccupation among urban social reformers, politicians, and writers with the subject of urban disorder. One of the causes of this growing disorder was believed to be the presence of women in the new industrial towns. She further suggests that the obsession of reformers with the issue of prostitution was, in a way, metaphorical. Prostitution served as "a metaphor for the whole new regime of nineteenth-century urbanism" (Wilson 1992: 105), a regime in which women—their bodies, their sexuality—were suddenly on the streets, potentially both tempting and threatening male order, male self-discipline, and the male disciplining of the city. Barbara Hooper's essay in this volume develops and deepens the themes raised by Wilson. Hooper focuses on nineteenth-century Paris and the texts of planners, public hygienists, sanitation engineers, and city fathers to show how female/female body became synonymous with disease, disorder, and pollution.

Recent work in cultural studies (Ross 1995), gay history (Chauncey 1994), and environmental studies (Stratford 1996) continues to illuminate the importance of discourses on hygiene and disorder as central to planning's history as a regulatory regime concerned to control the presence and activities of certain bodies in space. Kristin Ross's *Fast Cars, Clean Bodies* (1995) is a study of decolonization and the reordering of French culture during the period of intense modernization of the French economy in the two decades after World War II. She describes the "construction" of a new social geography of Paris during the second half of this century which involved expelling from the center of the city ("Paris intra-muros") more than two-thirds of its inhabitants, either by force or by means of successive rent increases. In this new social geography she identifies the political effects of the yoking together of modernization and a discourse on hygiene, effects that become "increasingly racial in nature in the form of a kind of 'purification' of the social/urban body" (Ross 1995: 150). Between 1954 and 1974 Paris underwent the demolition and reconstruction of 24 percent of its buildable surface, and modernity and hygiene served as the pretext for the demolition of entire *quartiers* (neighborhoods). In those years, Paris proper lost 19 percent of its population, but the number of workers declined by 44 percent, dispersed to the outlying suburbs. This modernization of Paris was built largely on the backs of Algerian immigrant labor, and the growing population of Algerians settled in the *bidonvilles* (shantytowns) on the outskirts or in the Goute d'or and other of what were called *ilots insalubres* (unhealthy blocks) inside the city. It was these areas that were specifically targeted for aggressive renovation in the early 1960s, "at a moment when de Gaulle is reported to have commented to his prefect of the Seine, Paul Delouvrier, that the Parisian region was a brothel. And that Delouvrier should proceed in 'making me some order in there' " (Ross 1995: 153).

Studies of the renovation of specific areas in France have shown that in many cases the very presence of immigrants was used by promoters and the interests favoring redevelopment as an indicator of the need for intervention. "The studies all show some degree of convergence between the discourses of hygiene and sanitation, on the one hand, and expulsion of foreigners, on the other. . . . Cultural stereotypes took on new vigor, . . . the cause of all the evils changed from the dilapidated housing to the presence of the immigrants: limiting their number becomes an act of 'social hygiene' " (Ross 1995: 155–156). What Ross's work points up is how the processes of urban renovation, requiring as they do active state intervention into the urban structure (that is, planning) for the purposes of changing both the function and the social contents of already existing spaces, were, in Paris at least, the logical outcome of capitalist modernization's adroit manipulation of the discourse of hygiene. And, just as nineteenth-century urban discourse used the language of hygiene and the metaphor of disease as a mask for patriarchal control of women's bodies in the city, so too has twentieth-century planning used the language of social hygiene as a rationale for removing immigrants and people of color from certain parts of cities. An extreme case of the practice of this discourse in the United States was the anti-Japanese campaign in California between 1900 and 1942, the logical culmination of which, Eugene Kim (1996) argues, was the mass incarceration of Japanese Americans in American "concentration camps," irrespective of their actual threat to national security.[5]

A parallel theme—that of concern with the maintenance of a particular kind of social and moral order in the city—is also pursued by George Chauncey in *Gay New York*. Chauncey argues that the thinking about the city that ultimately coalesced into urban planning theory in the early twen-

---

5. "Wherever Japanese have settled, their nests pollute the communities like the running sores of leprosy. They exist like the yellowed, smoldering discarded butts in an over-full ashtray, vilifying the air with their loathsome smells, filling all who have the misfortune to look upon them with a wholesome disgust and a desire to wash" (*American Defender,* April 27, 1935; quoted in Kim 1996: 1).

tieth century identified "sexual deviants" as one of the causes of social disorganization:

> Some theorists in the first generation of urban sociologists, who echoed many of the concerns of the reformers with whom they often worked, expressed similar anxieties about the enhanced possibilities for the development of a secret homosexual life that urban conditions created. Urbanization, they warned, resulted in the breakdown of family and social ties that kept an individual's behavior under control in smaller, more tightly organized and regulated towns. The resulting "personal disorganization," the sociologist Walter Reckless wrote in 1926, led to the release of "impulses and desires . . . from the socially approved channels," and could result "not merely in prostitution, but also in perversion." (1994: 132)

Chauncey's research places gays and lesbians at the center of this debate over threats to urban order. Taken together, the works of Rabinow, Wilson, Ross, and Chauncey, with their Foucauldian line of inquiry about the disciplining of bodies in cities, the control of bodies in space, provides the basis for a reinterpretation of planning history as a regulatory activity whose purpose has been the imposition of a particular kind of moral and social order with its attendant relations of power (patriarchal, heterosexual, and white) and whose origins were in part propelled by a pervasive fear of desire and of "disorder" in the city. Definitions of order and disorder, then, are necessarily a preoccupation not only of planning historians and theorists but also of people in cities, taking to the streets to claim their rights to public space and public resources. The stories of resistance to dominant definitions of "order" and "hygiene" and "pathology" become an important dimension of insurgent planning histories.

The emergence of Marxist urban studies in the 1970s gave rise to another retheorization of planning history, most notably in Richard Foglesong's *Planning the Capitalist City* (1986). Inspired by German and French theorists (Habermas, Offe, Castells, Poulantzas), Foglesong describes his task as to apply the structuralist model to the story of American city planning *and* to discover what the actual story of this planning has to teach us about the adequacy of this theoretical approach. His themes are the relationship between planning and the contradictions of capitalist development; the relationship between planners, class interests, and the state; and the question of the relative autonomy of planners from capital. The most significant contribution of Marxist approaches to planning history has been the focus on class and the deconstruction of the notion of "the public interest." In contrast to mainstream historians, Marxists have made transparent the class impacts of planning practices, bringing to the forefront the question of who gets what, and where, in the city through the planning process, and why.

There are a number of problems with existing Marxist histories (which should not, however, detract from their important contributions). The exclusive focus on class analysis has ignored or blurred the gender and race effects of planning. And the paradigm has a very tautological and determinist effect. Given the theoretical starting point—that planning is a function of the state, that the state in capitalist society is a capitalist state, and therefore in the final analysis every aspect of planning serves the needs of capital—then of course every idea and action of planners must be interpreted as "system maintaining." Either planning serves the accumulation needs of capital or it serves the legitimation function. This conclusion, a necessary one given the theoretical starting point, is a troubling one for those who wish to change the world through the planning profession and partially, at least, explains why Marxist urban scholarship is less influential now than it was a decade ago.

The overarching problem with such a macrotheoretical approach lies in the very search for a unifying theoretical framework through which everything can be explained. The search for such a totalizing theory seems a misguided one, pushing us toward some kind of universal generalizing in our work, predetermining what we are going to find in our researches, ignoring the Foucauldian insight that power begins in little places and in terms of little things, and closing off the possibilities of human agency. Unless we bring our analysis down from this level of grand theorizing and away from the search for the metatheory that will explain everything (for example, all planning is system reinforcing, or all planning is social control), we will never be able to imagine the potential for transformation inherent in any city at any time. This seems particularly important in planning history, a field that is inevitably concerned with questions of action, of change, of transformation, of empowerment—questions that emerge forcefully in the essays in this volume.

Theory is indispensable. It is how we make sense of the world. As planning historians, we need a range of theories at our disposal, and an open mind concerning their usefulness (remembering that our purposes shape our theoretical choices). We need theories of space and of place; theories of the state and of the role of planning within the state apparatus; theories of power and knowledge; theories of gender and race inequalities; theories of bodies as social constructions; and so on. The list can never be complete, or completed, for two reasons. First, because each new generation rewrites history according to its own interests and issues, choosing the lens or lenses that seem most appropriate at the time. Second, because the boundaries we draw around the object of planning history are determined in the first place by how we define planning. That is, and always will be, a political and strategic decision.

MAKING THE INVISIBLE VISIBLE

The emphasis of the essays in Part 1 is on histories of insurgent planning practices, stories of marginalized and oppressed groups excluded from or in resistance to state-directed, modernist planning. The focus of the chapters in Part 2 is the importance of theoretical tools in re-presenting the past. They are rereadings of some of the texts of planning history, readings that uncover new meanings in old practices and suggest new methodologies and new themes.

Opening this collection, the anthropologist James Holston takes on the fields of architecture and planning for their obsession with the design of objects and the execution of plans and policies. His historically based critique begins with the modernist doctrine of CIAM (the Congrès Internationaux d'Architecture Moderne), whose manifestos in the 1930s and 1940s "called for the state to assert the priority of collective interests over private interests by imposing on the chaos of existing cities the construction of a new type of city based on its master plans." Seeking to account for the disappearance of "the social" from the agenda of modernist planning and architecture, Holston deconstructs CIAM's assumptions, specifically its attempt to create "a plan without contradiction, without conflict," and its desire for a "rational domination of the future in which its total and totalizing plan dissolves any conflict between the imagined and existing society in the imposed coherence of its order." For Holston, the crucial question is how to include the insurgent forms of the social (which are outside the state and heterogeneous) that exist in grassroots mobilizations and in everyday practices that subvert state agendas. "If modernist planning relies on and builds up the state, then its necessary counteragent is a mode of planning that addresses the formations of insurgent citizenship." He urges us to study the sites of insurgent citizenship—including the realms of the homeless, networks of migration, neighborhoods of Queer Nation, ganglands, fortified condominiums, sweatshops, suburban migrant labor camps—because it is at these fault lines of urban existence that we perceive not only the dynamism of society but also new realms of the possible, rooted in the heterogeneity of lived experience.

Holston's challenge finds a response in the activist historiographies of the next four essays, by Dubrow, Woods, Jojola, and Kenney. As a planner and planning historian concerned with issues of social justice, Gail Dubrow argues that the tools of historic preservation are essential to any radical planning practice. She notes how two decades of change in the field of U.S. history—which have brought social relations of gender, race, class, ethnicity, and sexuality into the center of historical analysis—have finally begun to transform applied fields of history. Her essay outlines the potential for using historic preservation as an instrument of a democratic and inclusive approach to planning. For too long, she notes, places designated as landmarks reflected the distorted and incomplete picture found in standard historical narratives, erasing the historical experiences, contributions, and sometimes the very existence of women, ethnic communities of color, working people, and lesbians and gay men. Replete with examples from the recent literature of preservation planning as well as examples taken from her own practice, Dubrow shows us how historic sites and buildings can raise public awareness of the contributions of diverse groups to our heritage. For Dubrow, the very idea of a radical planning practice requires an insurgent planning history—one that acknowledges the erasures and repressions of previous (historic preservation) planning practice and actively seeks to confront and redress those erasures and silencings.

Clyde Woods's account of the failed effort at regional economic development planning embodied in the short history of the Lower Mississippi Delta Development Commission forges a new historiography of regional planning. His project is the recovery of the memory, voices, and visions of the African American community of the Delta. Drawing on Foucault's archaeological/genealogical method, he excavates a repressed African American tradition of resistance to the hegemonic definitions of planning and development in the Delta. What Woods makes visible is the existence of a regional epistemology grounded in African American experience, what he calls the "Blues Epistemology," which, he argues, embodies an alternative theory of social, economic, and cultural development and change. Woods describes how the blues has operated to instill pride in a people facing daily denigration, and has channeled folk wisdom, descriptions of life and labor, and critiques of bosses, sheriffs, planters, and the plantation regime. Woods argues that the blues operated as a self-referential system of social explanation, as an epistemology. This new epistemology proceeded from the assumption that the indigenously developed folk culture—its orature, its ethics, its tradition of social explanation, and its prescriptions for social action—was the basic representational grid of working-class African American consciousness. Woods also explains why those voices were systematically marginalized in the interests of a hegemonic modernization of which planning was and is a complicit partner.

The project of the Native American scholar and activist Theodore Jojola parallels that of Woods. While he emphasizes that tribal communities have been victims of modernization and urbanization—their histories and planning traditions rendered invisible by virtue of not being part of the narrative of modernization—the story he tells is nevertheless a story of hundreds of years of resistance and survival, of selective interaction and adaptation. He argues that this survival was possible precisely because of indigenous planning traditions, specifically the role of clans in community development and the tradition of consensus seeking among intertribal confederations. Together, these constitute traditions of community and regional planning with a much longer history than their parallels in mainstream (Euro-American) planning. Jojola's essay focuses on the history of these traditions among the Pueblo Indian nations of the Southwest but notes variations on these same models throughout Native America. Jojola's long march through the centuries could be described as a success story—albeit one with powerful tragic overtones. In the long view, in spite of decimation, assimilation, and alienation from their lands, tribal communities have survived and are being revitalized, and the indigenous planning traditions that have made this survival possible are being reasserted.

In recent years, a wealth of scholarship about the history of gay and lesbian experience in the city has revealed, on the one hand, extensive and systematic practices of discrimination and oppression targeting gays and lesbians as threats to the urban social order and, on the other, a century of resistance to this oppression. The scholar and activist Moira Kenney asks planning theorists and historians to acknowledge the importance and relevance of this research, as part of a broader shift away from a focus on the institutional responses to urban inequalities and toward the collective, street-level responses of those who are targets and subjects of discrimination. Like Woods and Jojola, Kenney shows us a repressed activist history. She also illumines the meaning of the city as the activator of social and political empowerment. And like Holston, she reminds us that what may appear today as marginal activity is more than likely evidence of a transformation that will openly shape our cities tomorrow.

The first four essays in Part 2 are critical reviews, although of very different subjects. The essay by Iain Borden, Jane Rendell, and Helen Thomas reflects on recent European writings on city and planning history. For any planning history to provide a critical interpretation of planning, these authors argue, a theoretical grounding must come from outside (mainstream) planning discourse. Theory's most important potential contributions to planning history come from challenging the objects of study and from the framing of interpretive questions. In questioning the nature of the object of study, they suggest, in line with Holston, that work on liminal and "other" spatial zones and practices (Holston's spaces of "insurgent citizenship") and on reconceptualized experiences of the city offers new suggestions as to what actually constitutes the city, its peoples, and its regulatory practices. And in challenging the questions we might ask of cities and planning (the interpretive framework), they suggest that works in feminist philosophical theory, geography, visual theory, and histories of various kinds offer a challenge to historical studies at their core, redefining the very epistemological grounds on which they are founded. The authors then illustrate the fertility of these new questions in an extensive review of recent literature, noting in particular the usefulness of the theoretical works of Henri Lefebvre, Michel Foucault, Pierre Bourdieu, and Jacques Derrida and of a broad spectrum of feminist theorizings.

The feminist historian Susan Wirka reminds us of the difference between merely adding various social groups to our canon of planning history and writing histories with transformative potential. Wirka's essay examines a single text, *City Planning for Girls,* written in 1928 by Henrietta Additon, a researcher and social worker in Philadelphia. How should such a text be read? *City Planning for Girls* argues the case for closer links between social work and city planning, insisting on the importance of *the social* in urban affairs. Thus it would seem to fall within the planning tradition of the City Social (an alternative to the dominant traditions of the time, the City Beautiful and the City Functional) in which many women were active and visible. Additon's text could be read as reinforcing the importance of that neglected tradition in the history of planning. It could also be interpreted within a "redemptive" historiographical framework—that is, redeeming for planning's memory the contributions of hitherto invisible women, the "foremothers of planning." But the central research question of Additon's text is "the girl problem"—that is, female juvenile delinquency in the city—and her stated aim is keeping girls "out of trouble," keeping the children of Philadelphia "as clean and beautiful in body and spirit as are the material symbols of human progress." Wirka suggests that perhaps a Foucauldian reading is more appropriate, in which case this text becomes a study in the micropractices of power, the production of "docile bodies" (Foucault 1975), an exemplar of the myriad ways in which patriarchal order is reproduced and enforced by repetition of the historic binary, the good woman and the whore, and, intriguingly, of the role of female planners in reproducing patriarchal values. Wirka uses this text as a way of exploring some of the ambiguities in "women's planning history" and reevaluating the very idea of redemptive histories and their transformative potential.

In this introduction I have argued that planning historians have remained oblivious to important developments in historiography in recent decades. This observation is the starting point of the contribution by Olivier Kramsch. Intrigued by the critique of traditional historiography offered by Hayden White (1985, 1987), Kramsch explores the implications of White's writings for the field of planning history. White rejects the idea of historical discourse as a mirror image of the set of events it purports to describe and the idea of the historian as a centered consciousness capable of looking out at the world and grasping it objectively. He has developed instead a notion of the poetic-mythical nature of historical discourse, positing a third level of meaning beyond both description and narrative interpretation. Kramsch applies this notion, and its associated analytical grid, to a group of planning history texts (Scott 1969; Boyer 1983; Hall 1988; Davis 1990; Wilson 1991) as a way of establishing a different typology of planning's historical discourses, and also, potentially, as a means of translating between alternative modes of representation. His excavations of the "constructive imaginary" of these texts yield some fascinating and surprising insights, not only into their authors' interpretive strategies and ideological implications, but also into some of the shortcomings of White's own attempt to construct an interpretive metalanguage.

Robert Beauregard shares Kramsch's fascination with how planning histories are written, but for Beauregard the key question is whether they are written in such a way as to be able to influence the ability of planners to invent ways of changing the world through practice. Acknowledging that we write in and for the present, Beauregard describes histories that undermine the possibility of effective action, that disempower, as subversive— subversive, that is, of the project of planning, effectively trivializing it. He advocates an approach to history that will give us a sense of ourselves as people who make history, who can make a difference. While all exclusionary histories are obviously disempowering for those people and social groups who are rendered invisible, or who appear only as attendants to or victims of those who make history, Beauregard takes us beyond the questions of inclusion/exclusion. He challenges us to think about how we construct narrative, how we frame explanation, to question how planners could have behaved differently and what they should have done. To illustrate his argument, he takes a collection of recent writings on South African planning history and demonstrates how and why he finds these writings disempowering.

The theme of empowerment is also central to the essay by June Manning Thomas, whose project is to place the issues of race and racism at the center of any analysis of the history of urban planning in the United States. Criticizing existing histories for their dismissive treatment of African Americans as invisible, as victims of urban policies, or, worse, as the carriers of social pathologies, Thomas gives us a fine-grained account of the historical links among race, racism, and planning. While not avoiding the extent to which planners have been complicit with oppressive policies in the past, she also gives a subtle reading of the difficulties of urban improvement efforts in a social context of racial oppression. She describes the consistent struggle by African Americans to plan their own communities, emphasizing (like Beauregard) how these stories can empower present and future generations. Her arguments are grounded in a discussion of a wide range of urban policies in the postwar period. Her message is the indispensability of the theoretical constructs of race and empowerment for understanding American planning history.

The two final essays in this section, by Dora Epstein and Barbara Hooper, take us into the hitherto unexplored territories of planning's hidden desires, fears, and fantasies, territories at once political, psychoanalytical, and literary. Epstein provides a fascinating deconstruction of what she calls planning's "pathology of solutions." The history of planning interventions since the Enlightenment carries a familiar tune—that of the promise to contribute to the betterment of physical and social conditions. Epstein's project is to shift attention away from the consequences of planning interventions in order to interrogate the psychological bases of those interventions. Taking as her theme the subject of "city-fear"—fear in and of the city—she asks how planning has handled this problem. The pathology of solutions (an implicit belief that built environments and social interactions can be made right), she argues, blurs or erases our memories of how the problem—fear—was socially constructed and signified in the first place. Planning's solution-oriented drive, which has resulted in the attempt to create safe spaces, misses two fundamental points. These "safe spaces" neither limit the perpetuation of fear nor seem to take into account the research that shows that city dwellers are most at risk of violence from people close to or known to them, rather than from the ubiquitously feared Stranger. Epstein then uses the lens of Lacanian psychoanalytic theory to help explore why the planning tradition of fear resolution through safety measures has failed, noting how city-fear has been reiterated through the norms of patriarchal power on the urban terrain. Without such an analysis and interrogation, "the historiographical project of learning from the past and making the invisible visible, remains incomplete." Insurgent planning histories, she argues, must critically examine the discourse not only of the city but also of planning itself. To decipher this discourse, we need to go beyond the visibilities implied by Other histories, to a much wider critique of power and repression.

Barbara Hooper's subject is the origins of planning in late-nineteenth-century Paris and its discourses of urban reform, specifically, its unannounced fantasies and desires. Her postmodern feminist analysis moves from critique of the modernist planning project to new ways of theorizing both planning and history, by foregrounding the subject of bodies and the body as subject. Hooper's essay takes us into the streets of nineteenth-century Paris, as well as into its planning mentality and planning texts, and shows us the relationships among all three: it is "a story of bodies, cities, and social order and more particularly of female bodies and their production as a threat to male/social order." Focusing on modern conceptual practices, Hooper explores how planning, in the moment of inventing itself as master, as knower, as producer of order in disorderly cities, took on the baggage of the dominant cultural tradition—a patriarchal tradition—and hence came to function not simply as the emancipatory practice it theorized but as a participant in new forms of social control directed at women. She "reads" the plans for the modern city (of Baron von Hauss-mann and his colleagues in adjacent professions and of Le Corbusier) as "poems of male desire," fantasies of control, written against the fears and upheavals of the nineteenth century which the female body comes to represent. Her approach is influenced by Lefebvre (the social production of social space), Foucault (the operation of knowledge and power organizing everyday practice into relations of subordination and domination), and feminism (insisting on embodying theory and therefore placing bodies at the center of analysis). Thus her project becomes the study of how bodies are ordered in social space—discursive, physical, and lived—through modern planning practices. Hooper reveals the unannounced fantasies and desires that have worked themselves unconsciously into the best intentions of planning's knowledges, histories, and plans.

This collection of insurgent planning histories holds in unresolved and unresolvable tension the transformative and repressive powers of state-directed planning practices and their mirror image, the transformative but also repressive potential of the local, the grassroots, the insurgent. It challenges the modernist paradigm in which the history of planning is synonymous with the history of the profession and its great men, great ideas, and great achievements. It also challenges the very idea of *a single* history of planning, emphasizing instead plural histories of planning practices and plural readings, according to the theoretical lenses in use. Nevertheless, dominant themes do emerge. For example, many of these essays are concerned with the theme of planning as an ordering tool, as a kind of "spatial police." While this idea first surfaced two decades ago in Marxist accounts of planning, it has taken on new meaning under the influence of postmodern attention to discursive practices and regulatory regimes. Rather than interpret all planning as social control, as a disciplinary practice essential to the maintenance of the modern social order (as earlier Marxist writings on the city tended to do), the authors in this collection are wary of such totalizing claims, ever alert to the resistances that arise in the face of such disciplinary/controlling practices. So a second theme recurs, from Woods to Jojola, Kenney to Dubrow, of marginalized groups contesting urban and regional spaces, which includes contesting the spaces of representation, as in historical preservation practices and historical narratives.

Traditional planning histories have presented planning as the voice of Reason in modern society, as the carrier of the Enlightenment mission of material progress through scientific rationality. The authors in this collection implicitly and explicitly challenge the accuracy of this representation of planning. Woods, Dubrow, Jojola, and Kenney represent subaltern consciousness as a rationality of its own, which has been subjected to erasure by those in power—which of course includes those in power in the academy. Each underscores ways in which, through resistance, the subaltern confronts the world and may transform it. Other chapters challenge the notion of rational planning in the public interest by deconstructing the class, gender, race, and ethnic origins, biases, and effects of the planning profession. And the theme of bodies, cities, and social order, running through the work of Hooper, Kenney, Wirka, and Epstein, offers a radically different way of understanding planning's intentions, stripping them of their emancipatory rhetoric, and planning practices, revealing them to be, at least in part, concerned with the production of docile bodies and the regulation of "threatening" bodies.

Still, there is no single theoretical framework that informs these essays, nor is there a dominant theme. My intention is not to produce a new, unified, radical interpretation of planning history, the new official story. Rather it is to present a diversity of stories and interpretations, with an emphasis on the insurrection of subjugated knowledges and the usefulness of new ways of theorizing history. I began by criticizing the inadequacies of modernist planning histories, what they have rendered invisible, their noir side. But the essays presented here go beyond deconstructing traditional histories. They offer ways of reconceptualizing the subject, challenging mainstream definitions of planning and the role of planners as well as disputing dominant definitions of who is a planner. Clearly we still need to see planning as, in part, a state-directed activity, an agency of city and region building, but this must not be seen as an exclusively expert-driven process. There have always been oppositional movements, within and outside of mainstream planning, from the City Social tradition dominated by women urban reformers to community-building traditions. Stories of resistance to planning by the state, we argue, are as important a part of the historical narrative as are the more familiar stories of master plans and master planners, of planning legislation and state planning agencies. There is a tradition of community resistance and community building (on the part of those excluded from or by the modernist project) that needs to be incorporated as a counterpoint to the modernist narrative.

In other words, planning by and through the state is only one story among many, rather than *the* story. Today, not all professionally trained planners work as agents of the state. Increasingly, planners work for diverse local communities, including communities of color, indigenous communities, and gay and lesbian communities, in a dialogic relationship that goes far beyond advocacy. And planning as a profession has spread its wings to include environmental policy, historic preservation, community development, antipoverty planning, and so on. There are many strands of plan-

ning, loosely held together through a common education and a professional culture that includes the teaching of some version of planning
history. We are concerned about whether the subject is taught in its full
richness and diversity, its noir as well as its triumphal versions. The diversi-
fying of planning education—the opening of its doors to women, people of
color, indigenous peoples—and the emergence of identity politics within
planning programs, which have been gradual processes over the past thirty
years, have brought to the forefront the need to re-present planning history as part of a contemporary project of rethinking planning's future.
That link between past and future, evoked in the opening quotation from
bell hooks, is something that every contributor to this volume is concerned
about. In the end, none of us is interested in the past for its own sake. The
essays presented here try to relate the investigation of the past to problems
that have not been transcended in the present. That is, we are concerned
with historiography as a transformative act.

THE FUTURE IMAGINARY OF PLANNING HISTORY

In the history of radical planning thought there have been two powerful
ideas, one addressing the material needs of the disadvantaged, for better
housing and community services, the other addressing people's need and
right to participate in decisions affecting their daily lives in cities and communities. These ideas are as relevant today as they were when Marx and
Engels wrote of the housing conditions of the working classes in the middle
of the nineteenth century, or when turn-of-the-century slum reformers
wrote their manifestos, or when advocacy planners in the 1960s incorporated civil rights issues into their expanding definition of planning's con-
stituency and project. But today, cities are experiencing yet another era of
dramatic changes. In the post-Fordist, postmodern cities of the turn of the
twenty-first century, the dominant features of the landscape are massive
economic and demographic restructurings, which have exacerbated economic inequalities and social polarities as well as ethnic and racial tensions. What kind of planning can address these deepening urban and regional problems in the multicultural cities of the next millenium?[6]
  Perhaps, to imagine the future differently, we need to start with history,
with a reconsideration of the stories we tell ourselves about the role of
planning in the modern and postmodern city. There is an important sense
in which history is, as Herodotus said 2,500 years ago, stories we tell ourselves around a campfire. In telling new stories about our past, our intention is to reshape our future. If we can uncouple planning history from its

6. This is the subject of my *Cosmopolis* (forthcoming).

obsession with the celebratory story of the rise of the planning profession, we may be able to link it to a new set of public issues—those connected with a dawning appreciation of a (Canadian, American, Australian, and so on) multicultural heritage and the challenge of planning for a future of multicultural cities and regions.

The multicultural city cannot be imagined without a belief in inclusive democracy and the diversity of social justice claims of the disempowered communities in existing cities. If we want to work toward a policy of inclusion, then we had better have a good understanding of the exclusionary effects of planning's past practices and ideologies. And if we want to plan in the future for heterogeneous publics (rather than a unitary public interest), acknowledging and nurturing the full diversity of all of the different social groups in the multicultural city, then we need to develop a new kind of multicultural literacy. An essential part of that literacy is familiarity with the multiple histories of urban communities, especially as those histories intersect with struggles over space and place claiming, with planning policies and resistances to them, with traditions of indigenous planning, and with questions of belonging and identity and acceptance of difference.

We have moved from planning history to planning's histories.

REFERENCES

Almaguer, T. 1994. *Racial Fault Lines: The Historical Origins of White Supremacy in California.* Berkeley: University of California Press.

Anderson, Kay. 1991. *Vancouver's Chinatown: Racial Discourse in Canada, 1875–1980.* Toronto: McGill-Queens University Press.

Appleby, Joyce, Lynn Hunt, and Margaret Jacob. 1994. *Telling the Truth about History.* New York: Norton.

Beauregard, Robert. 1993. *Voices of Decline: The Postwar Fate of U.S. Cities.* Cambridge, Mass.: Blackwell.

Birch, Eugenie. 1983. "From Civic Worker to City Planner: Women and Planning 1890–1980" In *The American Planner,* ed. Donald Krueckeberg. New York: Methuen.

Boyer, Christine. 1983. *Dreaming the Rational City: The Myth of American City Planning.* Cambridge, Mass.: MIT Press.

Camarillo, Albert. 1979. *Chicanos in a Changing Society: From Mexican Pueblos to American Barrios in Santa Barbara and Southern California, 1848–1930.* Cambridge, Mass.: Harvard University Press.

Caro, Robert. 1975. *The Power Broker: Robert Moses and the Fall of New York.* New York: Knopf.

Chan, Sucheng, ed. 1991. *Entry Denied: Exclusion and the Chinese Community in America, 1882–1943.* Philadelphia: Temple University Press.

Chauncey, George. 1994. *Gay New York: Gender, Urban Culture, and the Making of the Gay Male World, 1890–1940.* New York: Basic Books.

Davis, Mike. 1990. *City of Quartz: Excavating the Future in Los Angeles.* New York: Verso.

Dubrow, Gail Lee. 1991. "Preserving Her Heritage: American Landmarks of Women's History." Ph.D. dissertation, Urban Planning Program, University of California, Los Angeles.

———. 1992. "Women and Community." In *Reclaiming the Past: Landmarks of Women's History,* ed. Page Putnam Miller. Bloomington: Indiana University Press.

———. Forthcoming. *Planning for the Preservation of American Women's History.* New York: Oxford University Press.

Fitzgerald, Joan, and William Howard. 1993. "Discovering an African American Planning History." Paper presented to the American Collegiate Schools of Planning Conference, Philadelphia.

Fogelson, Robert M. 1967. *The Fragmented Metropolis: Los Angeles, 1850–1930.* Cambridge, Mass.: Harvard University Press.

Foglesong, Richard. 1986. *Planning the Capitalist City: The Colonial Era to the 1920s.* Princeton, N.J.: Princeton University Press.

Foucault, Michel. 1975. *Discipline and Punish: The Birth of the Prison.* Paris: Gallimard.

Gerckens, L. 1979. "The Historical Development of American City Planning." In *The Practice of Local Government Planning,* ed. F. So, I. Stollman, F. Beal, and D. Arnold. Washington, D.C.: International City Management Association.

Gilkes, Cheryl. 1988. "Building in Many Places: Multiple Commitments and Ideologies in Black Women's Community Work." In *Women and the Politics of Empowerment,* ed. Sandra Bookman and Elaine Morgen. Philadelphia: Temple University Press.

Goldsmith, William, and Edward Blakely. 1992. *Separate Societies: Poverty and Inequality in U.S. Cities.* Philadelphia: Temple University Press.

Grigsby, J. Eugene, III. 1994. "In Planning There Is No Such Thing as a 'Race Neutral' Policy." *Journal of the American Planning Association* 60(2):240–241.

Guha, Ranajit, and Gayatri Chakravorty Spivak. 1988. *Selected Subaltern Studies.* New York: Oxford University Press.

Hall, Peter. 1988. *Cities of Tomorrow: An Intellectual History of Urban Planning and Design in the Twentieth Century.* London: Blackwell.

Harvey, David. 1989. *The Condition of Postmodernity.* London: Blackwell.

Hayden, Dolores. 1981. *The Grand Domestic Revolution.* Cambridge, Mass.: MIT Press.

———. 1984. *Redesigning the American Dream.* New York: Norton.

———. 1995. *The Power of Place: Urban Landscapes as Public History.* Cambridge, Mass.: MIT Press.

Hines, Thomas. 1974. *Burnham of Chicago: Architect and Planner.* New York: Oxford University Press.

hooks, bell. 1994. "House, 20 June 1994." *Assemblage* 24:22–29.

Hooper, Barbara. 1992. " 'Split at the Roots': A Critique of the Philosophical and Political Sources of Modern Planning Doctrine." *Frontiers* 13(1):45–80.

Hunt, Lynn, ed. 1989. *The New Cultural History: Essays by Aletta Biersack.* Berkeley: University of California Press.

Kayden, J., and C. Haar, eds. 1989. *Zoning and the American Dream.* Chicago: Planners Press.

Kelly, Joan Gadol. 1984. *Women, History, and Theory*. Chicago: University of Chicago Press.

Kenney, Moira. 1994. "Strategic Visibility: Gay and Lesbian Place Claiming in Los Angeles, 1970–1994." Ph.D. dissertation, Department of Urban Planning, University of California, Los Angeles.

Khakee, Abdul, and Huw Thomas. 1995. "Ethnic Minorities and the Planning System in Britain and Sweden." *European Planning Studies* 3(4):489–510.

Kim, Eugene. 1996. "Understanding the Japanese-American Experience in California (1900–1945): The Logic of Racial Exclusion and the Purification of Urban Space." Term paper, UP210B, Department of Urban Planning, University of California, Los Angeles.

Krueckeberg, Donald, ed. 1983a. *Introduction to Planning History in the United States*. New Brunswick, N.J.: Center for Urban Policy Research, Rutgers University.

———. 1983b. *The American Planner: Biographies and Recollections*. New York: Methuen.

Kruger, B., and P. Mariani, eds. 1989. *Remaking History*. Seattle: Bay Press.

Leavitt, Jacqueline. 1980. "The History, Status, and Concerns of Women Planners." In *Women and the American City*, ed. Catherine Stimpson et al. Chicago: University of Chicago Press.

Lerner, Gerda. 1976. "Placing Women in History: A 1975 Perspective." In *Liberating Women's History: Theoretical and Critical Essays*, ed. Berenice Carroll. Urbana: University of Illinois Press.

Lingafelter, Teresa. 1996. "Ideas in Planning History: Bitter Tales of Great Men." Term paper, UP210B, Department of Urban Planning, University of California, Los Angeles.

Marcuse, Peter. 1980. "Housing in Early City Planning." *Journal of Urban History* 6, no.2 (February): 153–171.

Massey, D., and N. Denton. 1993. *American Apartheid: Segregation and the Making of the Underclass*. Cambridge, Mass.: Harvard University Press.

Rabinow, Paul. 1989. *French Modern: Norms and Forms of the Social Environment*. Cambridge, Mass.: MIT Press.

Reps, J. W. 1965. *The Making of Urban America: A History of Urban Planning in the United States*. Princeton, N.J.: Princeton University Press.

Reyes, Eric. 1993. "Queer Spaces: The Spaces of Lesbians and Gay Men of Color in Los Angeles." Master's thesis, Graduate School of Architecture and Urban Planning, University of California, Los Angeles.

Romo, Ricardo. 1983. *East Los Angeles: History of a Barrio*. Austin: University of Texas Press.

Ross, Kristin. 1995. *Fast Cars, Clean Bodies*. Cambridge, Mass.: MIT Press.

Sandercock, Leonie. 1990. *Property, Politics, and Urban Planning: A History of Australian City Planning, 1890–1990*. 2d ed. New Brunswick, N.J.: Transaction.

———. Forthcoming. *Dreaming Cosmopolis: Planning for Multicultural Cities and Regions*. London: Wiley.

Sandercock, Leonie, and Ann Forsyth. 1992. "A Gender Agenda: New Directions for Planning Theory." *Journal of the American Planning Association* 58(1):49–59.

Schaffer, Daniel, ed. 1988. *Two Centuries of American Planning*. Baltimore: Johns Hopkins University Press.

Scott, Mel. 1969. *American City Planning Since 1890*. Berkeley: University of California Press.

Stratford, Elaine. 1996. "Construction Sites: Creating the Feminine, the Home and Nature in Australian Discourses on Health." Ph.D. dissertation, University of Adelaide, South Australia.

Takaki, Ronald. 1993. *A Different Mirror: A History of Multicultural America*. Boston: Little, Brown.

Thomas, Huw, and V. Krishnarayan, eds. 1994. *Race Equality and Planning: Policies and Procedures*. Aldershot, England: Ashgate.

Thomas, June Manning. 1994. "Planning History and the Black Urban Experience: Linkages and Contemporary Implications." *Journal of Planning Education and Research* 14(1):1–10.

Vose, C. E. 1967. *Caucasians Only: The Supreme Court, the NAACP, and the Restrictive Covenant Cases*. Berkeley: University of California Press.

White, Hayden. 1985. *Tropics of Discourse: Essays in Cultural Criticism*. Baltimore: Johns Hopkins University Press.

———. 1987. *The Content of the Form: Narrative Discourse and Historical Representation*. Baltimore: Johns Hopkins University Press.

Wilson, Elizabeth. 1991. *The Sphinx in the City: Urban Life, the Control of Disorder, and Women*. Berkeley: University of California Press.

———. 1992. "The Invisible Flaneur." *New Left Review*, no. 191 (January–February): 90–110.

Wirka, Susan. 1989. "A Foremother of Planning: Mary Kingsbury Simkhovitch and the First National Conference on City Planning, 1899–1909." Master's thesis, Graduate School of Architecture and Urban Planning, University of California, Los Angeles.

———. 1994. "Housing." In *The American Planner*, 2d ed., ed. Donald Krueckeberg. New Brunswick, N.J.: Center for Urban Policy Research.

Woods, Clyde. 1993. "Development Arrested: The Delta Blues, the Delta Council, and the Lower Mississippi Delta Development Commission." Ph.D. dissertation, Urban Planning Program, University of California, Los Angeles. (Forthcoming, Verso, 1997.)

Yonemura, Ayanna. 1996. "Lessons from Ethnic Studies. Asian Americans in Planning History." Term paper, UP210B, Department of Urban Planning, University of California, Los Angeles.

PART I

Historical Practices

ONE

Spaces of Insurgent Citizenship

James Holston

Cities are plugged into the globe of history like capacitors: they condense and conduct the currents of social time. Their layered surfaces, their coats of painted stucco, their wraps of concrete register the force of these currents both as wear and as narrative. That is, city surfaces tell time and stories. Cities are full of stories in time, some sedimented and catalogued; others spoorlike, vestigial, and dispersed. Their narratives are epic and everyday; they tell of migration and production, law and laughter, revolution and art. Yet, although obvious, their registry is never wholly legible because each foray into the palimpsest of city surfaces reveals only traces of these relations. Once lived as irreducible to one another, they are registered as part of the multiplicity and simultaneity of processes that turn the city into an infinite geometry of superimpositions. Their identities, modes, forms, categories, and types recombine in the gray matter of streets. City narratives are, as a result, both evident and enigmatic. Knowing them is always experimental.

It must have been with extreme exasperation, therefore, that the Dutch architect Aldo van Eyck asserted in the mid-1960s that "we know nothing of vast multiplicity—we cannot come to grips with it—not as architects, planners or anybody else. . . . [But] if society has no form—how can architects build its counterform?" (quoted in Frampton 1980: 276–277). This confession of illiteracy is especially striking not only because it abandons the narrative of cities but also because it does so by declaring the dissolution of the social within the disciplines of modern architecture and planning. This declaration is particularly bitter because it signals the end of a century in which modernist doctrine posed the urban questions of our time precisely by advancing planning and architecture as solutions to the *social* crises of industrial capitalism. At least in its European and Latin American versions, modernism forged what we could call this imaginary of planning by developing its revolutionary building types and planning conventions as instruments of social change and by conceiving of change in terms of the imagined future embodied in the narratives of its master plans.[1]

But is van Eyck's inability to find form in society—that is, to read its multiplicity—a problem of society as he implies or a consequence of a theoretical position that rejects the redemptive claims and social engagements of modernism? Given the human capacity for narrative, and its ineluctable registry in artifact, I conclude the latter. Moreover, I would argue that van Eyck's consternation is representative of the estrangement of the social in modern architecture and its related modes of planning generally. I suggest that this estrangement is a consequence of a number of theoretical conditions that structure the current production of concepts in these fields about the urban landscape: (1) the rejection of the redemptive power of modernism deriving not only from the perceived failures of its utopian mode but also from the more general dissolution of the idea of the social itself in planning, architecture, government, and social science; (2) the inability of the professions of planning and architecture to move beyond that rejection to develop a new activist social imagination; and (3) the preoccupation in postmodern theory with aesthetic formalism, technologies of communication, and concepts of virtual reality which tends to disembody the social and rematerialize it as commodity images.[2] If my conclu-

1. Van Eyck's conjunction of "architect or planner" suggests a potentially confusing use of terms. I am grateful to John Friedmann for having urged, in a conversation about this essay, that I clarify my own sense of this problem. If we look at the use of the terms *planner* and *planning* in the various professions and disciplines that claim them, we see two distinct but, I argue, related meanings. On the one hand, planning is very generally used to refer to urban design, derived in large measure from architectural theory and practice. In this form, the dominant mode of planning in modern times is that developed by CIAM. As I discuss, this model is predicated on an idealist project of alternative futures. On the other hand, since the consolidation of the modern state, planning is also widely used to refer to the application of social science to the management of society. Indeed, some applied social scientists, like Friedmann, who call themselves planners, are deeply critical of modernist urban design and its modes of planning. Very often, however, these two senses of planning share a notion of alternative futures and a reliance on the state that relate them both historically and theoretically. It is this relation that interests me and that permits a broader argument about modernity and planning in its various forms. Thus, I use the CIAM model of urban design as paradigmatic of modernist planning. However, I also consider applied social science as a related version when it is based on a similar ideal of the future.

2. These concerns receive such extensive discussion in the literature on postmodernism that I cannot comment on them here without being superficial. In addition to the well-known studies of the glorification of consumption in postmodernist theory and description of contemporary society by Jean Baudrillard or Paul Virilio, for example, see the recent (and fun, if not always accurate) work by Celeste Olalquiaga (1992). For a recent attempt to dematerialize the city itself, see Sorkin 1992.

sion is correct, then the problem van Eyck poses is more anthropological than morphological. That is, it is a question of learning to interpret anew what appears to him now thoroughly defamiliarized; in a word, society itself, or, better, aspects of the social that indicate its dynamism.

As I do not believe that "society has no form" or that "we know nothing of vast multiplicity," I want to argue that one of the most urgent problems in planning and architectural theory today is the need to develop a different social imagination—one that is not modernist but that nevertheless reinvents modernism's activist commitments to the invention of society and to the construction of the state. I suggest that the sources of this new imaginary lie not in any specifically architectural or planning production of the city but rather in the development of theory in both fields as an investigation into what I call the spaces of insurgent citizenship—or insurgent spaces of citizenship, which amounts to the same thing. By insurgent, I mean to emphasize the opposition of these spaces of citizenship to the modernist spaces that physically dominate so many cities today. I also use it to emphasize an opposition to the modernist political project that absorbs citizenship into a plan of state building and that, in the process, generates a certain concept and practice of planning itself. At the heart of this modernist political project is the doctrine—also clearly expressed in the tradition of civil or positivist law—that the state is the only legitimate source of citizenship rights, meanings, and practices. I use the notion of insurgent to refer to new and other sources and to their assertion of legitimacy.[3]

THE ALTERNATIVE FUTURES OF MODERNISM

The spaces of an insurgent citizenship constitute new metropolitan forms of the social not yet liquidated by or absorbed into the old. As such, they embody possible alternative futures. It is important to distinguish this concept of the possible from the fundamentally different idea of alternative futures inherent in modernist planning and architectural doctrine. Both express the basic paradigm of modernity that emphasizes that alternative futures are indeed possible. But the insurgent and the modernist are competing expressions, which I will distinguish as ethnographic and utopian,

3. See Holston 1989 and 1995 for further discussion of, respectively, this modernist political and planning project and the notion of an insurgent urbanism. See also the collection of essays I edited (1996) for studies of contention to the state's monopoly of law and citizenship in various urban, national, and global contexts. I would like to thank the organizers of two conferences for inviting me to present early versions of this essay, "New Metropolitan Forms" at Duke University and "Art, Architecture, and Urbanism" in Brasília. I am grateful to Teresa Caldeira for her suggestions on the final version and to Leonie Sandercock for encouraging its publication.

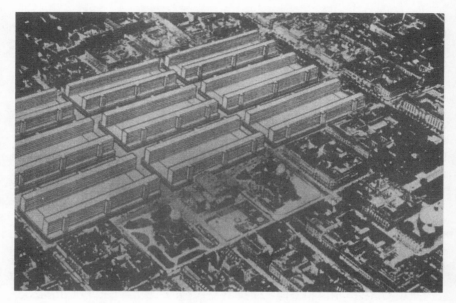

Figure 1.1. Berlin: Project for center city by Ludwig Hilberseimer, 1927.

respectively. In modern architecture and urban design, the latter derives specifically from the model city of the Congrès Internationaux d'Architecture Moderne (CIAM). Since the 1920s, its manifestos have called for the state to assert the priority of collective interests over private interests by imposing on the chaos of existing cities the construction of a new type of city based on its master plans (fig. 1.1). But that model derives in turn from the pervasive ideal of modernity that the state, usually in the form of a national government, can change society and manage the social by imposing an alternative future embodied in plans. In this Faustian sense, the project of modernist planning is to transform an unwanted present by means of an imagined future. Whether in the form of urban design or applied social science, this idea of planning is central to the identity of the modern state: it motivates political authorities to attempt to create and legitimate new kinds of public spheres, with new subjects and subjectivities for them. The instruments of these initiatives define not only the development agenda of the state but also its accredited liberal professions and social sciences—architecture, urban design, demography, bureaucratic administration, sociology, criminology, epidemiology, and so forth—by means of which governments try to forge new forms of collective association and personal habit as the basis of propelling their societies into a proclaimed future.

This ideology of planning is utopian not because it is critical of the present or because it has as its objective the disruption of taken-for-granted norms. It shares these characteristics with the ethnographic mode I propose. Rather, it is utopian because its notion of alternative futures is based on absent causes and its methods on a theory of total decontextualization. The CIAM version of modernist planning is an instructive example. The key features of its theory of alternative futures are four. First, it is based on a tension between existing social conditions and their imagined opposite. Second, this opposite is conceived in terms of absent causes, present nowhere in the world but existing only in plans and their technologies that are supposed to colonize the old and create the new in relation to which they then appear as natural offspring. Lúcio Costa, planner of Brasília, clearly expressed this concept of generative absent causes when he wrote the following in "Razões da nova arquitectura" (Reasons for the New Architecture) in 1930: "There exists, already perfectly developed in its fundamental elements . . . an entire new constructive know-how, paradoxically still waiting for the society to which, logically, it should belong" (1980: 15). Costa conceived of this technology as embodying the imagined principles of a society that did not yet exist but that it would help bring into being precisely by giving embodiment to those principles in built form.

The third and fourth aspects of the model constitute a theory of colonization to implement the new architecture-planning-technology. Its aim is to achieve both an objective and a subjective transformation of existing conditions. In terms of the former, colonization depends on the force of the state to create objective conditions for the imposition of a new order of urban life. The CIAM model appeals directly to state authority to institute the total planning of the built environment that, according to the theory, constitutes these conditions and permits the implementation of its blueprints of the future. This appeal privileges the development of the apparatus of the modern state itself as the supreme planning power. Precisely because of that emphasis, state-building elites of every kind of political persuasion have embraced the CIAM model of urban development, as the history of city planning around the world attests.

The model also relies on a subjective transformation of existing conditions. In this case, borrowing from other avant-garde movements of the early twentieth century, it uses techniques of shock to force a subjective appropriation of the new social order inherent in its plans. These techniques emphasize decontextualization, defamiliarization, and dehistoricization. Their central premise of transformation is that the new architecture/urban design would create set pieces within existing cities that would subvert and then regenerate the surrounding fabric of denatured social life. El Lissitzky explained this premise concisely in 1929: "The introduction of new building types into the old fabric of the city affects the whole

Figure 1.2. Brasília: South wing of the Plano Piloto, 1981. (Photograph: James Holston)

by transforming it" (1970: 52). It is a viral notion of revolution, a theory of decontextualization in which the radical qualities of something totally out of context infect and colonize that which surrounds it. This something may be a single building conceived as an instance of the total plan, that is, as a fragment of its radical aesthetics and social practices. Or it may be an entire city designed as an exemplar, as in the case of Brasília (fig. 1.2). Either way, the radical fragment is supposed to create new forms of social experience, collective association, perception, and personal habit. At the same time, it is supposed to preclude those forms deemed undesirable by negating previous social and architectural expectations about urban life.

This use of decontextualization ultimately springs from the conviction that it is possible to extract antithetically from existing conditions an absent ideal as a new positive entity—that is to say, to extract an imagined social and aesthetic order "from [the] estranged and splintered reality by means of the will and power of the individual," as Theodor Adorno once described this process in a discussion of Schönberg's music (quotes in Buck-Morss 1977: 57). This extraction is achieved, in other words, through subjective synthesis. Such synthesis is reached through the shock of defamiliarization during which the subject identifies with the ideal in the dialectic as the means necessary to bridge the now evident gap between his or her local and splintered situation and the proposed future plenitude.

CIAM doctrine maintained that these proposals of transformation would create a city embodying revolutionary premises of work, housing, transportation, and recreation. It argued that this embodiment would re-define the social basis of urban organization. These propositions were not, I would hold, wrong. Indeed, over the course of this century, CIAM's new building types, urban structures, and planning conventions triumphed to such an extent that they became standard practice in the professions of architecture and planning around the world. Moreover, I would argue that they remain so today, even where their derivation from the CIAM model is unrecognized and their use has nothing to do with its social agenda, as is often the case, for example, in the United States.[4]

However, if few promises for change have captured the world's imagina-tion to a greater degree than this idealist project of alternative futures, few have yielded greater perversity. A fundamental dilemma inevitably domi-nates this project if it is to have any substance beyond the imaginary world of plans. It is one inherent in all forms of planning—both as urban design and as applied social science—that propose an alternative future based on absent totalities: the necessity of having to use what exists to achieve what is imagined destroys the utopian difference between the two that is the project's premise. Worse, examples such as Brasília show that attempts to maintain the plan in spite of the corrosive effects of this utopian paradox

4. I cannot discuss more fully the CIAM model city here, but I refer readers to my 1989 study of Brasília for a historical and critical analysis (especially pp. 31–58). Nor can I discuss its relation to postmodernism, which I would have to do to substantiate my claim of its contin-ued dominance. The outline of my argument would be to distinguish the planned and em-bodied spatial logic of the built environment of the contemporary city—its patterns of urban-ization—from the architecture of its individual buildings. I would also distinguish the city's spatial logic from its modes of social change and capital accumulation, though the two are related. Many authors have described both recent architecture and modes of social change and capital accumulation in terms of new patterns of representing and consuming "space, time, and identity" which they call postmodern. Be that as it may, I would call the *urban* landscape postmodern only where I could identify new modes and processes of developing the city that generate both spatial and social counterformations to the modernist urbanism that already dominates most cities. From that perspective, I detect little in the spatial produc-tion of Los Angeles, for example, that could constitute a postmodern urbanism beyond lim-ited exercises in historical preservation or citation (often related to shopping or elite resi-dence). As I suggest later, there are some examples of what I call insurgent urbanism (i.e., the spaces of insurgent citizenship) that might qualify in this sense. But, overwhelmingly, I see the built Los Angeles metropolitan region as a consequence, more or less explicit, of modernist doctrines. Moreover, I would argue that recent patterns of urbanization—e.g., the downtown "renaissance" developments and the urbanization of suburbia into "edge cities"— are further consecrations of these doctrines.

Figure 1.3. Vila Chaparral, Brasília: Insurgent squatter settlement on the periphery of the Plano Piloto—near the legal housing track QSC of the satellite city Taguatinga, 1981. (Photograph: James Holston)

exacerbate the very conditions that generate the desire for change. Perversely, they tend to turn the project into an exaggerated version of what its planners wanted to preclude in the first place (figs. 1.3, 1.4).[5]

Consider, for example, the modernist system of traffic circulation. When we analyze it in terms of what it systematically set out to abolish—the traditional street system of public spaces, which was considered too congested and unhealthy for the modern machine age—its social consequence becomes clear. By eliminating this kind of street, it also eliminates the urban crowds and the outdoor political domain of social life that the street traditionally supports. Alienated from and fearful of the no-man's land of out-

---

5. In Brasília, for example, such attempts led urban designers and other kinds of planners to respond to the inevitable deformations of their plans (such as illegal squatter settlements, chaotic growth, and organized political opposition) with dystopic measures that characterized the rest of Brazil they wanted to exclude. These measures reproduced that Brazil at the foundations of Brasília. They included the denial of political rights, the repression of voluntary associations, and the restricted distribution of public goods, especially housing, on the basis of status discriminations (see Holston 1989: chaps. 6–8).

Figure 1.4. Vila Chaparral, Brasília: Internal street, 1981.
(Photograph: James Holston)

door public space that results, people stay inside. But the consequent displacement of social life from the outdoor public "rooms" of streets and squares to the indoor rooms of malls, clubs, homes, and cars does not merely reproduce the outdoor city public and its citizenry in a new interior setting. Rather, this interiorization encourages a privatizing of social relations. Privatization allows greater control over access to space, and that control almost invariably stratifies the public that uses it. The empty no-man's spaces and privatized interiors that result contradict modernism's declared intentions to revitalize the urban public and render it more egalitarian. This interiorization is not an extraneous consequence or a by-product of some other process. Rather, it is a direct entailment of the solid/void–figure/ground conventions of modernism's spatial logic, as I have demonstrated elsewhere (1989: 101–144). Significantly, it is this logic that motivates today's developers to use the vocabulary of modernist architecture and urban design to create the new fortified spaces of contemporary urbanism (see fig. 1.5 below).[6]

The imagined future of modernism raises a further dilemma. On the one hand, it always runs the risk of the utopian paradox I just described: either it remains without substance and thus disconnected from the conditions that generate a desire for it; or, in gaining history, it exacerbates the very issues it intends to negate. On the other hand, a second conclusion is also apparent: without a utopian factor, plans remain locked in the prison house of unacceptable existing conditions. Is not the elimination of the desire for a different future as oppressive as the modernist perversion of it? To exclude the imaginary and its inherently critical perspective in that way is to condemn planning to accommodations of the status quo, and I reject such paralysis. Hence, a difficult question remains: if the notion of alternative futures is both indispensable and yet, in its utopian form, perverse, what kind of intervention in the city could construct a sense of emergence without imposing a teleology that disembodies the present in favor of a utopian difference?

INSURGENT CITIZENSHIP

My criticism of modernist planning is not that it presupposes a nonexistent egalitarian society or that it dreams of one. To deny that dream is also to conceal or encourage a more totalitarian control of the present. It is rather that modernist planning does not admit or develop productively the paradoxes of its imagined future. Instead, it attempts to be a plan without contradiction, without conflict. It assumes a rational domination of the future in which its total and totalizing plan dissolves any conflict between the imagined and the existing society in the imposed coherence of its order. This assumption is both arrogant and false. It fails to include as *constituent* elements of planning the conflict, ambiguity, and indeterminacy characteristic of actual social life. Moreover, it fails to consider the unintended and the unexpected as part of the model. Such assumptions are common to master plan solutions generally and not only to those in urban planning. Their basic feature is that they attempt to fix the future—or the past, as in historical preservation—by appealing to precedents that negate the value of present circumstance. The crucial question for us to consider, therefore, is how to include the ethnographic present in planning, that is, the possibilities for change encountered in existing social conditions.

Not all master plans negate the present as a means to get to the imag-

6. See Caldeira 1992 and 1996 for a discussion of the reuse of modernist design in generating contemporary forms of segregation in Los Angeles and São Paulo.

ined future (or past) of planning. A powerful counterexample is the U.S. Constitution. It is certainly a master plan and certainly modern in proposing a system of national government "in order to form a more perfect union" (Preamble). Yet its great strength is precisely that its provisions are imprecise and incomplete. Moreover, it is distrustful of the very institutions of government it creates. As a blueprint, it does not try to legislate the future. Rather, its seven original articles and twenty-six amendments embody a few guiding principles—for example, federalism, separation of powers, and checks and balances—that not only channel conflict into mediating institutions but also protect against possible abuses of the governmental powers they create. Above all, they establish a trust that future generations of citizens have the ability and the right to make their own histories by interpreting what the master plan means in light of their own experience.[7]

The U.S. Constitution has, therefore, two kinds of planning projects: state building and citizenship building. The key point for our discussion is that the latter is conditioned by the former but not reducible to it because the Constitution secures for citizens a real measure of insurgence against the state. On the one hand, it designs a state with the *minimum* conditions necessary to institutionalize both order and conflict. On the other hand, it guarantees the necessary conditions for social mobilization as a means to include the unintended and the unforeseeable as possible sources of new constitutional interpretation.

This frame of complementary perspectives offers an important suggestion for thinking about a new production of the city. If modernist planning relies on and builds up the state, then its necessary counteragent is a mode of planning that addresses the formations of insurgent citizenship. Planning theory needs to be grounded in these antagonistic complements, both based on ethnographic and not utopian possibility: on one side, the project of state-directed futures which can be transformative but which is always a product of specific politics; and, on the other, the project of engaging planners with the insurgent forms of the social which often derive from and transform the first project but which are in important ways heterogeneous and outside the state. These insurgent forms are found both in organized grassroots mobilizations and in everyday practices that, in different ways, empower, parody, derail, or subvert state agendas. They are found, in other words, in struggles over what it means to be a member of the modern state—which is why I refer to them with the term *citizenship*. Membership in the state has never been a static identity, given the dynamics of

---

7. Thus, for example, the Supreme Court has at different times both upheld and prohibited race discrimination.

Figure 1.5. Morumbi, São Paulo: Guardhouse of residential building in a neighborhood where all street activity is suspect, 1994. (Photograph: Teresa Caldeira)

global migrations and national ambitions. Citizenship changes as new members emerge to advance their claims, expanding its realm, and as new forms of segregation and violence counter these advances, eroding it. The sites of insurgent citizenship are found at the intersection of these processes of expansion and erosion.

These sites vary with time and place. Today, in many cities, they include the realm of the homeless, networks of migration, neighborhoods of Queer Nation, constructed peripheries in which the poor build their own homes in precarious material and legal conditions, ganglands, fortified condominiums, employee-owned factories, squatter settlements, suburban migrant labor camps, sweatshops, and the zones of the so-called new racism. They are sites of insurgence because they introduce into the city new identities and practices that disturb established histories (figs. 1.5–1.7).[8]

8. Examples of such sites of insurgent citizenship may be found in the essays in Holston 1996. It is important to stress that both the elite and the subaltern mark urban space with new and insurgent forms of the social—that these forms are not, in other words, limited to the latter. For a view of this conjunction in one city, São Paulo, compare figures 1.5, 1.6, and 1.7; for further discussion, see Caldeira 1996 on closed condominiums and Holston 1991 on autoconstructed peripheries.

Figure 1.6. Morumbi, São Paulo: Elite urban periphery—a new urbanism of closed condominiums for the rich mixed with squatter settlements for the poor, 1994. (Photograph: Teresa Caldeira)

These new identities and the disturbances they provoke may be of any social group, elite or subaltern. Their study views the city as not merely the container of this process but as its subject as well—a space of emergent identities and their social organization. It concentrates on practices that engage the problematic nature of belonging to society. It privileges such disturbances, emergences, and engagements because it is at the fault lines of these processes that we perceive the dynamism of society—that is, the "multiplicity" that van Eyck could not discern. This perception is quite different, however, from a sociological accretion of data, and its register includes the litter and not only the monuments of urban experience.

This dynamism and its perception are the theoretical objectives of a planning linked to insurgent forms of the social. It differs from the modernist objectives of planning because it aims to understand society as a continual reinvention of the social, the present, and the modern and their modes of narrative and communication. What planners need to look for are the emergent sources of citizenship—and their repression—that indicate this invention. They are not hard to find in the wake of this century's important processes of change: massive migration to the world's major cities, industrialization and deindustrialization, the sexual revolution,

Figure 1.7. Jardim das Camélias, São Paulo: Working-class urban periphery—
auto-constructed houses with high security gates and yet lots of street life, 1994.
(Photograph: Teresa Caldeira/James Holston)

democratization, and so forth. The new spaces of citizenship that result
are especially the product of the compaction and reterritorialization in
cities of so many new residents with histories, cultures, and demands that
disrupt the normative and assumed categories of social life. This disruption is the source of insurgent citizenship and the object of a planning
theory that includes the ethnographic present in its constitution.

The distinction between formal and substantive citizenship is useful in
identifying this object because it suggests how the forms of insurgent citizenship appear as social practice and therefore how they may be studied.
Formal citizenship refers to membership in a political community—in
modern history, preeminently, the nation-state. Substantive citizenship
concerns the array of civil, political, and social rights available to people.
In a much-quoted essay, T. H. Marshall links these two aspects: "Citizenship
is a status bestowed on those who are full members of a community. All
who possess the status are equal with respect to the rights and duties with
which the status is endowed" (1977: 92). As new kinds of residents occupy
cities—southern blacks in Chicago, Turks in Frankfurt, Nordestinos in São
Paulo, Candangos in Brasília—these formal and substantive conditions

shape their urban experience. In turn, this experience becomes a principal focus of their struggle to redefine those conditions of belonging to society.

Notions of formal citizenship have become problematic especially in the context of the massive urban migrations of recent decades. As new and more complex kinds of ethnic diversity dominate cities, the very notion of shared community becomes increasingly exhausted. What now constitutes that "direct sense of community membership based on loyalty to a civilization which is a common possession" that Marshall (1977: 101) considered essential to citizenship—essential because only direct participation secures the rights, responsibilities, and liberties of self-rule? In the past, this sense has been a supralocal, indeed, national consciousness. But both national participation and community have become difficult notions for citizenship in the context of the new urban and, often at the same time, global politics of difference, multiculturalism, and racism. One indication of this problem is that in many cases formal citizenship is neither a necessary nor a sufficient condition for substantive citizenship. In other words, although in theory full access to rights depends on membership, in practice that which constitutes citizenship substantively (rights and duties) is often independent of its formal status. Indeed, it is often inaccessible to those who are formal citizens (e.g., the native poor), yet available to those who are not (e.g., legally resident "aliens"). These kinds of problems challenge the dominant notion of citizenship as national identity and the historic role of the nation-state as the preeminent form of modern political community.

But in so doing, they indicate a new possibility that could become an important focus for urban planning: they suggest the possibility of multiple citizenships based on the local, regional, and transnational affiliations that aggregate in contemporary urban experience. Although this possibility represents a significant change in the recent history of citizenship, it is not a new arrangement. Multiple and overlapping jurisdictions predominated in Europe until the triumph of national citizenship obliterated other forms, among them the urban citizenships that organized so many regions of the ancient and the premodern world. The modern state explicitly competed with the city for the primary affiliation of its citizens. Moreover, it usurped their differences, replacing the local management of history with the national. That is, the state reorganized local diversity under the banner of national heritage. One of the most widely shared projects of modern states, this nationalization of diversity legitimates a *singular* state citizenship as the best condition for securing a society of plural cultural identities. But the recent worldwide multiplication of "rights to difference" movements profoundly challenges this claim. Their new ethnocultural politics and violence are in large part a response to the perceived failures of a singular national citizenship. In this reevaluation, the local and the urban reappear as the crucial sites for articulating not only new fanaticisms and hooliganisms but also new transnational and diasporic identities. If planning theory, as I suggest, can conceptualize this collision between state citizenship and these insurgent alternatives, planning practice can respond to this articulation first by expressing its heterogeneity—the social condition we actually live—and then by developing some of the ethnographic possibilities that are, by definition, embedded in heterogeneous conditions.

In terms of substantive issues, the insurgence of new citizenship is no less dramatic. Over the last few decades, many societies have experienced great expansions and erosions of rights. The expansions are particularly evident in the new social movements of the urban poor for "rights to the city" and of women, gays, and ethnic and racial minorities for "rights to difference." These movements are new not only because they force the state to respond to new social conditions of the working poor—in which sense they are, indeed, one of the important consequences of massive urban poverty on citizenship. They are also unprecedented in many cases because they create new kinds of rights, based on the exigencies of lived experience, outside of the normative and institutional definitions of the state and its legal codes.

These rights generally address the social dramas of the new collective and personal spaces of the city, especially its impoverished residential neighborhoods. They focus on housing, property, sanitation, health, education, and so forth, raising basic questions about the scope of entitlements. Is adequate housing a right? Is employment? Moreover, they concern people largely excluded from the resources of the state and are based on social demands that may not be constitutionally defined but that people perceive as entitlements of general citizenship. The organization of these demands into social movements frequently results in new legislation, producing an unprecedented participation of new kinds of citizens in making law and even in administering urban reform and local government. Thus, as the social movements of the urban poor expand citizenship to new social bases, they also create new sources of citizenship rights and new forms of self-rule.

Yet if the city is in this sense an arena for a Rousseauian self-creation of new citizens, it is also a war zone for this very reason: the dominant classes meet the advances of these new citizens with new strategies of segregation, privatization, and fortification. Although the city has always been a place of such contestations, they have taken on new and especially intense forms in recent decades. Where the repressive structures of the state are especially effective, as in the United States, or especially murderous, as in Brazil, the resulting erosions of citizenship are particularly evident in the city's disintegrating public spaces and abandoned public spheres. This contemporary war zone includes not only the terror of death squads and gangs but also the terror of corporate fortresses and suburban enclaves (figs. 1.5 and 1.6). The latter too are insurgent forms of the social, subverting the proclaimed equalities and universals of national citizenship. Thus, the city-as-war-zone threatens the articulation of formal state membership as the principal universalizing norm for managing the simultaneity of modern social identities. As the war escalates, this threat ignites ever-deeper anxieties about what form such coordination might take if national citizenship no longer has that primary role. As much as optimism may radiate from the city's social movements, this anxiety hovers over its war zone, structuring its possible futures.

PLANNING THE ETHNOGRAPHICALLY POSSIBLE

In this essay, I have raised the problem of developing a new social imagination in planning and architecture. I have suggested that when citizenship expansions and erosions focus on urban experience, they constitute an insurgent urbanism that informs this development in several ways. First, they present the city as both the text and the context of new debates about fundamental social relations. In their localism and strategic particularism, these debates valorize the constitutive role of conflict and ambiguity in shaping the multiplicity of contemporary urban life. In a second sense, this heterogeneity works against the modernist absorption of citizenship into a project of state building, providing alternative, possible sources for the development of new kinds of practices and narratives about belonging to and participating in society. This "working against" defines what I called an insurgent citizenship; and its spatial mode, an insurgent urbanism (fig. 1.7). This insurgence is important to the project of rethinking the social in planning because it reveals a realm of the possible that is rooted in the heterogeneity of lived experience, which is to say, in the ethnographic present and not in utopian futures.

But in advocating a move to the ethnography of the present, I do not suggest that planning abandon the project of state building that modernist doctrine defined and that is basic to the notion of modernity itself. Excessive attention to the local has its own dangers. Although I argue, for example, that ethnographic investigation is the best way to establish the terms by which residents participate in the planning of their communities, such participation can be paradoxical: residents across the economic spectrum will often decide, by the most democratic of processes, to segregate their communities "from the evil outside," closing, fortifying, and privatizing their spaces in relation to those deemed outsiders. Hence, throughout the United States, it is common to find home-owner associations trying to use the powers and privileges of democratic organization to exclude and discriminate. Local enactments of democracy may thereby produce anti-democratic results.[9]

The lesson of this paradox is that planning needs to engage not only the development of insurgent forms of the social but also the resources of the state to define, and occasionally impose, a more encompassing conception of right than is sometimes possible to find at the local level. An example of this transformative power of the state comes from the conflict over legal segregation in the southern United States during the 1960s when the federal government eventually intervened in local affairs and acted against local authorities. Above all, planning needs to encourage a complementary antagonism between these two engagements. It needs to operate simultaneously in two theaters, so to speak, maintaining a productive tension between the apparatus of state-directed futures and the investigation of insurgent forms of the social embedded in the present.

In developing the latter as the counter of the former, planners and architects engage a new realm of the possible with their professional practice. But this realm requires a different kind of practice, different in both objective and method, and this difference amounts to a reconceptualization of the fields. In terms of methods, I mean to emphasize those of an urban ethnographer—or of a detective, which are similar: methods of tracing, observing, decoding, and tagging, at one moment of the investigation, and those of reconstructing, identifying, presenting, and rearticulating, at another. Both the trace and the reconstruction compose this engagement with the ethnographic present. In this proposal, I am not suggesting that planners and architects become anthropologists, for anthropology is not reducible to ethnography. Rather, I suggest that they learn the methods of ethnographic detection and also learn to work with anthropologists.

As for its objective, it is the very heterogeneity of society, that which baffles the architect van Eyck. To understand this multiplicity is to learn to read the social against the grain of its typical formations. The typical are the obvious, assumed, normative, and routine, and these are—as Poe illustrates so well in *The Purloined Letter*—hardest to detect. Rather, it is often by their deformations and counters that we learn about them. But countersites are more than just indicators of the norm. They are themselves possible alternatives to it. They contain the germ of a related but different development. Embedded in each of the facets of the multiple relations we live, such possibility accounts for the feeling we have that social life and its spaces are heterogeneous. This possibility is like a bog just beneath the surface of experience, at every step threatening to give way to something different if we let it. But generally we do not, because the technology of

9. For examples from Los Angeles, see Davis 1990.

the normative keeps us from doubting the taken-for-granted on which we depend. Reading the social against the grain of its typical formations means showing that this surface is indeed doubly encoded with such possibility, and it means identifying the sites at which it seeps through.

To understand society's multiplicity is to learn to recognize "its counterform" at these sites—to return to van Eyck's critical mission—and "to form a more perfect union" without sacrificing this double encoding that is the vitality of present circumstance. As I have suggested here, one path to this understanding is to hunt for situations that engage, in practice, the problematic nature of belonging to society and that embody such problems as narratives about the city. But this kind of investigation amounts to a redefinition of the practice of planning and architecture as long as these fields remain obsessed with the design of objects and with the execution of plans and policies. Even though very few architects or planners conduct their professional practice in ways that correspond to this obsession, it remains a powerfully seductive mirage. To reengage the social after the debacle of modernism's utopian attempts, however, requires expanding the idea of planning and architecture beyond this preoccupation with execution and design. It requires looking into, caring for, and teaching about lived experience as lived. To plan the possible is, in this sense, to begin from an ethnographic conception of the social and its spaces of insurgence.

REFERENCES

Buck-Morss, Susan. 1977. *The Origin of Negative Dialectics: Theodor W. Adorno, Walter Benjamin and the Frankfurt Institute.* New York: Free Press.

Caldeira, Teresa P. R. 1992. "City of Walls: Crime, Segregation, and Citizenship in São Paulo." Ph. D. dissertation, University of California, Berkeley. (Forthcoming, University of California Press.)

———. 1996. "Fortified Enclaves: The New Urban Segregation." In *Cities and Citizenship,* ed. James Holston. Special issue: *Public Culture* 8(2):303–328.

Costa, Lúcio. [1930] 1980. "Razões da nova arquitetura." *Arte em Revista* 4:15–23.

Davis, Mike. 1990. *City of Quartz: Excavating the Future in Los Angeles.* London: Verso.

Frampton, Kenneth. 1980. *Modern Architecture: A Critical History.* New York: Oxford University Press.

Holston, James. 1989. *The Modernist City: An Anthropological Critique of Brasília.* Chicago: University of Chicago Press.

———. 1991. "Autoconstruction in Working-Class Brazil." *Cultural Anthropology* 6(4):447–465.

———. 1995. "Insurgent Urbanism: Interactive Architecture and a Dialogue with Craig Hodgetts." In *Technoscientific Imaginaries,* ed. George E. Marcus, 461–505. Chicago: University of Chicago Press.

———, ed. 1996. *Cities and Citizenship.* Special issue of *Public Culture* 8(2).

Lissitzky, El. [1929] 1970. *Architecture for a World Revolution*. Cambridge, Mass.: MIT Press.

Marshall, T. H. [1950] 1977. "Citizenship and Social Class." In *Class, Citizenship, and Social Development*, 71–134. Chicago: University of Chicago Press.

Olalquiaga, Celeste. 1992. *Megalopolis: Contemporary Cultural Sensibilities*. Minneapolis: University of Minnesota Press.

Sorkin, Michael. 1992. "Introduction: Variations on a Theme Park." In *Variations on a Theme Park: The New American City and the End of Public Space*, ed. Michael Sorkin, xi–xv. New York: Noonday Press.

TWO

Feminist and Multicultural Perspectives on Preservation Planning

Gail Lee Dubrow

Planners concerned with issues of social justice have rarely viewed historic preservation as a very engaging issue or considered the tools of preservation planning to be essential to their practice. The history of the preservation movement generally would support their perception that it has been a rather elite concern, combining elements of naive patriotic fervor and aesthetic preoccupation with a narrow view of what is significant about the built environment and the past. Two decades of change in the field of U.S. history, which have brought social relations of gender, race, class, ethnicity, and sexuality into the center of historical analysis, finally have begun to transform applied fields of history, including historic preservation. The time has come to reexamine the potential for using historic preservation as an instrument of a democratic and inclusive approach to planning.

For too long the places designated as landmarks and chosen for preservation reflected the distorted and incomplete picture found in standard historical narratives. Far from random, the gaps tend to erase the historical experiences, contributions, and sometimes the very existence of women, ethnic communities of color, working people, and lesbians and gay men. Emerging currents in historical scholarship have corrected omissions and distortions in the historical record where these groups are concerned and have framed new questions. Historic sites and buildings have the potential to bring these intellectual developments to a wider audience and to raise public awareness of the contributions of diverse groups to our heritage.

The literature of preservation planning, recent directions in practice,

This is a revised and expanded version of my essay "Redefining the Place of Historic Preservation in Planning Education and Practice," which originally appeared in the Symposium on Planning History and Theory guest edited by Leonie Sandercock in *Planning Theory* (Summer 1995): 89–103.

and the new agendas of preservation organizations bear witness to a growing concern for making preservation a more democratic and culturally
inclusive sphere of activity. Antoinette Lee's writings, calling for action to
preserve the multicultural heritage of America, are the first to be embraced by the preservation establishment (Lee 1987, 1992a, 1992b; Lee
and Lyon 1992). Likewise, Dolores Hayden's work on the Power of Place
project has earned widespread applause within the preservation, planning,
and design professions for demonstrating that the multicultural dimensions of urban history are relevant to the art of placemaking (Hayden
1983, 1988a, 1988b, 1990, 1995; Hayden, Dubrow, and Flynn 1985). The
preservation movement has come a long way from its early preoccupation
with "George Washington Slept Here" to current efforts to protect landscapes sacred to Native Americans.

The greatest recent gains in the protection of the nation's multicultural
heritage have come through efforts to reinterpret existing historic properties and identify overlooked ones to more effectively plan for their preservation. Figuratively speaking, perhaps the bloodiest battlefield in the war
of contested interpretations is the southeastern Montana site of Lieutenant
Colonel George Armstrong Custer's "last stand" against the Sioux and
Northern Cheyenne in 1876 (Linenthal 1991: 129–171). Although the
Seventh Cavalry lost the battle, this unit of the National Park system was
named for Custer and for decades its interpretive programs were shame-
lessly biased in his favor. Fifteen years of Native American demands for
change prodded the U.S. Congress to rename the site in 1991, and it is
now known as the Little Bighorn Battlefield National Monument. For years
the only memorial at the site honored the cavalry. At long last the National
Park Service has sponsored a competition to design a memorial to the
Native Americans who were there, one of a number of changes intended
to foster greater balance and accuracy in the site's interpretive programs.[1]
Custer buffs, who have resisted these changes, have not recovered from
what they perceive to be a double defeat at the hands of the Indians (Pulley
1990).

Both the federal government and a number of State Historic Preservation Offices have commissioned surveys of sites and buildings significant
in the history of African Americans,[2] and increasingly these agencies have

1. This competition has been managed by Barbara Booher, Indian Affairs Coordinator,
National Park Service, Rocky Mountain Region, 12795 West Alameda Parkway, P.O. Box
25287, Lakewood, CO 80225–0287.
2. National studies include Afro-American Bicentennial Corporation December 1973
and August 1976. The National Park Service presently is engaged in a continuation of this
earlier theme study. Statewide projects include Merritt 1984 and California Office of Historic
Preservation December 1988.

launched surveys of cultural resources associated with other ethnic groups, such as immigrants from Asia and the Pacific Islands (Hattori 1991; Dubrow, Nomura, et al. 1994; Dubrow, Meisner, et al. 1995). The act of extending official recognition to historic sites can have profound implications for the politics of public memory, as in the case of the designation of World War II internment camps for Japanese Americans, which bear witness to their claims for redress. In many respects, however, the encounter between the United States and tribal governments over the protection of places significant in Native American cultural and religious practices has presented the most profound challenge to standard preservation and planning practices.

The popular periodical *Historic Preservation,* sponsored by the National Trust, recently carried the story of Curley Bear Wagner's leadership in the struggle of the Blackfeet tribe to protect some 1,750 square miles in Montana's Sweetgrass Hills from gold mining (Gillette 1994). The degradation of the landscape through mining threatens the sacred practices of the Blackfeet, who have used the Sweetgrass Hills as fasting, ceremonial, and prayer areas for thousands of years. There and elsewhere throughout the United States, the emerging concept of traditional cultural properties has proven to be a powerful tool for protecting places essential to the survival of traditional cultural practices (Parker and King n.d.; "Traditional Cultural Properties," 1993).

In western Washington, Snoqualmie Falls' determination of eligibility as a traditional cultural property and 1992 listing in the Washington State Register of Historic Places (Garfield 1992) provided the Snoqualmie tribe with a counterweight to the Puget Power and Light Company's overarching jurisdictional claims. Ironically, the Snoqualmie Falls Project, encompassing nineteen buildings and engineering structures associated with the hydroelectric facility, was designated a Historic District that same year and listed in the National Register of Historic Places. Yet this reading of Snoqualmie Falls' significance as a hydroelectric facility fails to address the concerns of Native American inhabitants, for whom the power of the place does not derive from the Falls' capacity to generate electricity but rather from the creation myth associated with that landscape as well as the traditional practices that are anchored in place and critical to the tribe's cultural survival.

Securing Snoqualmie Falls' designation as a traditional cultural property has provided the tribe with a point of entry into negotiations with the Puget Power and Light Company in an effort to maintain the integrity and seclusion of the Falls and plunge pool. It has strengthened the tribe's case for mitigating the cultural impact of the hydroelectric facility and has provided them with the leverage needed to displace economic values, even slightly, from the center of the debate over the future of the place. Viewed from a broader perspective, National Park Service guidelines for the preservation of traditional cultural properties, coupled with recent amendments to the National Historic Preservation Act,[3] have strengthened Native American participation in historic preservation and environmental planning processes. In response to these shifts in power, the conservative property rights movement has come to regard National Park Service efforts to protect traditional cultural properties as a threat to the rights of individual property owners. Mount Shasta, California, recently became the focus of just such a debate when the National Park Service declared it a traditional cultural property on the basis of its significance to Native people. Pressure exerted by local property owners at Mount Shasta, like the force of the mining companies at Montana's Sweetgrass Hills, has tended to result in a reduction in the total area granted protection.

Still, while significant progress has been made in identifying the landmarks of ethnic history and many cities have made great strides in protecting the historic districts that contribute to their unique character, there have been some glaring omissions in preservation planning for ethnic communities of color in American cities. The process of inventorying historic sites and buildings in Seattle's Central District, the historic center of the city's African American community, lagged a decade and a half behind other neighborhoods. In 1979, when many other Seattle neighborhoods were surveyed, the modest vernacular buildings in the Central District were not perceived to be architecturally significant. Increased awareness of the richness inherent in the city's ethnic diversity and a growing appreciation for the commonplace architectural forms that contribute to its physical character set the stage for a second and more appreciative look at the multiplicity of undocumented cultural resources associated with Seattle's African American community. A federal pass-through grant to Certified Local Governments allowed the surveyor, Marilyn Sullivan, to add three hundred Central District properties to the Seattle Landmark Board's citywide inventory of historic places, although thousands more remain undocumented for lack of adequate funding (Sullivan 1991–1992). Past plans for the economic development of the Central District have been impoverished by a lack of information on and a failure to appreciate the cultural resources that constitute community assets. The updated inventory provides those planning for the future of the Central District with an opportunity to reframe questions so that instead of a pervasive emphasis on what

3. For a concise overview of U.S. federal agency historic preservation responsibilities, see the entire issue of *CRM Bulletin* 15, no. 3 (1992), "The Federal CRM Mandate: Responses to the Challenge," especially Bruce J. Noble, Jr., "Federal Agencies and the National Historic Preservation Act: An Overview," pp. 1, 3–5.

is lacking, there is a new appreciation of those aspects of the community's tangible heritage worth celebrating and preserving.

A wider range of property types associated with ethnic communities of color are now gaining recognition as a result of systematic preservation planning efforts. Recently completed statewide and local plans for protecting Asian Pacific American heritage in the state of Washington suggest that a rich array of previously neglected property types await those who look beyond the familiar terrain of urban districts, such as Seattle's International District or Walla Walla's Chinatown (Dubrow 1994, forthcoming a; Dubrow, Nomura, et al. 1994; Dubrow, Meisner, et al. forthcoming). They include historic settlements of Chinese and Japanese workers at the periphery of fishing, mining, railroad, and lumber mill towns. In Kalama, a boomtown by virtue of its selection as the terminus of the Northern Pacific Railroad in 1870, 1,300 Chinese workers established a neighborhood known as China Garden. Selleck, created by the Pacific States Lumber Company, contained a cohesive Japanese settlement. These sites, which have few above-ground remains, are primarily of interest for archaeological reasons. Urban properties associated with Asian Pacific Americans, such as Chinatowns, have been more thoroughly surveyed than rural ones. Yet farms associated with market production are important in the history of Japanese Americans, particularly the commercial dairy farms of the White River Valley, which reportedly supplied half of Seattle's milk during the 1920s, and horticultural operations associated with the strawberry industry in the White River Valley, on Vashon and Bainbridge islands.

Canneries are among the most significant industrial properties associated with Asian Pacific Americans in Washington. Major fish packers typically maintained racially segregated bunkhouses, such as the 1905 example of a "China House" that still stands in South Bend. Asian Pacific Americans also can be linked to major engineering structures, such as a three-mile system of ditches and flumes along the Methow River known as China Ditch. Built by Chinese placer miners, it carried water to gold-bearing sandbars on the west side of the Columbia River. In addition to their imprint on the built environment, immigrants from Asia and the Pacific Islands shaped the land through aesthetic preferences, horticultural techniques, and dietary traditions that combined to create distinctive cultural landscapes. They range from the subsistence gardens of Chinese Americans in Walla Walla to traditional sites for gathering mushrooms prized in Japanese cooking to the well-recognized Japanese American influence on the design of formal gardens.

Ironically, it also may be necessary to reexamine historic properties long recognized as significant in the heritage of various ethnic communities because of features that were overlooked when they were originally documented, as the example of Seattle's Panama Hotel doubly illustrates. A

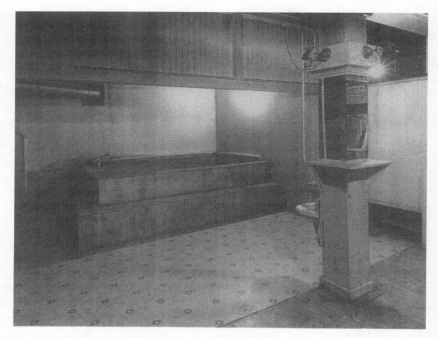

Figure 2.1. Seattle, Washington: Panama Hotel. The oldest known intact example of an urban *furo*, or Japanese bathhouse. (Courtesy of John Stamets)

single-room occupancy workingman's hotel built in 1910, the Panama is one of many contributing structures to Seattle's International District. As has been common practice in many places, the surveys conducted in preparation for the historic district nomination did not extend into the building's interiors. As a result, the district nomination overlooked two significant features in the Panama Hotel's basement. One is an extraordinarily well-preserved example of an urban *furo*, or Japanese American bathhouse (fig. 2.1). The other more haunting feature is a significant number of fully packed trunks stored by Japanese Americans on the eve of internment which were never reclaimed (fig. 2.2). Important cultural resources such as these have no recognition or protection unless they are documented in the preservation planning tools of cultural resource managers. The example of the Panama Hotel suggests that state and local preservation planning initiatives can bring long-overlooked ethnic cultural resources into public view, building new constituencies for their protection.

In another western Washington city, Tacoma, where the University of Washington is establishing a new branch campus, the presence of one des-

Figure 2.2. Seattle, Washington: Panama Hotel. Dozens of fully packed trunks left by Japanese Americans on the eve of World War II internment. (Courtesy of Gail Lee Dubrow)

ignated historic district and another unrecognized one may mean the difference between preservation and demolition for the historic buildings associated with them, with devastating consequences for the few tangible remains of the city's Japanese American heritage. The decision to locate the new campus in Tacoma's designated Union Depot/Warehouse Historic District required a commitment to preserving the rather ordinary buildings associated with the city's development "as an early commercial, distribution and manufacturing center in the Pacific Northwest" (Sias and Gallacci 1979: 3); consequently, the architects have integrated industrial structures such as warehouses and the Snoqualmie Falls Power Transformer Building into the design of the campus. No doubt Tacoma's historic preservation officials would have found it more difficult to secure the university's commitment to preserving these buildings without public awareness of their significance and the controls over development that are conferred by the historic district designation.

In purchasing properties to assemble the campus, the university acquired a historic property listed on the Tacoma and National registers, the Nihongo Gakko, or Japanese Language School, which once was an important center for the city's Japanese American community (fig. 2.3).

Figure 2.3. Tacoma, Washington: Japanese Language School. In recognition of its importance as a community institution prior to World War II, the Japanese Language School has been listed on the National Register of Historic Places and has been designated a City of Tacoma Landmark. (Courtesy of the National Register of Historic Places)

As a University of Washington planning student, Susan Morrison, explained in her thesis research on the property,

> It was at Nihongo Gakko in the early twentieth century where the children of Japanese immigrants were formally taught the language, traditions, and cultural values of their parents as well as the English language and other skills that might help them compete in the United States. The building served as a common meeting ground for Japanese Americans of all religions and affiliations. Whether they were Buddhist, Baptist or Methodist, the children of shopkeepers, house cleaners or dentists, they came to Nihongo Gakko to study and celebrate their common Japanese heritage. This education was a vital link in maintaining a sense of cultural and community identity for second generation children in a new land. (1994: 1–2)

The university was not predisposed to saving this large and somewhat dilapidated wood frame building and considered its status as a historic property a nagging obstacle to plans for demolition. Thus far the university's efforts to clear the way for demolition have met with little community resistance,

Figure 2.4 Tacoma, Washington: Japanese Language School. The decline of Tacoma's Nihonmachi, or Japantown, has eroded the base of support for preserving individual landmarks such as the Japanese Language School. (Courtesy of the National Register of Historic Places)

since the World War II internment of Japanese Americans on the Pacific Coast decimated the Nihon Machi, or Japantown, in which the language school was set and which never again regained its prewar population or vitality. In essence, the long history of exclusion and discrimination has undermined the possibility of finding vocal advocates for the preservation of Tacoma's Japanese American heritage.

The city's failure to perceive the significance or officially recognize the remains of what once was a thriving Japanese American community in the immediate vicinity of the University of Washington's Tacoma campus has left the surviving buildings associated with it more vulnerable than they otherwise would be to the vicissitudes of development, since the fate of each building is now considered in isolation from the historical, cultural, and physical contexts that give it meaning (fig. 2.4). Meanwhile, the cumulative result of each independent development decision has been to erode the remaining historic fabric of Tacoma's Nihon Machi. Although state and local preservation agencies thus far have resisted the university's efforts to de-designate the language school, it is unlikely to be saved. If a Nihon Machi Historic District had been established earlier, the landmarks of Tacoma's Japanese American community might have enjoyed the same level of protection as the Historic Warehouse District.

This example suggests that it is the planner's responsibility not only to enforce existing regulatory controls but also to determine whether the protections they confer are equitably distributed. It also suggests that planners have a special ethical, moral, and political responsibility to advocate for the preservation of cultural resources when systematic inequalities have weakened the power of particular groups to defend their own tangible heritage. Finally, this example suggests that a multicultural and inclusionary approach to historic preservation planning has a vital, if neglected, place in the planner's tool kit. It has the potential to provide planners with the combination of skills and awareness needed to identify, document, and protect neglected aspects of our cultural heritage.

During the past two decades the National Park Service has acquired new historic properties and engaged in efforts to reinterpret existing landmarks that collectively have produced a more balanced and inclusive portrait of the American past. The establishment of Lowell National Historical Park in 1978, which uses both the cotton mills and the boardinghouse to depict the daily lives of workers in America's first industrial city, signifies progress in the incorporation of both women's history and labor history into the mainstream of preservation activity. The 1980 establishment of the Woman's Rights National Historical Park in Seneca Falls, New York, marking the 1848 convention that launched the women's rights movement, advanced the preservation movement light-years beyond its well-established conventions for depicting women in the domestic sphere, as the wives of notable men or anonymous homemakers in demonstrations of archaic folkways, or, more rarely, as accomplished literary ladies.

A lively discussion of the possibilities for using historic preservation to increase public awareness of women's history finally has emerged in the scholarly literature (Spencer-Wood 1987; Huyck 1988; Dubrow 1989, 1991, 1992, forthcoming b; Howe 1990; Miller 1992, 1993; West 1992). Sensing widespread interest in the subject, Philadelphia-area women successfully organized the first national conference, "Reclaiming Women's History Through Historic Preservation," in 1994 which attracted more than three hundred participants.[4] Several themes clearly emerged from

---

4. "Reclaiming Women's History Through Historic Preservation: A National Conference," held at Bryn Mawr College, Bryn Mawr, Pennsylvania (June 17–19, 1994), convened by the Alice Paul Centennial Foundation, the Preservation Coalition of Greater Philadelphia, and Women's Way.

the meeting: a renewed appreciation for women's vital contributions to the history of the preservation movement; a concern for developing a more accurate and complete picture of women's lives at existing historic properties; the search for a wider array of property types, beyond the ubiquitous historic houses, as sites for marking women's history; and a well-placed concern for transforming institutional policies and practices that are barriers to identifying, interpreting, and protecting places significant in the history of women (Dubrow and Goodman forthcoming). Taken together, these developments suggest that the combined force of feminists well placed in the preservation community and scholars in the field of U.S. women's history are prepared to counter male biases in historic preservation.

A second national conference on women and historic preservation was hosted by Arizona State University in March 1997 which attracted more than two hundred participants. This gathering brought greater attention to the preservation and interpretation of women's history in the western region. It also reflected a closer working relationship among academic and public historians, universities, and the National Park Service, which fully participated in the conference planning and provided a significant portion of the funding. A special issue of the journal *CRM* is an important resource for those who were unable to attend, since it includes brief accounts of some of the conference papers (Huyck 1997). Future gatherings on the subject of women and historic preservation are likely to be held every two or three years.

To date, the most ambitious attempt to reinterpret women's history at existing landmarks is the project "Raising Our Sites: Women's History in Pennsylvania." Initiated by the Pennsylvania Humanities Council, this three-year project, funded by the National Endowment for the Humanities, is dedicated to improving the representation of women's lives at fourteen well-established historic sites and organizations (Moon et al. 1994). One of the sites involved in the Pennsylvania project is Pennsbury Manor, the Morrisville summer home of William Penn. Until Jean Soderlund, a local scholar, became involved, the interpretive spotlight narrowly focused on William Penn, as if he had lived there alone. Her research in late-seventeenth-century probate records, wills, inventories, and court records fueled the development of a broader interpretive program that now includes information about the women who lived and worked at Pennsbury Manor, including "Sue, an enslaved African American woman and her daughter, little Sue, as well as housekeeper Mary Lofty and her assistant Abigail Pemberton" (" 'Raising Our Sites,' " 1995: 6). "Raising Our Sites" merits recognition as a model of cultural planning for its systematic approach to remedying omissions and distortions in the coverage of women's history on a statewide basis and for its emphasis on collaboration between scholars

and museum professionals to increase the capacity of resource-poor organizations and institutions to effect the desired changes ("Raising Our
Sites," 1993: 6). Cultural resource managers searching for ways to enrich
the interpretation of women's history at properties under their jurisdiction
would benefit from studying the approaches developed by participants in
the Pennsylvania project.

Existing landmarks offer abundant opportunities for reinterpreting
women's history. However, significant gaps still remain in the coverage of
women's history on national, state, and local registers of historic properties. In her 1990 analysis Page Putnam Miller found that less than 2 percent of National Historic Landmarks, the "honor roll of the nation's historic properties," had been designated because of their association with
women (1992: 13). The computerized database for the National Register
contains no category for women's history, so it is difficult to assess the coverage of this subject within its more than 100,000 listings (Shull 1997). A
review of historic property listings for selected states suggests that Miller's
figure for National Historic Landmarks is also a relatively accurate estimate
of the status of women's history on the National Register.[5] Houses and club
buildings appear to be the most frequently designated types of properties
associated with women's history in these states. As might be expected, only
a handful of properties illuminate the lives of women of color.

Additional data from a study of five major cities reveal women's history
to be better represented in some places than others, from a high of 8
percent of Miami historic sites to the startling discovery that the Boston
Landmarks Commission has not designated a single property significant in
women's history during its seventeen years in existence.[6] This is a mind-
boggling proposition in a city that is otherwise fanatical about celebrating
its history and that has access to the Schlesinger Library at Radcliffe College, which contains a world-class collection of books and manuscripts on
women's history as well as abundant materials specifically on women's history in Boston. In other cities the norm was closer to 3 percent. In sum,
the few designated properties associated with women on the National Register, and parallel listings at the state and local level, suggest that major
themes and property types have been overlooked. For that reason new
statewide and local surveys are needed to identify previously undocumented properties significant in the history of women.

5. I have completed an analysis of National Register data for three states, New York, Virginia, and Florida, and the news is not good. Women's history is best represented in Virginia,
where 2.1 percent of National Register listings are directly related to women's history, and
most poorly represented in New York State, at 1.2 percent. I am convinced there will be other
contenders for both titles—best and worst—by the time this project is done.
6. I studied five American cities: Boston, New York, Miami, Chicago, and Los Angeles.

Figure 2.5. Roxbury, Massachusetts: New England Hospital for Women and Children. The Women's Landmark Project succeeded in gaining National Historic Landmark designation for this hospital now known as the Dimock Community Health Center, because it is the oldest existing example of the hospitals developed by and for women in the second half of the nineteenth century. Shown is the Zakrewska Building, named for its founding physician, Marie Zakrewska. (Photograph: Gail Lee Dubrow)

The four-year National Women's History Landmark Project, which was funded by congressional appropriation, succeeded in gaining National Historic Landmark designation for nearly forty properties, in the process demonstrating that gaps in the coverage of women's history can be closed when resources are allocated to solve the problem (figs. 2.5, 2.6). To identify potential landmarks, the project director, Page Putnam Miller, drew on a network of scholars and preservation professionals, culled tours and guidebooks, and identified nationally significant properties already listed on the National Register. But what resources will enable those working at the local level to increase the number of properties associated with women's history on the National Register as well as state and local registers of historic places?

Widespread interest in identifying women's history sites has resulted in the publication of quite a few tours and guidebooks that identify properties that might be added to the landmark registers. These include the

Figure 2.6. Fort Pierce, Florida: Zora Neale Hurston House. Despite its modest appearance, the Women's Landmark Project gained National Historic Landmark status for the home of writer, folklorist, and anthropologist Zora Neale Hurston, the most noted African American woman writer of the mid-twentieth century. (Courtesy of the National Register of Historic Places, photograph by Hal Kelly)

newly revised guide to U.S. properties, *Susan B. Anthony Slept Here* (Sherr and Kazickas 1994), tour books for London, Paris, Boston, Chicago, and the Twin Cities, and a new guide to women in the City of Brotherly Love, among others.[7] These guidebooks indirectly contribute to the preservation of women's history landmarks by increasing public awareness of their significance; but public appreciation alone will not protect properties from damaging alterations or outright demolition. Clearly there is a need for bringing together the skills of women's historians and preservation planners, since many of the properties identified in women's history tours and guidebooks would benefit from being officially designated as landmarks, especially in localities where preservation ordinances have some teeth.

In recent years State Historic Preservation Offices have used the tools of preservation planning to enhance their ability to protect cultural resources

7. Sherr and Kazickas 1976, 1994; Rights of Women and Davin 1978; Domer et al. 1981; Mason and Lacy 1982; Gehman and Ries 1985; Tinling 1986; Clarke 1986; Sturtevant 1991; Cullen 1993; Belford 1993; and Samuels, Beard, and Libby 1994.

associated with ethnic communities of color as well as properties grouped by other themes (such as Transportation, Politics, and Agriculture). Yet they have generally failed to take the initiative in planning for the protection of cultural resources associated with women. Lobbying efforts are needed to make women's history more of a priority within the limited budgets State Historic Preservation Offices have available for comprehensive preservation planning.

Strong interest in improving the protection of cultural resources associated with women's history on a statewide basis has surfaced in several places, including New Jersey and Arizona, though lack of funding has stalled some efforts to develop historic contexts and initiate statewide surveys. Still, incremental progress is being made. A 1996 regional conference, "Telling Her Story: Expanding the Past of Georgia's Women Through Historic Preservation," launched the Women's History Initiative in Georgia (Sharpe 1997). A historic context document is planned which will link the history of Georgia women to historic properties, fostering new listings on the National Register along with the reinterpretation of existing landmarks. The importance of this study is not only its potential to improve the protection of places significant in women's history on a statewide basis; it also has the potential to serve as a model for other State Historic Preservation Offices seeking to undertake similar initiatives. Given the limited funding most state offices have at their disposal, successful projects will likely require partnerships with community groups, nonprofit organizations, and universities with strong programs in fields such as planning, preservation, public history, ethnic studies, and women's studies.

Many recently published works in gay and lesbian history have untapped potential for the purposes of preservation planning. One such work is George Chauncey's *Gay New York* (1994), with its rich descriptions of the urban institutions critical to the emergence of gay culture and community, from the explicit sexuality of bathhouses to the moralistic facade maintained at mainstream institutions frequented by gay men, such as the Young Men's Christian Association. Systematic planning efforts are needed to identify the range of historic property types likely to be found in cities with substantial gay and lesbian communities and to analyze the problems and possibilities associated with their preservation and public interpretation. The time has come to bring together those engaged in documenting the history of gay and lesbian communities in Manhattan (Lustbader 1993), Buffalo (Kennedy and Davis 1993), Fire Island (Newton 1993), Provincetown and San Francisco (D'Emilio 1989; Stryker and Van Buskirk 1996), and many other cities with skilled preservation planners, to consider the wide range of historically significant gathering places that might be identified in surveys, designated as landmarks, and chosen as sites for public interpretation, including vacation destinations, neighborhoods, bars, parks, beaches, residences, and meeting halls. There is also much work to be done in challenging bland and misleading interpretive programs at historic homes open to the public, where the gay or lesbian sexual orientation of the prime subject has yet to be acknowledged, much less given the emphasis it merits. An emerging body of scholarship has reclaimed such luminaries as Willa Cather, Emily Dickinson, and Walt Whitman as part of the gay and lesbian literary heritage (Summers 1995). The sexual orientation and affectional preferences of leading figures in American political history, such as Jane Addams, Francis Willard, and Eleanor Roosevelt, similarly have been the subject of recent scholarly inquiry, raising new and difficult questions about the presentation of the past at historic house museums dedicated to their memory.

Advocacy for the protection of sites and buildings associated with gay and lesbian history has lagged behind other cultural diversity initiatives by nearly a decade. One can only speculate on the forces that have discouraged lesbian and gay male preservationists from organizing to promote the interests of their own communities: a powerful combination of fear, isolation, caution about being pigeonholed, and an alienating ethic of professionalism that shuts its practitioners off from aspects of their own identity at least during working hours, if not for longer periods. As a result the few efforts to develop itineraries of gay and lesbian landmarks have stemmed from community history projects nurtured outside the preservation mainstream, such as the tour of historic sites and buildings included in the cultural programs associated with the Gay Games, held in New York City during the summer of 1994 (fig. 2.7).[8]

"Out and About in the City," a 1997 article in *Preservation* magazine (Drabelle 1997), represented the National Trust for Historic Preservation's first step toward gaining greater visibility for gay and lesbian heritage within the broader preservation movement. By focusing on Trevor Hailey's lively San Francisco tour, "Cruisin' the Castro" and Jay Gifford's "Victorian Home Walk," National Trust members were introduced to places of historical significance in the formation of the gay and lesbian communities, as well as contemporary landmarks, from a comfortable distance as armchair tourists. Gradually, gays and lesbians within the staff and membership of

8. Duggan 1986 documents a number of community-based projects. Various heritage-oriented projects have emerged since Duggan's publication, including a map identifying many gay and lesbian landmarks in New York City, which was researched, designed, and published by the Organization of Gay and Lesbian Designers; maps of Boston and Los Angeles; and a signage project entitled "Queer Spaces," by the public art collective RepoHistory. These maverick projects generally have not engaged in the process of nominating properties associated with gay and lesbian history for formal listing on landmark registers.

Figure 2.7. New York City: Bonnie and Clyde's, a popular lesbian bar of the 1970s, located at 82 West Third Street. Pink masonite triangles served as temporary historical markers at nine sites that RepoHistory, an artists' collective, designated as significant in New York City's gay and lesbian history. The project, "Queer Spaces: Places of Struggle, Places of Strength," was commissioned by the Storefront for Art and Architecture from June 18 to July 30, 1994. (Courtesy of RepoHistory, photograph by Jim Costanzo)

the National Trust have succeeded in gaining more space for addressing their concerns. The 1996 annual conference featured the first social gathering for gay and lesbian preservationists, followed by the organization's approval of an educational session on gay and lesbian historic resources at the 1997 annual meeting in Santa Fe. These events have seeded the development of an informal network that is likely to generate future projects aimed at improving the protection and interpretation of so-called lavender landmarks.

Ken Lustbader's 1993 graduate thesis at Columbia University, "Landscape of Liberation: Preserving Gay and Lesbian History in Greenwich Village," is one of many signs that a radical revision is under way in the scope and content of history deemed relevant to the preservation and planning professions. So too the essays in this collection suggest that the dull and insular version of history that has come to occupy a central place in planning education finally has begun to yield to livelier and more expansive approaches that are responsive to inquiries about race, class, ethnicity, gender, and sexual identity in urban history. One key force for change in the relationship of history to the preservation and planning professions is a new and more diverse generation of planning students and educators, whose pride in their identity is coupled with a stubborn insistence on its relevance to their work in the world. It is their presence in the classroom and their growing visibility as practitioners and educators that has "called the question" about race, justice, gender, and power. This confrontation has revealed the incapacity of the canonical version of planning history to accommodate their interests and agendas, both because it is too narrow in focus and because it is cut off from a meaningful connection to praxis. I have suggested that a democratic and inclusive approach to historic preservation planning has the potential to translate many of their intellectual, cultural, and political concerns into effective action, by providing them with the tools needed to better understand, honor, and protect the tangible heritage of the many communities that have shaped the landscape.

REFERENCES

Afro-American Bicentennial Corporation. 1973. *A Summary Report of Thirty Sites Determined to Be Significant in Illustrating and Commemorating the Role of Black Americans in United States History.*
———. 1976. *Summary Report of a Three-Year Study by the Afro-American Bicentennial Corporation of Sites Determined to be Significant in Illustrating the Role of Afro-Americans in United States History.*
California Office of Historic Preservation. December 1988. *Five Views: An Ethnic Sites Survey for California.* Sacramento: Department of Parks and Recreation.
Chauncey, George. 1994. *Gay New York: Gender, Urban Culture, and the Making of the Gay Male World, 1890–1940.* New York: Basic Books.
Clarke, Jennifer. 1986. *In Our Grandmothers' Footsteps: A Walking Tour of London.* New York: Atheneum.
Cullen, Catherine. 1993. *Paris: The Virago Woman's Travel Guide.* Berkeley: Ulysses Press.
D'Emilio, John. 1989. "Gay Politics and Community in San Francisco since World War II." In *Hidden from History,* ed. Martin Duberman, Martha Vicinus, and George Chauncey, Jr. New York: New American Library.
Domer, Marilyn A., Jean S. Hunt, Mary Ann Johnson, and Adade M. Wheeler. 1981. *Walking with Women through Chicago History: Four Self-Guided Tours.* Chicago: Salsedo Press.
Drabelle, Dennis. 1997. "Out and About in the City," *Preservation* 49, no. 1 (January–February): 74, 76–78.
Dublin, Thomas, Nancy Grey Osterud, and Joy Parr, eds. 1994. Special issue on public history. *Gender and History* 6, no. 3 (November).
Dubrow, Gail Lee. 1989. "Restoring a Female Presence." In *Architecture: A Place for*

Women, ed. Ellen Perry Berkeley with Matilda McQuaid, assoc. ed., 159–170. Washington, D.C.: Smithsonian Institution Press.

———.1991. "Preserving Her Heritage: American Landmarks of Women's History." 2 vols. Ph.D. dissertation, Urban Planning Program, University of California, Los Angeles.

———. 1992. "Claiming Public Space for Women's History in Boston: A Proposal for Preservation, Public Art, and Public Historical Interpretation." *Frontiers: A Journal of Women's Studies* 13, no. 1 (Winter): 111–148.

———.1994. "Celebrating Washington's Asian Pacific American Heritage." *Preservation Washington* (Spring): 1–2.

———. Forthcoming a. "Asian American Imprints on the Western Landscape." In *Preserving Cultural Landscapes in America,* ed. Arnold R. Alanen and Robert Z. Melnick. Baltimore: Johns Hopkins University Press.

———. Forthcoming b. *Planning for the Preservation of American Women's History.* New York: Oxford University Press.

Dubrow, Gail Lee, and Jennifer Goodman, eds. Forthcoming. *Restoring Women's History through Historic Preservation.* Baltimore: Johns Hopkins University Press.

Dubrow, Gail Lee, and Jennifer Meisner et al. Forthcoming. *A Plan for the Protection of Asian Pacific American Heritage in King County.* Seattle: Preservation Planning and Design Program of the University of Washington in cooperation with the King County Landmarks Commission.

Dubrow, Gail Lee, and Gail Nomura et al. 1994. *The Historic Context for the Preservation of Asian/Pacific American Resources in Washington State.* Olympia, Wash.: Office of Archaeology and Historic Preservation.

Duggan, Lisa. 1986. "History's Gay Ghetto: The Contradictions of Growth in Lesbian and Gay History." In *Presenting the Past: Essays on History and the Public,* ed. Susan Porter Benson, Stephen Brier, and Roy Rosenzweig, 281–292. Philadelphia: Temple University Press.

Exploring a Common Past: Interpreting Women's History in the National Park Service. 1995. Washington, D.C.: National Park Service.

"The Federal CRM Mandate—Responses to the Challenge." 1992. *CRM Bulletin* 15(3).

Gehman, Mary, and Nancy Ries. 1988. *Women and New Orleans: A History.* New Orleans: Margaret Media.

Gillette, Jane Brown. 1994. "Sweetgrass Saga." *Historic Preservation* (September–October): 28–33, 90–92.

Hattori, Eugene. 1991. "Chinese and Japanese." In *Nevada Comprehensive Preservation Plan,* ed. W. G. White and R. M. James. Carson City, Nev.: Division of Historic Preservation and Archaeology.

Hayden, Dolores. 1983. "The Meaning of Place in Art and Architecture." *Design Quarterly* 122:18–20.

———. 1988a. "Placemaking, Preservation, and Urban History." *Journal of Urban History* 41, no. 3 (Spring): 45–51.

———. 1988b. "The Power of Place: A Proposal for Los Angeles." *Public Historian* (Summer): 5–18.

———. 1990. "The Potential of Ethnic Places for Urban Landscapes." *Places* (Fall): 10–17.

————. 1995. *The Power of Place: Urban Landscapes as Public History.* Cambridge, Mass.: MIT Press.

Hayden, Dolores, Gail Dubrow, and Carolyn Flynn. 1985. *The Power of Place: Los Angeles.* Los Angeles: The Power of Place.

Howe, Barbara J. 1990. "Women in Historic Preservation: The Legacy of Ann Pamela Cunningham." *Public Historian* 12, no. 1 (Winter): 31–61.

Huyck, Heather. 1988. "Beyond John Wayne: Using Historic Sites to Interpret Women's History." In *Western Women: Their Land, Their Lives,* ed. Lillian Schlissel, Vicki L. Ruiz, and Janice Monk, 303–329. Albuquerque: University of New Mexico Press.

————, ed. 1997. "Placing Women in the Past." *CRM* 20(3).

Kennedy, Elizabeth Lapovsky, and Madeline D. Davis. 1993. *Boots of Leather, Slippers of Gold: The History of a Lesbian Community.* New York: Routledge.

Lee, Antoinette. 1987. "Discovering Old Cultures in the New World: The Role of Ethnicity." In *The American Mosaic,* ed. Robert E. Stipe and Antoinette Lee. Washington, D.C.: U.S./ICOMOS.

————. 1992a. "Multicultural Building Blocks." In *Past Meets Future: Saving America's Historic Environments,* ed. Antoinette Lee. Washington, D.C.: Preservation Press.

————. 1992b. "Cultural Diversity and Historic Preservation." *CRM Bulletin* 15(7).

Lee, Antoinette, with Elizabeth Lyon. 1992. "Cultural and Ethnic Diversity in Historic Preservation." *National Trust for Historic Preservation Information Series,* no. 65.

Linenthal, Edward Tabor. 1991. *Sacred Ground: Americans and Their Battlefields.* Urbana: University of Illinois Press.

Lustbader, Ken M. 1993. "Landscape of Liberation: Preserving Gay and Lesbian History in Greenwich Village." Master's thesis, Historic Preservation Program, Columbia University.

Mason, Karen, and Carol Lacy. 1982. *Women's History Tour of the Twin Cities.* Minneapolis: Nodin Press.

Merritt, Carole. 1984. *Historic Black Resources: A Handbook for the Identification, Documentation, and Evaluation of Historic African American Properties.* Atlanta: Historic Preservation Section, Georgia Department of Natural Resources.

Miller, Page Putnam. 1993. "The Women's History Landmark Project: Policy and Research." *Public Historian* 15, no. 4 (Fall): 82–88.

————, ed. 1992. *Reclaiming the Past: Landmarks of Women's History.* Bloomington: Indiana University Press.

Moon, Kimberly, Emma Lapsansky, Beverly Sheppard, and Stephanie Wolf. 1994. " 'Raising our Sites': Women's History in Pennsylvania." Paper presented at Reclaiming Women's History through Historic Preservation: A National Conference.

Morrison, Susan E. 1994. "Tacoma's Nihongo Gakko: The Center of a Once Vibrant Community." Master's thesis, Department of Urban Design and Planning, University of Washington.

Newton, Esther. 1993. *Cherry Grove, Fire Island: Sixty Years in America's First Gay and Lesbian Town.* Boston: Beacon Press.

Parker, Patricia L., and Thomas King. n.d. *National Register Bulletin 38: Guidelines for the Identification and Evaluation of Traditional Cultural Properties.* Washington, D.C.: U.S. Department of the Interior, National Park Service.

Pulley, Breit. 1990. "Indian Tribute Sparks New Battle at Little Bighorn; Native American Park Chief Seeks a Balanced Exhibit, Outraging Custer Buffs." *Wall Street Journal,* October 15, A1.

Raising our Sites: Women's History in Pennsylvania. 1993. Proceedings of the Project Implementation Conference, June 28–29.

" 'Raising our Sites' at Pennsbury Manor." 1995. *Pennsylvania Humanities* (April–June): 6.

Rights of Women and Anna Davin. 1978. *The London Feminist History Walk.* London: Community Press.

Samuels, Gayle Brandow, with Lucienne Beard and Valencia Libby, 1994. *Women in the City of Bortherly Love . . . and Beyond: Tours and Deturs in Delaware Valley Women's History.* Philadelphia.

Sharpe, Leslie N. 1997. "The Role of Women in Preservation: A Georgia Perspective." *CRM* 20(3):18–19.

Sherr, Lynn, and Jurate Kazickas. 1976. *The American Woman's Gazetteer.* New York: Bantam.

———. 1994. *Susan B. Anthony Slept Here: A Guide to American Women's Landmarks.* New York: Times Books, Random House.

Shull, Carol D. 1997. "Women's History in the National Register and the National Historic Landmarks Survey." *CRM* 20(3):12–15.

Spencer-Wood, Suzanne M. 1987. "A Survey of Domestic Reform Movement Sites in Boston and Cambridge, Mass., ca. 1865–1905." *Historical Archaeology* 21 (2):7–37.

Stryker, Susan, and Jim Van Buskirk. 1996. *Gay by the Bay: A History of Queer Culture in the San Francicso Bay Area.* San Francisco: Chronicle Books.

Sturtevant, Katherine. 1991. *Our Sisters' London: Feminist Walking Tours.* Chicago: Chicago Review Press.

Summers, Claude J., ed. 1995. *The Gay and Lesbian Literary Heritage: A Reader's Companion to the Writers and their Works, from Antiquity to the Present.* New York: Holt.

Tinling, Marion. 1986. *Women Remembered: A Guide to Landmarks of Women's History in the United States.* Westport, Conn.: Greenwood Press.

"Traditional Cultural Properties." 1993. Special issue. *CRM Bulletin* 16.

West, Patricia. 1986. "The 'New Social History' and Historic House Museums: The Lindenwald Example." *Museum Studies Journal* 2(3):22–26.

———. 1992. "The Historic House Museum Movement in America: Louisa May Alcott's Orchard House as a Case Study." Ph.D. dissertation, Department of History, State University of New York at Binghamton.

———. Forthcoming. *Domesticating Clio: The Origins of the Historic House Museum Movement in America.* Washington, D.C.: Smithsonian Institution Press.

THREE

Regional Blocs, Regional Planning, and the Blues Epistemology in the Lower Mississippi Delta

Clyde Woods

This essay tells the story of the conception, life, and early death of the Lower Mississippi Delta Development Commission (LMDDC). In the process it forges a new historiography of regional planning, using new theoretical tools: a fusing of regional political economy, cultural studies, and regional epistemology. The object of this history is to provide new and multiple foundations for new regional orders, a more egalitarian and democratic planning practice, and regional restructuring based on indigenous concepts of sustainability and of social, cultural, and economic justice. Central to this task is the Blues epistemology, that is, the use of the Blues as a theory of social, economic, and cultural development and change (Woods 1993).

Planning plays a central role in preserving specifically regional forms of development and the language, aesthetics, and relations of power that support it. The banners of objectivity, rationality, expediency, and historic advantage are often used to devalue and make invisible the generational debates between and within communities over the distribution of power and resources. Consequently, the remembrance of alternative development theories and voices resonates within regionally constructed popular cultures to a much greater extent than in official planning discourse.

The creation of the federal Lower Mississippi Delta Development Commission in 1988 marked the beginning of a new era for the poorest and the most heavily African American region in the United States. Chaired by Bill Clinton, then governor of Arkansas, the official purpose of the LMDDC was to develop a ten-year economic development plan for a region consisting of 219 Lower Mississippi River Valley counties and parishes located in seven states: Arkansas, Illinois, Kentucky, Louisiana, Mississippi, Missouri, and Tennessee. Simultaneously hailed and condemned by many observers within the region and the nation, the commission was believed to mark the rebirth of federally funded multistate regional planning. Yet the model of economic development finally adopted by the commission could not significantly reduce persistent poverty, establish the infrastructure for sustainable production, or expand the parameters of social and economic justice.

This account of regional economic development planning history in the Lower Mississippi Delta is concerned as much with the future of the region as with its past. A regional future that promises social, cultural, and economic justice requires a method capable of accomplishing two tasks: recovering those historical memories, voices, and visions that imagined such a future and analyzing the institutional and intellectual structures deployed to systematically marginalize those voices.

I seek to understand this contemporary crisis by exploring three of the development traditions present in the region: the plantation tradition, the New South tradition, and the African American Blues tradition. The purpose of such an exploration is to demonstrate the existence, importance, and vitality of the popular and official intellectual traditions that continue to mold development debates, movements, and practices long after they were supposedly relegated to the scrap heaps of modernism. Comprehending these hidden traditions enables us to understand the renewed power of state and regional blocs, the cannibalization of federal authority, and the abandonment of urban and regional planning. Yet such explorations also allow us to identify and resurrect those marginalized yet persistent regional networks of knowledge and practice capable of creating a just society, that is, sustainable epistemologies. Therefore, my discussion of the LMDDC focuses primarily on instances in which the marginalized working-class African American conception of sustainable development insistently emerges time and again in the midst of debates dominated by blocs that are significantly more politically, economically, and institutionally powerful.

DELTA DEVELOPMENT TRADITIONS

The Plantation Tradition

The reproduction and expansion of plantation bloc hegemony is organized around several related tenets: an economic monopoly over agriculture, manufacturing, banking, land, and water; a fiscal, administrative, and regulatory monopoly over local and county activities; and an authoritative monopoly over the conditions and regulation of ethnic groups and labor. Although restructured and contested on numerous occasions, through intra- and interregional alliances the plantation bloc has successfully transported its system of representation, coordinating institutions, and development practices into the twenty-first century.[1]

"Plantation" is a sixteenth-century term used to describe a particular English colonial expansion policy. As opposed to the "conquest and civilization" policy, the plantation "was an adventure officially sponsored by the nation-state and involved the transfer of an entire package of personnel, laws and materials into a new territory" (Robinson 1984: 1). During the Elizabethan period, in the 1570s, state-sponsored plantations were increasingly reorganized as private entrepreneurial firms. Early in the seventeenth century, English and Scottish Protestants were the principal personnel for the plantations established in Irish Catholic Ulster and along the east coast of North America. Thus the plantation can be conceptualized as a military intervention, as an entrepreneurial activity, as a colonizing institution, and as an engine of enduring ethnic conflict.[2]

Typically, in plantation and plantation bloc-dominated regions, vertically integrated firms produce and process commodities for export. This particular concentration and combination of land, capital, and technology usually require the recruitment of designated ethnic groups as laborers; the construction of distinctive firm, sectoral, and state institutions to regulate and regiment labor; and the denial of access to land and to basic civil and human rights. For these reasons Edgar Thompson (1968) has referred to plantation systems as a military form of agriculture while George Beckford (1983) argued that they were, and are, the flip-side of Western "modernism" and "modernization."

In the Western Hemisphere, the distinctiveness of regional relations was structured by the patterns and institutions of colonization and settlement. During the Native American removal in the United States, a clear regional distinction emerged between those northern and southern areas identified with settler colonialism and subsistence farming and production for local and regional markets, on the one hand, and those (primarily southern)

---

1. Regional blocs can be best understood as place-based development alliances, bargains, contracts, compacts, conventions, or traditions. Their origins lie in movements that espouse various values or norms to promote solidarity between often disparate class, ethnic, gender, religious, sectoral, and political factions. To reproduce their control over resources, blocs create institutions designed to secure the conditions necessary for stable and profitable accumulation. To marginalize competing alliances, blocs describe its leadership, its adherents, and the complex it created as being morally, psychologically, biologically, and intellectually superior (Boyer 1983; FitzSimmons 1987; Gilbert 1988; Hadjimichalis 1987; Mudimbe 1988; Said 1979; Soja 1989; Williams 1973). According to Antonio Gramsci, "when one succeeds in introducing a new morality in conformity with a new conception of the world, one finishes by introducing the conception as well" (quoted in Forgacs 1988: 192).

2. "Plant," the shortened version of the term "plantation," was later used instead of "shop" to describe the increasingly hierarchical production of goods within a single facility.

areas identified by plantation-based colonization and cash crop production for the world market, on the other. In the latter, enslaved Africans became a nonwage proletariat while much of the rest of the country was engaged in subsistence production. In the South, they toiled within the distinct boundaries of a settlement institution with all the characteristics of a company town, a prison, and a small state.

Before the Civil War, plantation-based cotton production in the South served as the foundation of the British industrial revolution, and after the war it served the same role for the American industrial revolution. Despite these and more recent transformations, and despite being declared dead and an anachronism on numerous occasions, the Delta plantation bloc has been able to preserve its dominant position in the region. Its agility, and its ability to persist through modernism and Fordism, can be explained only if we conceive of it as a highly coordinated regional ethnoclass alliance that is actively engaged in the monopolization of resources, power, historical explanation, and social action.

The plantation classificatory grid has at its center the planter, the heroic master of a "natural" ethnic, class, gender, and environmental hierarchy. African Americans in general, and African American women in particular, are at the bottom of this Platonic order. The guarantee of absolute autonomy of the planter over labor resulted in the emergence of a state development tradition that was minimalist in terms of social progress and interventionist regarding the organization of production and the regulation of ethnic, labor, and gender relations.

The New South Tradition

The New South tradition of social explanation and development practice emerged out of the dominant bloc in the predominantly white rural areas on the periphery of the plantation region. After the Civil War this region was increasingly integrated into the sphere of northern capital by the construction of a northern-oriented commercial and rail system that connected emerging distribution centers and mill towns. These new centers grew at the expense of the older urban centers organized around the shipment of people, cotton, and other commodities by sea. The new rail network sped the flow of cotton and other raw materials north and manufactured products south.

By the early nineteenth century the ongoing crisis in southern agriculture led many rural leaders to adopt subsidy-laced community preservation programs designed to attract northern-based manufacturing plants. This strategy created an even stronger alliance between northern capital and the South's banking, commercial, educational, legal, press, utility, and political leadership. In this bargain, the New South bloc assumed responsibility for preserving the region's "competitive advantage": the availability of cheap and easily exploited resources and the preservation of a nonunionized, low-wage, easily exploitable labor force (Cobb 1984; Grantham 1979).

Many of these communities are now facing bankruptcy even though they have benefited from a half century of industrial development and industrial redlining that typically excluded African American workers and predominantly African American regions. The seemingly endless rounds of rural plant closures since the early 1980s, combined with a crisis in small- and medium-size farming, pushed New South rural communities, their leaders, and their alliances into a state of perpetual turmoil. Unable to recruit new industries that now prefer international locations, representatives of this multiclass bloc first looked toward an eroding federal government for relief. In desperation, they now look toward eliminating any program, regulation, institution, or party that interferes with a state's right to cannibalize ethnic, labor, youth, senior citizen, gender, and environmental protections (Beaulieu 1988; MDC, Inc. 1986; Rosenfeld, Bergman, and Rubin 1989).

African American Affirmation: The Blues Epistemology

As defined here, the third tradition of southern political-economic explanation is centered on resistance to plantation monopoly and on African American social, economic, and cultural advancement. The resistance to the plantation regime and attempts to preserve and create a community-centered social order finds expression among several regional groups. It emerged first from the Native American communities that experienced both genocide and exile as the plantation complex moved south and west. It also arose among several of the manifestations of Populism in the predominantly white communities. And it is clearly one of the central organizing principles of the new African American communities that were trapped inside the boundaries of the expanding plantation complex.

Although often represented by the other blocs as culturally, economically, morally, and intellectually immature or ruined, African Americans in the rural South actively constructed a system of explanation that continues to inform daily life, social institutions, and movements. This central tradition is referred to here as the Blues epistemology.

The Blues as a form of social explanation finds its origins in the processes of African American cultural construction within and resistance to the antebellum plantation regime. This tradition was crystallized during the establishment of Reconstruction governments throughout the South and their violent overthrow. During the Mississippi elections of 1872 African American voters were met with cannon fire while militias roamed the countryside eliminating their organizations and leaders. This model for "restoration" was then implemented throughout the South. After two hundred years of censorship and ten short years of open communication, the resurrected plantation bloc thoroughly demonized all autonomous forms of African American thought and action for another century. The Blues became the channel through which the Reconstruction generation of African Americans grasped reality in the midst of disbelief, critiqued the plantation regime, and organized against it. According to Willie Dixon, the late Delta-born Blues musician and cultural leader, "had it not been for the blues, the black man wouldn't have been able to survive through all the humiliations and all the various things going on in America. . . . [H]e had nothing to fight with but the blues. . . . [T]he blues is the facts of life" (1992: 47).

The Mississippi Delta is the home of the Blues tradition in music, popular culture, and social explanation. It is therefore fitting that this regional ontology and epistemology be used to interpret the continuous crisis in the Delta and African American attempts to create a new reality that places economic, social, and cultural justice at its center. Inherent in much of the Blues is the self-critical author speaking for a self-critical audience.

The Blues instilled pride in a people facing daily denigration, and it channeled folk wisdom, descriptions of life and labor, travelogues, medicinal and spiritual practices, and critiques of friends, relatives, mates, bosses, sheriffs, planters, and the plantation regime. The men and women who performed the Blues served as sociologists, reporters, counselors, advocates, preservers of language and customs, healers, and much more. Ralph Ellison observed that the Blues operated as a self-referential system of social explanation, as an epistemology: "Bessie Smith might have been a 'Blues Queen' to the society at large, but within the tighter Negro community where the blues were a total way of life, and major expression of an attitude toward life, she was a priestess, a celebrant who affirmed the values of the group and man's ability to deal with chaos" (1964: 78).

The Blues epistemology as a theory of African American aesthetics was formally developed beginning in the 1920s and 1930s by Richard Wright, Zora Neal Hurston, Sterling Brown, Margaret Walker, Langston Hughes, Romare Bearden, and other African American intellectuals actively engaged in studies of daily life. This new epistemology proceeded from the assumption that the indigenously developed folk culture, its orature, its ethics, its tradition of social explanation, and its prescriptions for social action were the basic representational grid of working-class African American consciousness (Baker 1984; Barlow 1989; Ellison 1989; Flynn 1986; Harrison 1988).

Writing from exile in Paris in 1959, Wright argued that the Blues became a global phenomenon because they spoke to the alienated everywhere in a manner combining materialism and faith:

> Their descendants, freed and cast upon their own in an alien culture, cre-
> ated the blues, a form of exuberantly melancholy folk song that circled the
> globe. In Buenos Aires, Stockholm, Copenhagen, London, Berlin, Paris,
> Rome, in fact, in every large city on earth . . . the orgiastic wail of the blues,
> and their strident offspring, jazz, can be heard. Yet the most astonishing
> aspect of the blues is that, though replete with a sense of defeat and down-
> heartedness, they are not intrinsically pessimistic; their burden of woe and
> melancholy is dialectically redeemed through sheer force of sensuality, into
> an almost exultant affirmation of life, of love, of sex, of movement, of hope.
> No matter how repressive was the American environment, the Negro never
> lost faith in or doubted his deeply endemic capacity to live. All blues are a
> lusty, lyrical realism charged with taut sensibility. (1990: xiii, xv)

The recognition of the Blues as an aesthetic epistemology also informed
the Black Arts movement of the 1960s and 1970s. One of its key figures,
Larry Neal, remarked on this phenomenon in an essay entitled "The Blues
Ethos": "The blues, with all of their contradictions, represent, for better or
for worse, the essential vector of Afro-American sensibility and identity. . . .
They are, therefore, lyrical responses to the facts of life. The essential motive behind the best blues song is the acquisition of insight, wisdom" (1989:
107–108).
     More recently, the critic Richard Powell has argued that the Blues and
Blues-derived musical forms are the aesthetic foundations of African American art and life throughout the nation:

> The term "blues" is an appropriate designation for this idea because of its
> association with one of the most identifiable black American traditions that
> we know. Perhaps more than any other designation, the idea of a blues aes-
> thetic situates the discourse squarely on: 1) art produced in our time; 2)
> creative expression that emanates from artists who are emphatic with Afro-
> American issues and ideals; 3) work that identifies with grassroots, popular,
> and/or mass black American culture; 4) art that has an affinity with Afro-
> U.S. derived music and/or rhythms; and artists and/or statements whose
> raison d'etre is humanistic. (1989: 21–23)

According to the African American folk critic Stephen Henderson, "the
Blues continues as its own reference point, speaking the truth to the people in the language of the people" (1983: 11). Like other working-class,
peasant, regional, and other censored representational systems, it has been
denigrated by hegemonic institutional structures and by African American
scholars, artists, professionals, entrepreneurs, and political figures hoping

to put some distance between them and their demonized working class.

The Blues epistemology is socially embedded, necessary, and reflective. It is a self-referential explanatory tradition among working-class African Americans in which development debates occur. It directly challenges those social science epistemologies that investigate African American communities by relying on theories of deviance and pathology. These approaches beg the question of indigenousness and the construction of new ethnic groups and of new ethnic-, class-, and region-based visions of development in the "New World." When questions about normalcy are left unaddressed, views on deviancy can only be cut from the whole cloth of myth; collective pathology then better denotes the observer than the observed (Taussig 1980).

The question remains, how can we bridge the gap between the Blues as a widely recognized aesthetic tradition and as a theory of social, economic, and cultural development? To answer this question, a new form of critical regional studies is required. This question was first fully broached by the Mississippi-born author Richard Wright and others of the Chicago Renaissance in 1937. Wright developed the Blues as an epistemology for social research as part of his studies on African American daily life. His novels, literary criticism, and urban and rural community studies all proceeded from the position that orature, especially music, was a central feature of African American folk-based social theory. My work attempts to extend his method into the field of regional studies by integrating five related discourses.

The first discourse consists of a theory of social change and a method of periodization based on a relational concept of regional construction, mobilization, reproduction, crisis, and historical blocs. The second centers on identification and analysis of the representational traditions of African Americans found in the social sciences, public policy, the humanities, and popular culture. The third identifies the material basis of this tradition in the plantation political economy. The fourth is structured by African American development theories and related forms of explanation and social practices. The last rests on an archaeological approach to the reinterpretation of literature, orature, social policies, and social movements.

In my forthcoming book, *Development Arrested,* these components are examined individually and then are used collectively to review development theory and practice in the Mississippi Delta. This examination is important for current debates on African American poverty and demonization for several reasons. First, it actively attempts to dispel the notion of poverty as a natural phenomenon; poverty is a consciously and violently enforced societal practice. Second, within the debates on African American poverty, African American theories of development are portrayed as being either

unimportant or nonexistent, even though a very intense development debate has been raging within this community from the beginning of enslave-
ment to the present. This raises the question of the division between recognized and privileged discourses, on the one hand, and denigrated,
marginalized, and censored voices and traditions, on the other. As a working-class epistemology, the thrust of the Blues tradition centers on collective emiseration, collective empowerment, redistribution, and equality.
This is perhaps the reason why Blues and its jazz, rock, soul, and rap deriva-
tions have struck such a popular chord and operate as one of the preeminent globally organized discourses.

The traditions of regional culture and social explanation possessed and
made use of by each bloc must also be understood in terms of how they
produce, reproduce, or contest daily practices, public policies, and movements (Blee and Billings 1986; Boyer 1983; Foglesong 1986). Therefore,
regional study becomes the story of how one bloc and its allies attempt
to restructure the political economy through social mobilization and the
establishment of institutions for the reproduction of these new relationships. It is also, however, the story of how seemingly marginalized regional
blocs continue to press their development agenda in daily life, cultural
work, and institutional development and through both unofficial theories
of development and countermobilizations. The story of the LMDDC reveals these historic tensions at work. Before we turn to the LMDDC itself,
however, we need to outline the roots of the regional crisis that led to its
creation. These roots lie within the long and tortured history of continued
planter bloc movements to preserve and expand their monopoly and in
the sustained and monumental countermobilizations of African Americans to preserve community and expand social and economic justice.

THE DELTA GREEN REVOLUTION AND THE ROOTS
OF THE NEW REGIONAL CRISIS

The post–World War II interregional social contract was partially founded
on the basis of two economic processes that transformed southern agriculture: appropriation and substitution. First, technical innovations such as
tractors and chemical fertilizers undermined segments of the agricultural
production process by transforming discrete elements into industrial activities that were then reincorporated into the production process as com-
modified inputs. The second process entailed the centralization and regulation of production based on the elimination of rural activities and
products and their replacement by chemical, synthetic, and other fabricated products. The intensification of production combined with massive
expulsion of African Americans from the Delta led to what Jack Temple

Kirby and others argue was the clearest example of a state-sponsored Green Revolution occurring in the United States (Kirby 1987: 338; Mann 1990).

The Green Revolution had two results: the ruination of African American communities and individual lives, and the emergence of a new production complex centered on neoplantations. The centuries-old push for ethnic, political, and economic democracy in the South which reemerged under the banner of civil rights in the 1950s was effectively hollowed by this revolution, typically summarized as "mechanization." According to Gavin Wright (1986), ethnic relations were not transformed by the civil rights revolution, but by the "pre-revolution in the countryside," between 1930 and 1960, which reorganized production and reduced both the workforce and the control of planters over the political and economic life of the region.

The culmination of what several southern historians are now calling a "rural enclosure movement" displaced several million African Americans and destroyed their homes, social networks, institutions, livelihood, and several centuries of agricultural and environmental knowledge and skills. Enclosure came through several stages, beginning with the New Deal Agricultural Adjustment Administration cotton acreage reduction programs after 1933. Between 1933 and 1955 approximately two-thirds of the African American workforce in the Delta were evicted from their plantation homes through acreage reduction and expanded use of tractors. The rural farm population in ten Mississippi Delta counties fell by 19 percent between 1940 and 1950, from 316,000 to 257,000, and by 54 percent between 1950 and 1960, from 257,000 to 119,000. During the next decade the remaining population was evicted (Day 1967: 442–443).

Labor shortages, labor strife, civil rights mobilizations, and the specters of desegregation and voting led the plantation bloc to eliminate 95 percent of the sharecropping families and seasonally employed workers by the mid-1960s. Writing in 1967, Michael Piore made the following observation:

> Suddenly, in the space of two years, the Negro part of the economy has been eliminated. In the Spring of 1960, seasonal employment in the Mississippi Delta totaled 30,510; in the spring of 1965, it was 32,328. Last year spring seasonal employment was cut almost in half, from 32,328 to 16,571. This spring it fell by over half again to 7,225. . . . Incomes of Negroes in the Delta have always been among the lowest in the nation, but today, numbers of families have no income at all. What was once malnutrition and accumulated diseases has become virtual starvation. Even in the summer months, many families were begging from door to door. . . . The beginnings of the agricultural displacement follow upon Civil Rights Summer of 1964 and coincide with the Voting Rights Act [1965] and the shift in tactics of the white community from outright violence to reliance upon economic retaliation. . . .

> Since the agricultural displacements are now probably irreversible, the issue
> of their cause is largely academic. (1968: 366–368)

As described by the geographer Merle Prunty in the mid-1950s, the
sharecropping plantation was transformed into the mechanized neoplantation. Instead of houses being scattered across the landscape, the cabins
were razed or bulldozed and all that was visible was row upon row of crops
stretching from one end of the property to the other. The only worker
housing remaining were the homes of the tractor drivers on the very edge
of the fields. The social and physical landscape had been redesigned to
meet the requirements of a production system restructured and integrated
with the Fordist mass production manufacturing and chemical sectors
(Prunty 1962).

Consequently, proceeding from a populist and class-based analysis, a
growing number of southern development historians have rejected the
view that the New Deal was progressive. In a 1973 statement made to the
First National Conference on Land Reform, Donald Grubbs made the following observation: "The new deal was seldom progressive and certainly
not radical; it strengthened both the traditional incentives and traditional
institutions. . . . Eventually millions drifted out of the South altogether,
probably the largest government-impelled movement in all our history . . .
[and] the course of our history was wrenched to the right" (1973: 2).

In the preface of his 1971 work on the Southern Tenant Farmers Union,
Cry from the Cotton, Grubbs explained the social implications of New Deal
policies: "Through the Agricultural Adjustment Administration, Franklin
Roosevelt gave southern planters the means and the incentives to substi-
tute machines and unemployed casual labor for their tenants. . . . [Y]ester-
day through ignorance and greed, the propertied drove the propertyless
off the land; tomorrow, Harlem and Watts and the South Side will be burn-
ing" (xii).

In a 1987 book review, "The Southern Enclosure Movement," Numan
Bartley poses the question of why the depression era New Deal rural transformation is receiving so much scholarly attention after forty years of neglect. He attributes the emergence of this new era of explanation to the
intellectual movement away from the "modernization as progress paradigm" in southern historiography:

> The academic tendency to ignore the tribulations associated with the col-
> lapse of traditional rural society was probably most directly the result of pre-
> vailing interpretations of southern history. . . . Plantations continued to exist
> and southern agriculture suffered from a variety of social and economic ail-
> ments, but according to accepted interpretive theory, a new capitalist class
> along with the remnants of the old order who "found ways of merging with
> the new middle class through the avenue of supply merchant" had trans-

formed the ideology of the region's rural establishment. Informed observers impatiently awaited the completion of the modernization process in the rural South. Thus, mechanization of southern agriculture and the displacement of the rural population marked the culmination of long developing trends. (1987: 440–441).

Major economic historians such as James Fite, in his 1984 work *Cotton Fields No More,* and Gavin Wright, in his 1986 work *Old South, New South,* continued to put forward a linear evolution argument that the federally funded cotton enclosure movement and mechanization were the progressive underpinnings of a New South in which the plantation bloc and racial discrimination were rapidly receding. This argument was countered by the 1985 work of Pete Daniels, *Breaking the Land,* and by Jack Temple Kirby's 1987 work, *Rural Worlds Lost,* both of which dispute the claim that African American expulsion was necessary and beneficial. Kirby argues that the federally subsidized enclosure, mechanization, depopulation, and Green Revolution in the Black Belt cotton economy led to the creation of federally subsidized neoplantations.

A recent contribution to the revision of post–World War II southern development history was James C. Cobb's 1992 work on the Mississippi Delta, *The Most Southern Place on Earth.* It follows in the tradition of neoplantation critique developed by Grubbs, Daniels, and Kirby. Focusing on the alliance between the Delta planters and the federal government from the New Deal through the civil rights movement, Cobb argues that the displacement of more than 100,000 African Americans and the current crisis in the region are both attributable to the replacement of planter paternalism with federal paternalism:

> Those who explained the failure of blacks in the Delta and elsewhere in the southern plantation belt to make more progress during the civil rights era often cited the enduring influence of paternalism, referring to the historic dependence of black tenants on their white landlords. . . . In reality, however, many of the human and material extremes that were the keys to the Delta's identity either as the "South's south" or "America's Ethiopia" were shaped not by its isolation but by pervasive global and national influences and consistent interaction with a federal government whose policies often confirmed the Delta's inequities and reinforced its anachronistic social and political order as well. (1992: 253, 333)

The above studies represent a significant theoretical advancement, yet they tend to examine regional transformation primarily as an outcome of federal policy while deemphasizing the role of conscious and coordinated regional mobilizations in designing and shaping the federal response. For example, none of the above studies contains an examination of the organization of planters known as the Delta Council that was formed in 1933 by the most important planters, bankers, merchants, academics, and industrialists in the Mississippi Delta. Absent from many of the works cited is a discussion of how the Delta Council spawned the National Cotton Council. Dedicated to accelerated mechanization, Green Revolution technologies, expanded federal subsidies, and strict labor control and displacement, this body became one of the Sunbelt's most powerful economic blocs and a major actor in the global agricultural complex of international research, financial, chemical, machinery, and commodity institutions (Cash and Lewis 1986; Russell 1980).

The Delta Council's de facto administration of local, county, state, and federal agencies in the region has also received scant attention. Similarly, little mention is made of how the Citizens' Council emerged from the Delta Council's membership in 1954 to resist school desegregation, expanded throughout the South and the Southwest, and then mobilized to restructure the national two-party political order. Also unaddressed was the role of this organization in the creation of the Sovereignty Commission, a Mississippi intelligence agency designed to disrupt both the civil rights movement and community development initiatives (Johnston 1990; McMillen 1971).

The rapid mechanical, chemical, biological, and genetic agricultural and social transformation that occurred in the region between 1932 and 1965 thoroughly destroyed and reordered African American community life. Homelessness, hunger, ill health, pesticide poisoning, and violence intensified in the Delta to a degree not found in other predominantly African American areas of the South. The African American countermobilizations were also monumental. First, evictions transformed the southern rural crisis into a nonsouthern urban crisis that continues to have significant ramifications. Second, the desegregation and voting movements of the 1950s and 1960s, and the attacks against them, increasingly drew a reluctant federal government into an era of active and continuous intervention.

By 1962 the Mississippi chapters of the Congress of Racial Equality (CORE), the National Association for the Advancement of Colored People (NAACP), the Southern Christian Leadership Conference, and the Student Nonviolent Coordinating Committee formed the Council of Federated Organizations (COFO) to push for voter registration. With the assistance of COFO, the Mississippi Freedom Democratic Party (MFDP) was formed in the Delta in 1964 to historically challenge the legality of the segregated practices of the national Democratic party. Out of this mobilization emerged Fannie Lou Hamer and many other Delta residents who moved the civil rights agenda closer to the historic African American rural reform agenda and its focus on resource redistribution, representative democracy, active participation in institutional decision making, and human and cultural rights. After what he believed was a revelation in the Delta town of Marks, Dr. Martin Luther King, Jr., adopted this rural reform agenda, allied himself with the Delta's Poor People's Committees formed in 1967, and dedicated himself exclusively to leading the National Poor People's March on Washington (Abernathy 1990; Morris 1984).

Throughout the 1970s and 1980s the African American communities of the Delta remained politically mobilized, yet the specifically regional economic crises associated with enclosure, mechanization, and a Green Revolution had been institutionalized, and continue to devastate their daily lives. In the 1990s an increasing number of rural families and communities are either barely surviving or have expired. Additionally, several recent studies have predicted the "extinction" of black farmers in the next fifteen years.

Since the early 1980s endless rounds of plant closures and farm foreclosures, combined with Republican and African American mobilizations, have withered the New South bloc's legitimacy and its ability to act as the linchpin of regional stability. The response of this bloc to global restructuring has been to accelerate the deregulation and subsidization of manufacturing and agriculture and the gutting of an already minimal social service infrastructure, on the one hand, and the attainment of more federal subsidies to continue this process, on the other. Consequently, the six-decade-old principal development strategy, the recruitment of manufacturing plants, had spawned a new era of fiscal cannibalism as impoverished rural towns and counties competed with each other by reducing local services in order to provide greater relocation and retention incentives to a declining number of interested firms.

On another front, collapsing social services and expanded chemical production have created a health crisis of enormous proportions. The Louisiana legislator Avery Alexander sarcastically asked the following question during an LMDDC hearing: "Should we celebrate or mourn the fact that among African American women, near St. James [parish], . . . the vaginal cancers are 36 times the national average. . . . [H]ere in Louisiana . . . we have found the job promises empty and the risk of poisoning inevitable" (LMDDC 1990c).

According to Earl Moore, a farmworker counselor, progress, the rhetoric of progress, and the effectiveness of programs designed to promote progress have all come to an end: "We said back in the 1960s when we started OEO that we wanted to teach people how to fish and that if we gave them fish they'd be back every day. So we came up with JTPA or CETA. Ladies and gentlemen, folks, the pond is dry. . . . [W]e are teaching people to fish in a pond that does not have fish" (LMDDC 1990a).

THE LOWER MISSISSIPPI DELTA DEVELOPMENT COMMISSION

Rather than view the LMDDC as good or bad, a success or a failure, it is more valuable to conceptualize it as an intersection where competing historic blocs and their development traditions meet, or refuse to meet, to negotiate the future of the region. It provides a window through which one can critically observe the evolution of development debates, practices, and movements in one specific place.

On one level, the LMDDC was the attempt of a dominant regional bloc confronted by global competition and crisis to consciously restructure their control over capital, labor, ethnic, cultural, and political relations. In a 1989 letter to President George Bush, Governor Bill Clinton of Arkansas, the commission chair, argued for a program of regional convergence and integration that would benefit residents of both the Delta and the nation: "Our goal is ambitious but *simple—to make the Delta and its people a full partner in America's future.* . . . By any objective economic, educational and social measurement, the 8.3 million people in the Delta region are the least prepared to participate in and to contribute to the nation's effort to succeed in the world economy" (LMDDC 1989).

The presence of massive and persistent poverty was constantly used by LMDDC advocates to gain federal and regional funding and other forms of support. Most of the officials testifying in support of the commission provided evidence of rural and regional exhaustion. Typically, the region's deepening crisis was explained as a product of global restructuring without any reference to the internal institutional structures of ethnic, class, and gender inequality. As Buddy Roemer, then Louisiana governor and LMDDC commissioner, warned at the outset, "the commission's work is not to criticize the past" (*Daily Town Talk,* January 24, 1990). Instead the LMDDC would focus on how to profitably restructure the historic entente between the planters and the New South modernization school. Additionally, according to then Governor Clinton, another high priority of the LMDDC was the restoration of interregional and international competitiveness: "We want to develop the Mississippi River from Memphis to New Orleans along the same lines as the Rhine River in Germany. . . . That is, we want to have industry and agriculture side by side. . . . [W]e want to diversify agriculture and take advantage of the fact that out west, in California, there will be more and more pressure on water, more and more pressure on land, which will open vast new markets for vegetable and fruit production in this part of the country" (*White River Journal,* March 16, 1990).

This New South vision of development ran headlong into challenges from both the planation bloc and the African American community. After emerging as a formal bill from the offices of Arkansas's U.S. Senator Dale

Bumpers, hearings were held on the creation of the LMDDC during the summer of 1988.

The boundaries and appointments of the LMDDC were immediately attacked by African American leaders. With the stroke of a pen, the creators of the commission had reduced the African American proportion of the region's population from 40 percent to 20 percent. Although later redrawn, the proposed boundaries were denounced for excluding the major cities that are both black population and political centers in their respective states: Baton Rouge and New Orleans, Louisiana; Jackson, Mississippi; Little Rock, Arkansas; and Memphis, Tennessee.

Moreover, while African Americans and women comprise 40 percent and 50 percent of the region's population, respectively, only white males were appointed as commissioners: the governors of Arkansas, Louisiana, and Mississippi appointed themselves; the governors of Illinois, Kentucky, and Missouri appointed cabinet officers; and the governor of Tennessee appointed a former congressman with strong ties to the neoplantation bloc. President Ronald Reagan appointed a conservative lawyer from St. Louis and, to heighten antagonism, the Mississippi Delta's former Republican congressman, Webb Franklin. Just several months earlier Franklin had been defeated by the African American majority after several exceedingly bitter campaigns.

Calls for a boycott of the LMDDC soon followed and the appointment of Governor Clinton as chairperson was immediately accompanied by calls for his removal. In his defense, Clinton stated that while the lack of blacks was "terrible," legitimacy was not the final consideration: "If we all got off tomorrow and appointed blacks . . . would the commission be more effective, or would it be less effective, but more credible with the black community? I mean it's a dilemma" (*Memphis Commercial Appeal*, January 11, 1989).

Although an African American was appointed the executive director, a significant section of this community viewed the LMDDC as another disempowering mobilization by the dominant regional leadership which was to be boycotted from beginning to end. Rev. Ellihue Gaylord, the president of the Phillips County, Arkansas, NAACP, explained the reasoning behind this action: "By participating in a discredited process, you lend it credibility or some hint of credibility. These people are going to fall on their face because you can't have credibility with nine white people on a commission. They have no blacks, no women and one token hanging from nine strings" (*Memphis Commercial Appeal*, February 21, 1989).

Those African Americans who did testify before the LMDDC advised the commissioners to focus on reforming the existing structures of exclusion before pressing forward with a new modernization program. This point was clearly made by Rev. Carl Brown of Marks, Mississippi: "And so you're about to approach Congress . . . and I'm wondering how effective will that report be. . . . [I]t needs to be understood that blacks are still not part of this process. . . . [I]n the final analysis, when this report is in, the same agenda will proceed and I hope not because we've been the victims of studies for a long time. You've done studied us to death!" (LMDDC 1990b).

During the same hearing in Mississippi, a Reverend Gwynn argued that exclusionary practices in the region were numerous, personal, and generational and that any proposed development program must explicitly confront them. In the same vein, Dr. Ronald Meyers, a physician who practices in Belzoni and Tchula, Mississippi, explained how even blacks who represented powerful institutions in the African American community were shunned and silenced when it came to economic development planning: "I mean here you've got an industrial development foundation who has applied, applies, for grants, federal grants, state money to improve the community and they won't meet. They will not meet . . . with what they call political and religious groups [African American political, community, and religious leaders]. And these are the same people that the money is being channeled through for community development, but the black community is not even allowed to talk to them" (LMDDC 1990b).

For some of the economic development officials there was nothing to talk about. According to the director of the Arkansas Industrial Development Commission, Pat Harrington, black workers had nothing to aspire to: "The workforce is not culturally adapted to industrial work. They don't have the history, a background, to work in factories. . . . They do what they have always done well" (LMDDC 1990b).

However, in his testimony before the commission, a Louisiana planter, Carl Bater, suggested several other ways to resolve African American unemployment: "Think about using these people that are idle to develop an . . . efficient energy system. . . . I'm tired of these prisoners sitting on their behinds and doing nothing; they should be creating their own power by either pumping an air tank with pressure or elevating water to turn a wheel. . . . Now that'll give them something to do and it'll be fruitful" (LMDDC 1990c).

When one of the region's major planters was asked to render his vision of the region's future, he took the opportunity to advocate a policy of accelerated displacement: "Ten years down the pike, I see beautiful fields of cotton and soybeans, the growth of industry, and a program to encourage out-migration, which will solve a lot of problems" (Porter 1992: 307).

Conflicts over the exclusion of ideas also emerged within the LMDDC. African American staffers inserted two paragraphs in the interim report which promised an investigation of issues high on their community's agenda:

Strained race relations have historically compounded the problems associated with poverty in the Delta. The Delta's economic, social and cultural structure of life has often reinforced tensions between ethnic groups and worsened the economic subjugation of African Americans. This reality has stood in the way of economic development efforts. The changes brought on by the civil rights movement and recent reforms in educational policies and spending have helped to make up for decades of low investments in human development. However, much work remains if the region is to overcome the legacy of the past.

Industrial redlining, a practice by which industries avoid locating in certain areas, has been widely perceived as an impediment to recruitment efforts in the Delta.... At the Commission's meeting, Clarence Wright ... requested that the Commission address the impact of industrial redlining in those instances in which industries avoid locating in areas where the African American population is 30 percent or higher. The extent to which this policy has adversely affected the Delta is a concern which has subsequently been raised by other citizens. In preparation for its final report, the Commission plans to conduct research to assess the incidence and impact of industrial redlining on economic development efforts in the Delta. (LMDDC 1989: Appendix A)

These two subjects were not what the commissioners wanted to address, and the idea of studying industrial redlining was quickly abandoned after outraged white commissioners and congressmen denounced this breach in the development code of silence. In many ways the LMDDC was doomed from this point forward because it appeared that even handpicked African Americans would raise the most sensitive of subjects. For those viewing the region from an African American perspective, these issues meant the difference between leaving and staying, living or dying, in the region. However, those operating from the dominant plantation bloc tradition objected to any serious discussion of how to address poverty and ethnic relations outside a discussion of what they saw as the region's principal problem, the crisis affecting agriculture. Another bloc, operating within the New South modernization school's focus on the future and industrial recruitment, objected to any full explorations of the past as too divisive.

To appease the latter two perspectives, the LMDDC embarked on a road that limited debate on what was and what will be. Instead it focused on a future, a federally subsidized future, in which the historic structures of regional inequality are neither mentioned nor addressed. Therefore, a comprehensive evaluation of the LMDDC must examine the historical origins and current manifestations of planter bloc hegemony, the appeasement of it, resistance to it, and the roads still open to regional development based on existing traditions of economic democracy and social justice. Such a study has implications for other regions. First, the problems that the LMDDC presented for the region's African American community are emblematic of those faced by similar communities in the rural South. Second, the LMDDC is part of a larger mobilization faced by communities during this period of crisis and restructuring. Commissions, summits, compacts, and other efforts to "reinvent" government are part of an attempt by numerous regional blocs to restructure alliances, relations, and communities. However, the mounting restrictions on participation and alternative visions of development bode ill for the future.

CONCLUSION

The plantation-based leadership of the region felt that it was being battered by plant closures, threatened reductions in agricultural subsidies, expanding environmental regulation, and urban and rural African American communities still actively pressing for still denied economic opportunities, public services, participatory governance, and labor, voting, and human rights. The presence of several simultaneous crises meant that, above all else, the purpose of the LMDDC was to identify mechanisms for protecting, preserving, and restructuring a dominant regional bloc, its central institutions, its hierarchy of supporting cultural symbols, and other structures of inequality.

Therefore, it is not surprising that the voices of ethnic and working-class communities trapped in the structures of inequality created by previous mobilizations were marginalized and silenced during the eighteen-month life of the commission. What was surprising was the plantation bloc's continued ability to silence those New South leaders who aspired to restructure the region while slowing the deepening social polarization. The recent designation of the northern part of the Mississippi Delta as an Empowerment Zone by the Clinton administration represents a partial resolution of this particular conflict; the Delta Council was named as the lead development agency.

This research grew out of my long-standing interest in African American community development issues, labor studies, and political economy. On examining these fields, it became obvious that the new wave of restructuring has been accompanied yet again by the marginalization of the African American development voice. The social science portrayals of African Americans as inarticulate statistics mask their rich traditions of development discourse and policy. The planning literature has also, for the most part, avoided questions of local voices and knowledge in favor of the modernization-as-progress paradigm and other universal models of growth.

To construct societies based on democratic participation and social and economic justice, a new form of planning has to occur during this period of transformation. Planning at the scale of historically constructed regions allows the creation of new social relations based on economic integration, environmental sustainability, respect for human rights, and cultural democracy. The origins for this new form of regional development planning are to be found within the region itself among the scattered, misplaced, and often forgotten movements, projects, and agendas of African American and other marginalized communities. Generation after generation, ethnic and class alliances arose in the region to expand democracy while eliminating inequality—only to be ignored, dismissed, and defeated. However, even in defeat these movements transformed the policies of the plantation bloc and informed daily life, community building activities, and subsequent movements. Within the oral and written record of these arrested agendas and movements rests the regionally indigenous knowledge on which to construct new relationships and new regional structures of equality.

Finally, I hope this study will spark a renewed interest among concerned individuals in the horrific implications of social collapse in the heavily African American counties and parishes of the rural South.

REFERENCES

Abernathy, Ralph David. 1990. *And the Walls Came Tumbling Down: An Autobiography.* New York: Harper Perennial.

Anderson, Benedict. 1983. *Imagined Communities: Reflections on the Origins and Spread of Nationalism.* London: Verso.

Baker, Houston. 1984. *Blues, Ideology, and Afro-American Literature: A Vernacular Theory.* Chicago: University of Chicago Press.

Barlow, William. 1989. *Looking Up at Down: The Emergence of Blues Culture.* Philadelphia: Temple University Press.

Bartley, Numan V. 1987. "The Southern Enclosure Movement." *Georgia Historical Quarterly* 71(3):438–450.

Beaulieu, Lionel, ed. 1988. *The Rural South in Crisis: Challenges for the Future.* Boulder: Westview Press.

Beckford, George. 1983. *Persistent Poverty: Underdevelopment in Plantation Economies of the Third World.* London: Zed Books.

Blee, Kathleen, and Dwight Billings. 1986. "Reconstructing Daily Life in the Past: A Hermeneutical Approach to Ethnographic Data." *Sociological Quarterly* 27(4).

Boyer, Christine. 1983. *Dreaming the Rational City: The Myth of American City Planning.* Cambridge, Mass.: MIT Press.

Cash, William M., and R. Daryl Lewis. 1986. *The Delta Council: Fifty Years of Service to the Mississippi Delta.* Stoneville, Miss.: Delta Council.

Cobb, James C. 1984. *Industrialization and Southern Society, 1877–1984.* Chicago: Dorsey Press.

———. 1992. *The Most Southern Place on Earth: The Mississippi Delta and the Roots of Regional Identity.* New York: Oxford University Press.

Daniels, Pete. 1985. *Breaking the Land: The Transformation of Cotton, Tobacco and Rice Cultures since 1880.* Urbana: University of Illinois Press.

Day, Richard H. 1967. "The Economics of Technological Change and the Demise of Sharecropping." *American Economic Review* 57(3):427–449.

Dixon, Willie. 1992. "A Tribute to Willie Dixon." *Living Blues* 103.

Ellison, Mary. 1989. *Extensions of the Blues.* New York: Riverrun Press.

Ellison, Ralph. 1964. *Shadow and Act.* New York: Random House.

Fite, Gilbert. 1984. *Cotton Fields No More: Southern Agriculture, 1865–1980.* Lexington: University of Kentucky Press.

FitzSimmons, Margaret. 1987. "The New Industrial Agriculture: The Regional Integration of Specialty Crop Production." *Economic Geography* 62(4):334–353.

Flynn, Julio. 1986. *The Bluesman: The Musical Heritage of Black Men and Women in the Americas.* London: Quartet Books.

Foglesong, Richard. 1986. *Planning the Capitalist City: The Colonial Era to the 1920s.* Princeton, N.J.: Princeton University Press.

Forgacs, David. 1988. *The Antonio Gramsci Reader: Selected Writings, 1916–1935.* New York: Schocken Books.

Gilbert, Anne. 1988. "The New Regional Geography in English and French Speaking Countries." *Progress in Human Geography* 12(2):209–228.

Grantham, Dewey. 1979. *The Regional Imagination: The South and Recent American History.* Nashville: Vanderbilt University Press.

Grubbs, Donald H. 1971. *Cry from the Cotton: The Southern Tenant Farmers' Union and the New Deal.* Chapel Hill: University of North Carolina Press.

———. 1973. "The Progressive Character of the New Deal." Paper presented at the First National Conference on Land Reform, San Francisco.

Hadjimichalis, Costis. 1987. *Uneven Development and Regionalism: State, Class, and Territory in Southern Europe.* London: Croom Helm.

Harrison, Daphne Duval. 1988. *Black Pearls: Blues Queens of the 1920s.* New Brunswick: Rutgers University Press.

Henderson, Stephen. 1983. "Blues Poetry and Poetry of the Blues Aesthetic." *Sagala* 3.

Johnston, Erle. 1990. *Mississippi's Defiant Years: 1953–1973.* Forest, Miss.: Lake Harbor.

Kirby, Jack Temple. 1987. *Rural Worlds Lost: The American South, 1920–1960.* Baton Rouge: Louisiana State University Press.

Lower Mississippi Delta Development Commission (LMDDC). 1989. *Body of the Nation: Interim Report of the LMDDC.* Memphis: LMDDC.

———. 1990a. *Arkansas Public Hearing, September 5, 1989.* Memphis: LMDDC.

———. 1990b. *Mississippi Public Hearing, November 28, 1989.* Memphis: LMDDC.

———. 1990c. *Louisiana Public Hearing, January 24, 1989.* Memphis: LMDDC.

MDC, Inc. 1986. *Shadows in the Sunbelt.* Chapel Hill: MDC, Inc.

Mann, Susan. 1990. *Agrarian Capitalism in Theory and Practice.* Chapel Hill: University of North Carolina Press.

McMillen, Neil. 1971. *The Citizens' Councils: Organized Resistance to the Second Reconstruction, 1954–1964.* Urbana: University of Illinois Press.

Morris, Aldon D. 1984. *The Origins of the Civil Rights Movement: Black Communities Organizing for Change.* New York: Free Press.

Mudimbe, V. Y. 1988. *The Invention of Africa: Gnosis, Philosophy, and the Order of Knowledge.* Bloomington: Indiana University Press.

Neal, Larry. 1989. *Visions of a Liberated Future: Black Arts Movement Writings.* New York: Thunder's Mouth Press.

Piore, Michael J. 1968. "Negro Workers in the Mississippi Delta: Problems of Displacement and Adjustment." *Industrial Relations Research Association Series.* Madison: Industrial Relations Research Association.

Porter, Judith. 1992. "What Works and What Doesn't: Perceptions of Economic Development among Delta Leaders." In *A Social and Economic Portrait of the Mississippi Delta,* ed. Arthur Cosby. Mississippi State: Social Science Research Center, Mississippi State University.

Powell, Richard. 1989. "The Blues Aesthetic: Black Culture and Modernism." In *The Blues Aesthetic: Black Culture and Modernism,* ed. Richard Powell. Washington, D.C.: Washington Project for the Arts.

Prunty, Merle C., Jr. 1962. "Deltapine: Field Laboratory for the Neoplantation." In *Festschrift: Clarence F. Jones,* ed. Merle C. Prunty, Jr. Studies in Geography, no. 6. Evanston, Ill: Northwestern University.

Robinson, Philip S. 1984. *The Plantation of Ulster: British Settlement in an Irish Landscape, 1600–70.* New York: St. Martin's Press.

Rosenfeld, Stuart, Edward Bergman, and Sarah Rubin. 1989. *After the Factories: Changing Employment Patterns in the South.* Research Triangle Park, N.C.: Southern Growth Policies Board.

Russell, Albert R. 1980. *The First Forty Years: The National Cotton Council, 1939–1979.* Memphis: National Cotton Council.

Said, Edward. 1979. *Orientalism.* New York: Vantage Books.

Soja, Edward. 1989. *Post-Modern Geographies: The Reassertion of Space in Critical Social Theory.* London: Verso.

Taussig, Michael. 1980. *The Devil and Commodity Fetishism.* Chapel Hill: University of North Carolina Press.

Thompson, Edgar. 1968. "The Plantation: The Physical Basis of Traditional Race Relations." In *Race Relations and the Race Problem,* ed. Edgar Thompson. Durham, N.C.: Duke University Press.

Williams, Raymond. 1973. *The Country and the City.* New York: Oxford University Press.

Woods, Clyde. 1993. "Development Arrested: The Delta Blues, the Delta Council, and the Lower Mississippi Delta Development Commission." Ph.D. dissertation, Urban Planning Program, University of California, Los Angeles. (Forthcoming, Verso 1997.)

Wright, Gavin. 1986. *Old South, New South: Revolution in the Southern Economy since the Civil War.* New York: Basic Books.

Wright, Richard. 1990. Preface. In *Blues Fell This Morning: Meaning in the Blues,* by Paul Oliver. Cambridge: Cambridge University Press.

FOUR

Indigenous Planning

Clans, Intertribal Confederations, and the History of the All Indian Pueblo Council

Theodore S. Jojola

INTRODUCTION

The history of Western civilization has become synonymous with urbanization and modernization. Much of the preindustrial impetus for modernization evolved from the desire to unify vast colonial holdings through economic interdependency and political integration. Tribal communities were largely ignored in this path toward Westernization. Instead their histories were subsumed as inconsequential; historiographers wrote them off as casualties of Western civilization. Tribal communities were dismissed as impediments to progress.

Yet in spite of the overwhelming odds faced by these tribes, our communities continue to survive. Many exist as semisovereign nations. The largest grouping among these are the 333 federally recognized American Indian tribes of the forty eight contiguous states. Another 246 tribal governments are in the state of Alaska. Together, we are characterized by our own styles of government, our own languages, our own cultures, and our own land and resource bases. We maintained these, not in isolation as many social scientists lead us to believe, but through our abilities to selectively interact with others and to adapt to outside change. Survival was accomplished through decisive action using indigenous planning models that were integrated into our own cultural patterns.

This chapter discusses only two aspects of these traditions: the role of the clans in community development and the role of consensus modeling among intertribal confederations. Together, these two indigenous traditions constitute what are considered to be community and regional planning traditions within the dominant mainstream society. Although the discussion focuses on only one cultural group, the Pueblo Indian nations of the geographic Southwest, there are variations of these same models throughout what is known as Native America.

THE CONTEXT

Planning as a tradition was not a concept imposed on indigenous peoples by Euro-Americans. Indigenous communities existed in myriad highly coordinated and planned towns and villages. As witnessed by great native civilizations, such as those of the Aztec and the Inca, indigenous peoples of the so-called New World established urban centers equal to any European centers of the same period. Unfortunately, these native empires were not resilient to European invasion, and their native denizens succumbed in the hundreds of thousands to both warfare and foreign diseases.

The invention of the image of America by romanticists of the nation-building era minimized the contributions of Native Americans. Instead the achievements of indigenous people were superseded by the populist revisions of the political and philosophical literature of Western civilization. Romantic images of the American wilderness after the decimation of native populations and a purposeful discourse of the state of the savage Indian after their communities had been uprooted by aggressive land campaigns abound throughout popular literature.

James Fenimore Cooper's *The Last of the Mohicans,* published in 1826, and Francis Parkman's *Conspiracy of Pontiac,* of 1851, were about the noble savages who refused to change. Of course, such beings never existed. The poetic and literate mind refused to acknowledge that Indians could successfully adapt and transform. Quite simply, the European colonizers made the land and the aboriginal peoples into an image that was consistent with their actions. The colonialist of the Americas glorified the devastation they wreaked on the natives. Doubtless, they were extolled for having brought "civilization" to the "wilderness" and "intelligence" to the "heathens."

The notion of civilization was sustained by a powerful myth. Christian Caucasians were holy, white, and civilized. Indians were idolatrous, dark, and savage. The Greeks had invented the term "barbarian" to apply to outsiders. By the time it had been translated to apply to the New World, it also meant morally inferior. Thus America was a virgin wilderness, inhabited by stupid and barbaric nonpeople called savages.

Such imagery has wrought more than a harmless stereotype on American Indians and their communities. By consigning them to a primitive status, historians and popular writers also refused to recognize that their communities also were occupied with such fundamental social principles as government, philosophy, and economics. Instead, in exchange for the appropriation of the fruits of the New World, European sovereigns simplemindedly bestowed their own values of civilization and Christianity. This was deemed just compensation for colonizing native people.

Such was the belief that nurtured Western scholarship. The gist of this misconception was embodied in attitudes of social scientists of the latter 1800s. In an essay written in 1876, "Montezuma's Dinner," Lewis Henry Morgan, the founding father of anthropology, denounced the idea that the Aztec and Inca empires were equal to those of European civilizations. This discussion was intended to refute the historian William H. Prescott, who thirty-three years earlier in his treatise *History of the Conquest of Mexico and History of the Conquest of Peru* (1843), concluded that the Aztecs and the Incas were higher-order civilizations.

The anthropological debate was about whether the Aztec ruler Montezuma behaved like a barbarian. In his essay Morgan reasserted the importance of the accounts of Spanish soldiers and chroniclers of the dinner given by Montezuma for the conquistador Hernán Cortés (hence, "Montezuma's Dinner"). Had Montezuma behaved in a manner that befitted European nobles?

Prescott, who died in 1859, was no longer around to champion the idea that the Aztec empire was civilized. This task, however, was doggedly assumed by another prominent historian of that era, H. H. Bancroft. In 1875 Bancroft had written a five-volume work, *Native Races of the Pacific States*. Beginning with "Montezuma's Dinner," Morgan renewed his scathing attack by denouncing Bancroft for bestowing "civilized" terminology on the primitive Aztecs. The misuse included Bancroft's reference to Aztec nobles as "kings" and, particularly, the labeling of the Aztec empire as a "nation."

Morgan used his essay to advance his own theory of the "Red Race" and ancient society. His approach was to divide social development into "ethical periods": the savagery (hunter) phase, the barbarian phase, and the civilized phase. Barbarism was exemplified by the lower barbarians (Iroquois), the middle barbarian (Zuni and Aztecs), and the upper barbarian (use of iron). Morgan further contended that the latter stage was never attained in the Americas. Rather, the Indian tribes had become "arrested" societies, due largely to the displacement of the ancient tribes because of Old World conquest and colonization.

It was Morgan's contention that the Aztecs—because they functioned at the middle barbarian stage—were incapable of politically organizing themselves at the regional level. To cite Morgan: "So long as we apply to their social organizations and domestic institutions of civilized society, we caricature the Indians and deceive ourselves. There was neither a political society, nor a state, nor any civilization in America when it was discovered; and excluding the Eskimos, but one race of Indians, the Red Race" (1876: 308).

As for other tribes of the Americas, they were held in even lower political esteem than the Aztecs. It was concluded that the term "tribe" was by definition nothing more than a designated unit, or clan, that was totally responsible to a single leader. Furthermore, leaders were not chosen because of intelligence but on account of their brute strength and cunning. In essence, Morgan's concepts were a simple extension of the notions embodied in the popular theory of the era, the Darwinian survival of the fittest. The basic tenet of that interpretation is that modern society could also trace itself to a primitive origin. Western civilization, as such, evolved from the hunter-gatherer tribe. The indigenous tribes of the New World were considered to be the remnants of the primitive links that had long ago devolved in Europe.

The political philosopher Friedrich Engels said of Morgan, "Anthropologists, even in England, now generally appreciate, or rather appropriate, Morgan's discoveries. But hardly one of them has the honesty to admit that it is Morgan that we owe this revolution in our ideas" (1972: 83). His sentiment reflected that of the majority of scholars, who believed that political states did not exist in aboriginal America and that tribal societies could not be differentiated by political jurisdictions. Such scholars inculcated the social sciences with the notion that the tribal societies of the Americas were not capable of creating and maintaining their own polities much less organizing and planning their own communities.

Mainstream scholarship in the United States, as exemplified in the later writings of the archeologist Edgar L. Hewett (1930), continued to advance the stance promulgated by Morgan, and this stance remained unchallenged until another anthropologist, Franz Boas (1932), developed the concept of cultural relativism. Boas argued that tribal societies were not associated as one "Red Race" but were composed of independent entities that evolved parallel to each other based on their own relative political, historical, and economic situations. Considered a minor theory in the United States, it was fostered by a few vocal cultural anthropologists such as Robert Redfield, Ruth Benedict, and Margaret Mead.

The most fruitful debate, however, continued outside the United States. More specifically, the debate became centered around identity issues associated with Mexican nationhood. The *indigenistas* embraced the concept that the Aztecs were a civilization and that the modern nation-state of Mexico was an amalgam of Indian and Spanish, owing, in fact, its political origins to the Aztec empire. The *hispanistas,* however, continued to contend that the only origins of civilization were those brought to the New World by the Iberians of Spain.

In spite of such debates, the role of tribal cultures in contributing to the process of nation-state building was summarily dismissed. Western scholars denounced the role that tribal societies played and reinvented a history that was consistent with a popular Eurocentric ideology. The development of a primitivistic classification scheme became the basis for a type of anthropological fascism. Historical revisionists gave an allegedly scientific basis for categorically eliminating the role of Native America in the process of nation-state development, and this was widely employed by policy makers to dismiss tribal leadership and their abilities to plan for themselves.

By affirming that primitive societies were incapable of political behavior, such founding principles as the Doctrine of Discovery became an indelible fixture in Indian treaty rights and in the evolution of paternalistic public policy toward the indigenous tribes in North America. First articulated in an 1823 Supreme Court decision by the Chief Justice of the United States, John Marshall, the Doctrine of Discovery was defined as a right claimed by the superior civilizations of Europe and assumed by the Americans. "But power, war, conquest, give rights, which, after possession, are conceded by the world" he concluded (*Johnson v. M'Intosh*).

President Theodore Roosevelt, in *The Winning of the West*, used the same ideology to justify the aggressions waged against the tribes: "Whether the whites won the land by treaty, by armed conquest or, as was actually the case, by a mixture of both, mattered comparatively little so long as land was won. It was all-important that it should be won, for the benefit of civilization and the interests of mankind. It is indeed a warped, perverse, and silly morality which would forbid a course of conquest that has turned whole continents into the seats of mighty and flourishing civilized nations" (1883: 44). The taming of the west thus was based on a simple but flawed premise: tribal people were uncivilized and therefore had no sense of community. Rather, their towns, villages, and habitations were to be destroyed or removed and replaced by Christian compounds. Baptism or renaming became a euphemism for "taking possession." In this manner, aboriginal communities were transformed in a manner that was consistent with the Doctrine of Discovery.

In fact, "possession" became the foundation of Americanism. With the creation of the United States in the late eighteenth century, the term "American" became the embodiment of a great social experiment designed to make every individual economically independent. The ideals of that period equated life and liberty with private property. America's bountiful and cheap land, which was really Indian land, became a world symbol for individual prosperity—a land of opportunity.

The General Allotment Act of 1887 was based on this notion of land-ownership. The act was designed to force Indian people into becoming landed farmers. By consigning heads of Indian families to 80- and 160-acre parcels of land, the U.S. government fabricated a surplus from the vast acreages that were left undistributed within the Indian territories. The policy transplanted the American ideal of civilized life to the Native American and fragmented native societies and their territories even further.

From the chaos exacted by policy makers on native people, the Bureau of Indian Affairs, created in 1824, was reorganized in 1880 for purposes of domestic intervention. Its basic tenet was that native people were devoid of planning skills for their communities and incapable of managing their own internal affairs. Hence a policy framework of dependency was created and the internal affairs of tribal governments were controlled externally by non-Indians. Their communities were purposely repressed by a policy of forced cultural assimilation. From the ashes of tribal community genocide arose the great mythological phoenix of Western paternal benevolence.

CLANS AND CONFEDERATIONS

Prolonged contact between the two worlds created interdependence. Native societies were transformed in significant ways, but so too were Europeans. To this day the concept of reciprocal discovery has continued to elude the Euro-Western mind.

At the time of European contact, the tribes of the Americas had evolved their own building traditions that were and continue to be characterized by specific worldviews. These worldviews were made distinctive through the evolution of specific archetypes that were the embodiment of generations of peoples developing a direct relationship to their environment. In a greater sense the basic elements of their societies, their clanships, served as the basic social unit for mobilizing their communities.

So in this regard the clan is more than a matrilineal system for ordering blood relationships. Being educated in this group determines how children will determine their role in life. They are taught to interact with others not simply in a social way but in a more philosophical and cosmological way. To know a clanship is to understand both the spatial and social relationships of many tribal communities. It is the superstructure on which many tribal societies base their most well founded plans. The clan is akin to a neighborhood in planning theory. But it supersedes mere boundaries; people in tribal clans are united in time and space as well.

Today, clanships are still regarded as being inconsequential in tribal community development. They are seen as merely informal bonds or affinal relationships to which individuals are unwittingly born. This is but an anthropological mask. Indeed, the clans of various cultural communities came together in a cohesive fashion to form even greater regionally based groupings. These groupings, or tribal confederations, became a superstructure on which native society remodeled their own political societies, and these, in turn, orchestrated and commanded even larger regions.

Tribal confederations abounded both in tribal oral histories and in the historical literature. They were part of the cultural geographic landscape that the European explorers first encountered. Today, this same system would be called a regional planning model. Tribal confederations usually consist of two or more tribal communities who entered into a compact or who made formal statements of principles to govern collective concerns. The confederations are composed of designated leaders from respective tribes that form a supreme council. It is a representative government whose members were traditionally delegated by clans from the respective cultural groups.

As members of the supreme council, the individual tribes surrendered certain powers and rights that they had exercised individually. The most important of these was to guarantee mutual protection as groups of travelers entered other territories. Another was the establishment of a peace-justice system that mitigated intertribal conflicts. They essentially solidified accords through intertribal compacts. The incentive was the mutual protection of their territories and their communities.

Such regional matters superseded cultural differences such as language and customs. Many confederations were thus composed of tribes who spoke mutually unintelligible languages, and communication was made possible through a lingua franca or through translators. Meetings were held on a regular basis at a neutral or centralized location, and were not interrupted by warfare. Councils of war were secondary to the intent of these meetings. Rather, the issues were much broader and an agenda was developed for the benefit of the entire region. The common bond that these confederations ultimately established was an interdependent economic system, which, in turn, was tied to managing and sustaining a shared ecosystem. This ecosystem represented a diversity of environments ranging from desert to woodland. The tribal confederations linked themselves regionally with adjoining confederations as trade expanded along a network of streams and trails.

Some of the frequently mentioned confederations were the Red and White Towns of the Cherokee Confederacy as well as others of the Creek Confederacy; the Chippewa, Ottawa, and Potawatomi Alliance; the Seven Council Fires of the Dakota; the Powhatan Confederacy; the Caddo Confederacy; and the Iroquois Confederacy. A few have survived into contemporary times. Those confederations that are now desegregated are repositioning themselves to revive an ancient polity.

Of the tribal confederations that have survived, one in particular has been instrumental in defining the emerging nation-state: the All Indian Pueblo Council (AIPC) of the American Southwest. The AIPC has historical roots that predate European contact.

THE ALL INDIAN PUEBLO COUNCIL

The Pueblo Indians of the southwestern United States were considered peaceable primarily because of their sedentary agricultural lifestyle. At the time of first contact in 1540, Spanish chroniclers recorded more than seventy-five Pueblo villages in limited forays through the major river basins. Together, their combined territories represented nearly the whole of all major river basins in New Mexico. At the height of the Spanish occupation, the Pueblo nations occupied 87,000 square miles and extended from the Salinas Pueblos of east central New Mexico to the Hopi Pueblos of Arizona.

It was estimated by some accounts that these regions were inhabited by as many as 248,000 people. The combination of aggressive Spanish intrusion, increased nomadic raiding, and a lack of resistance to foreign disease quickly decimated their populations. By the Pueblo Revolt of 1680 the population had declined to 30,000. In 1821 the Pueblo population declined to only 9,034. Habitation had been reduced to only twenty villages. In spite of the drastic population decline, however, territories had been delineated in accordance with Spanish usufruct property law. Usufruct, or common lands, was deeded through land grants, and the Pueblo governments were given status equal to those of other Spanish colonial townships (hence *pueblos*) or to other landed estates (*encomiendas*).

Once colonial rule was secured in New Mexico, the designation *pueblo* went far beyond mere description. Under a royal ordinance issued by King Philip II of Spain in 1573, New World towns were to be planned and laid out around an exacting set of specifications (Stanislawski 1947). Under the ordinance a village could not petition the Crown for formal recognition until all township elements were in place. Lengthy descriptions that attested to the fulfillment of such requirements and a roster of Catholic converts served as documents necessary for petitioning the *Audiencia* (head town authority), which was located at Mexico City. On review by the appropriate officials and clergy, the petition was forwarded to the court of the king of Spain for concurrence.

The designation *pueblo*, therefore, was a legal one. A formal royal proclamation attesting to a township's authority was issued. More significant, as part of this proclamation, the king alienated his title to the land encompassed by the town plaza and turned it over to the community (*fondo legal*). Canes of authority, called *varas*, were issued to the town officials as a symbol of their acceptance into Spanish governance. On a more functional level, the canes also became a standard unit of physical measurement, comparable to an American yardstick. The *fondo legal*, in fact, was often designated as the area bounded by measuring 1,000 *varas* from the church door, in each cardinal direction.

The designation *pueblo* under Spanish authority spared the natives from being devastated by the brunt of the relocation policies (*repartimientos*). The *repartimiento* was widely enforced among other natives who had neither *pueblos* (towns) nor *villas* (villages). That the Pueblos had villages physically similar to Spanish townships served to quickly incorporate them into colonial sovereign rule. It only remained that the Pueblo populations be converted to Catholicism and that the churches be built, preferably, fronting on the village plaza.

In a sense the Pueblos were opportune for conversion. The indigenous villages had already evolved a high degree of community organization by the time of first Spanish contact. Fray Marcos de Niza, who was the first Spaniard to venture as far as the Zuni village of Háwikuh, described it as having "the appearance of a pretty [Spanish] pueblo." A few years later, Francisco Vasquez de Coronado bequeathed it the name of Granada, because "it resembles the Albanicín," one of the sections of old Granada near the Alhambra (Bolton 1949: 118).

At the time of the first encounter with Coronado's expedition in 1540, the area continued to intrigue the Spaniards. In his report to Coronado, Captain Alvarado narrated the first foreigner's description of the middle Rio Grande valley region with its "fields of maize and [which lay] dotted with cottonwood groves." He went on to indicate that "there are twelve pueblos, whose houses are built of mud and are two stories high" (Bolton 1949: 118).

In the winter of 1540, Coronado's expedition used this Province of Tiguex (variant of Tiwa) as its base of operations. They described the villages, one of which they occupied, as being greatly fortified, enclosed by palisades, with small houses lacking entryways at the ground level. They negotiated among *caciques* (theocratic leaders), and it soon became apparent to the explorers, and later the Spanish colonialists, that the Pueblo world had its own sophisticated philosophies. It was significant, for example, that the first Catholic church established in 1498 by the Spanish colonial Juan de Oñate was constructed inside an abandoned *kiva* (ceremonial house). It was quickly obliterated, however, after outside clerics criticized the colonialists for worshiping in a heathen and blasphemous space. But it was the same for many other aspects of Pueblo ceremonial life. For every Christian concept, the Pueblo people had a parallel one. And in many regards it was these parallel concepts that threatened ecclesiastical efforts at conversion.

At the nexus of these concepts was the emergence place. Pueblo people believe that their origin is within the earth. This is characterized in various ways, but the emergence is described as a journey from the center and through a series of levels that ultimately lead toward the earth's crust and the sky. The first beings to emerge were the sacred clowns. And from the sequence of other beings that followed, a strict order or protocol was established. It is from these origins that a pantheon of moieties and clan-ships were ordered in succession.

What is remarkable, and what seems to have escaped the appreciation of the Spanish, was that the Pueblo societies used such progression to order all aspects of their universe as well as to plan their communities. Sacred architecture, such as the *kiva,* symbolically replicated the cyclical time dimensions of this cosmological relationship by its circular shape. The *sipapu,* or center navel, was a distinctive feature that symbolically represented the hole of emergence. The building often straddled the surface of the earth, with the floor at the subterranean level and the roof above the ground. This symbolized the threshold between the inner and outer worlds. In other words, the *kiva* was an archetype representing the Pueblo universe, which came as a result of the Pueblo society's preoccupation with ordering their relationships with the cosmos and with each others' clans.

Other relationships were specified as well. Moieties are designated according to the cycles of the season. Clans are designated by direction. Most Pueblos have seven directions (cardinal directions, up and down, and center), and they occupied or were responsible for corresponding sections of the *kiva.* Clanships too were as numerous as they were varied. A typical village will have a dozen or more clans. To cite a Hopi village elder:

> You have to remember that a good many of those clan groups that arrive here weren't Hopis as we know them today. They came in with different customs, different traditions, even different languages. They brought ceremonies that the Hopis didn't know about, and they brought whatever guiding spirits, or deities, they happened to have. Before you can even begin to understand the inner relationships among the Hopis, you have to know a lot about the beliefs that the clans hold to. If clans are having a dispute of some kind, they might argue their cases by recalling something that happened back at the *sipapuni* [emergence place] or during migrations. (Yava 1978: 48–49)

Ceremony characterized much of how the Pueblo societies conducted their affairs as well. In particular, the order of things and events was paramount to decision making. Consensus was an operative element of decision making in the sense that leaders were allowed to speak in the order of their symbolic emergence. The concept of order in this respect was equated with the male side; specifically, those clans that emerged first were considered the "younger" brothers. In the assembly they were the ones who spoke first. The "older" brothers, therefore, would preside over the proceedings, and it was also their duty to synthesize and formulate a consensus.

Consensus also helped to explain the human settlement patterns of the Pueblos. After centuries of occupation in the geographic Southwest, thousands of abandoned village sites dotted the landscape. Some of these undoubtedly were not simply the result of relocation but of certain clans not being able to attain consensus among the others. For in this mode of decision making, those who were unwilling to conform to the overall consensus had only one recourse—to save their political face by relocating elsewhere and establishing villages anew.[1]

Clanships also determined land tenure. Certain areas were reserved only for the use of members of a particular clan. These included agricultural lands and demarcated where individual houses were constructed, not only the ground floor, but also each successive level of a multistoried complex. Often, clans were associated with specific skills, and trade and barter zones were created to coordinate the production of goods among villages. Overall, the village community reflected a complex interplay of social affinities with the overarching structure being the clanships.

The evolution of the regionally based tribal confederation was a natural extension of this clan ordering. For reasons that are lost in antiquity, the heterogeneous cultures that converged on the Southwest and that became the Pueblo nations formed regional alliances for their mutual benefit and aid. These were evident as soon as the Spanish entered the region, and they continued unabated throughout the contemporary periods.

The first written account of a meeting of the All Indian Pueblo Council was with the Spanish colonial governor, Juan de Oñate, at the Pueblo of Santo Domingo on July 7, 1598. At that momentous occasion Oñate met with seven Pueblo leaders, or *caciques,* who were said to represent thirty-four villages. Thereupon it was agreed by these representatives that Spain could occupy the region and, furthermore, that the Pueblos would give their allegiance to the king of Spain.

AIPC was composed of a confederation of distinct cultural communities belonging to disparate language groups. Even today, the surviving AIPC membership of nineteen Pueblos continues to be linguistically diverse. The basic language alliances are the Keresan-speaking Pueblos of Ácoma, Laguna, Zia, Santa Ana, Cochiti, Santo Domingo, and Santa Felipe; the Tiwa-speaking Taos, Picuris, Sandia, and Isleta pueblos;[2] the Tewa-speaking Pojoaque, San Juan, Santa Clara, Nambe, San Ildefonso, and Tesuque

---

1. The most dramatic contemporary example of this phenomenon was the factional dissolution of the Hopi village of Orabi in 1904. As a result of clan infighting, the matter was settled only after opposing clans moved away from Orabi to establish two new adjacent villages. Hotevilla embodied those clans that held steadfastly to older belief systems, whereas the village of Bacavi was established among those clanships that embraced Western educational values.

2. In 1989 the historically removed Tiwa Pueblo group known as Ysleta del Sur whose small reservation is located on the outskirts of El Paso, Texas, was also officially recognized by the AIPC.

pueblos; and the Pueblos of Zuni and Jemez, which maintain their own separate language groups of Zunian and Towa, respectively.

Although there are no specific Spanish records attesting to the formal existence of the AIPC, the unified actions of the Pueblos in resisting Spanish intrusion continued throughout the period. In spite of their township status, tremendous unrest among the Pueblos was evident. And in spite of their linguistic and cultural differences, tribes exhibited a pattern of regional unity in their attempts to stave off Spanish exploitation. In 1650, for example, six Pueblos united with their traditional adversary, the Apaches, to oust the Spanish. Their plot was discovered before they could implement their plan; nine leaders were hanged, and others were given into slavery.

Political bickering between civil and ecclesiastical officials continued and caused much discontent. In 1660 reports emerged from civil authorities that religious authorities were abusing their powers over the natives. These actions were attributed to the widespread abuse of the *permicia* (tithes). At the same time, the civil authorities were dissatisfied with what they perceived as meager returns from Indian labor.

Civil taxation and ecclesiastical tithes became especially burdensome in the face of a regional drought. In 1650 and again in 1670 severe droughts that lasted for several years resulted in widespread famine and death. Epidemics of smallpox further decimated hundreds and even thousands of Pueblo lives. To make matters worse, nomadic raiding dramatically increased and the kidnapping of women and children from Spanish colonial settlements prompted the government to establish buffer villages in an attempt to control regional strife.

As a result of these problems, on August 10, 1680, a combined and coordinated assault by the members of the AIPC was launched against the Spanish. Colonial settlements and missions were attacked throughout the region. Although many priests and colonialists were killed, survivors were able to regroup at several sites, and Pueblo warriors allowed an estimated 1,500 Spanish colonialists to flee unharmed southward along the Camino Real. After several weeks the Spanish reached a major juncture where the Rio Grande shifted its course eastward. There the survivors founded the settlement of El Paso.

It took another twelve years for the Spanish to successfully reenter the territories of the Pueblos. At that time they found the various remaining Pueblos factionalized and weakened by intertribal warfare. Many villages had been abandoned, and vast acres of adjacent agricultural lands lay fallow. Although the Spanish government attempted to repatriate a few of these villages, the whole of the region had been disrupted beyond repair. The Spanish took advantage of this situation and wooed back the original colonizers with land grants. In the end, the 1680 Pueblo Revolt was an unmitigated disaster for the land tenure of the Pueblos.

Despite these setbacks, the AIPC continued to resist foreign intrusions. Barely four years after the Spanish reestablished their presence in New Mexico, the combined forces of the Pueblos attempted another revolt. In this foray five missionaries were killed. Many of the remaining Rio Grande Pueblos fled to Hopi where they were to further consolidate their remaining ranks. The result of such regrouping was the establishment of new Pueblos such as the present-day village of Laguna.

But resistance continued even well after this episode. Even after the 1821 transfer of Spanish authority to the Mexican government, regional resistance continued. In 1837 Pueblo villages in northern New Mexico combined with other *genizaro* (nomadic tribal people of Christian conversion) communities to stage a short-lived coup against the new Mexican regime. And after the American occupation of New Mexico in 1846, the Pueblos organized against the intruders. In 1847 forces numbering over one thousand Pueblos, Apaches, and Mexicans were amassed in an attempt to overthrow U.S. rule. The leader, Tomasito, a Pueblo Indian from Taos, deposed the newly appointed territorial governor, Charles Bent, who was killed in an ambush. In retaliation, American troops routed this resistance by barraging Taos Pueblo with mortars and by arresting and subsequently killing Tomasito.

Soon after the American territorial government was established in New Mexico, though, the courts reaffirmed that the Pueblos had a unique status among its residents. The Supreme Court of New Mexico Territory, in the case of *United States v. Lucero,* established the following interpretation: "A law made for wild, wandering savages, to be extended over a people living for three centuries in fenced abodes and cultivating the soil for the maintenance of themselves and families, and giving an example of virtue, honesty, and industry to their more civilized neighbors, in this enlightened age of progress and proper understanding of the civil rights of man, is considered by this court as wholly inapplicable to the pueblo Indians of New Mexico" (1869: 442).

Pueblo communities were equivalent to "incorporated townships," to sue or be sued like any other territorial denizen. The steady westward movement by Anglo settlers into the territory, however, resulted in encroachment on Pueblo lands. The American territorial government did not intervene and used the "equal status" of the Pueblo people to undermine tribal authority. The result was the legal and illegal transfer of individual deeds to outsiders and the gradual erosion of Pueblo territories. Such contentions were supported by the territorial courts, and in 1864 it was further determined that Pueblo people could not vote in state elections because of the common lands they held. Suffrage, in fact, was not reinstated until 1948 and only under the threat of legal duress by the federal government.

Beginning with New Mexico statehood in 1912, the Pueblos continued to mobilize against the unjust practices of local authorities. In 1913 the constitutionality of U.S. government control over the Pueblos was upheld in the case of *United States v. Sandoval*. As a result of this ruling the Pueblos became federally recognized as "American Indians," subject to the provisos and protection of the U.S. government. More important, interference from the newly constituted state government was stopped. Illegal land cessions were temporarily curtailed, and the Spanish land grant was established as the foundation for the Pueblo Indian reservation system in New Mexico.

Nonetheless, a major issue that remained to be resolved concerned the claims of non-Indians within Pueblo territories. In 1922 Senator Holm O. Bursum, supported by the Harding administration, introduced the Act to Quiet Title Lands Within Pueblo Indian Lands. Unfortunately, the intent of this act was to place the burden of proof for all non-Indian land claims on the Pueblos. This essentially reversed the procedure and threatened to deplete the meager resources of the Pueblos by forcing them to spend years in court litigating non-Indian claims.

With the support of the General Federation of Women's Clubs, the Committee on Indian Welfare was created to oppose this act. Under the guidance of John Collier, a defense for the Pueblos was organized.[3] At a meeting of the AIPC in 1922, one of the Pueblo elders exclaimed, "We must call all the Pueblos together. We must organize as we did long ago, when we drove the Spaniards out" (Collier 1963: 132).

The confederated Pueblos were successful in defeating the Bursum Act. It was replaced by a more favorable bill in 1924, The Pueblo Lands Act, which, unlike the Bursum Act, placed the burden of proof on the non-Indian claimants. More important, organized opposition during this period served to officially endorse the All Indian Pueblo Council as a legitimate tribal confederation, a gain not to be underestimated at the national level.

And AIPC continued to be decisive in other major threats against Pueblo sovereignty. In the early 1950s AIPC took a major role in the repeal of Indian termination legislation that had been enabled by Congress. In the 1960s its leaders were also actively participating in civil rights efforts that served to reframe tribal interrelationships nationwide. Spearheaded

3. John Collier eventually built a career on advocating Indian causes. As commissioner of Indian affairs (1933–1945), he was the chief policy architect of the 1934 Indian Reorganization Act.

by pan-Indian organizations like the American Indian Movement, occupations at Alcatraz in 1969, at the Department of Interior in Washington, D.C., in 1972, and at Wounded Knee in 1973 stemmed the tide of termination injustices and brought valuable public sentiment to bear on public policy.

As a result of increasing pressure, a formal governing body was seen as necessary for building consensus and for coordination of economic development at a regional level. Water rights, land rights, and mineral extraction, for example, became paramount concerns for many Pueblos. The sharing of resources to pursue costly litigation and the competition for scarce resources by neighboring non-Pueblo communities spurred the need to consolidate.

On October 19, 1970, the All Indian Pueblo Council adopted a formal constitution and bylaws. Its charter was relatively straightforward and exacting. Its membership continued to be the designated officials from each of the respective nineteen Pueblos. In most cases this was the tribal governor, although in situations in which this individual was unavailable, the lieutenant governor was designated. Its officers were elected and limited to a chairman, vice-chairman, secretary, and treasurer. Among the legislative powers deeded in the constitution were the following provisions: the right to employ legal counsel and to negotiate with other governments; and the power to enter into outside contracts, to arrange for the maintenance of law and order, to promote and conduct educational, health and publicity campaigns, to foster programs for the welfare of members, and to raise revenues. Moreover, its meetings were regularized, and the executive officers were responsible for formulating an official agenda.

Such formal reorganization barely anticipated a major shift in U.S. Indian federal policy. On December 15, 1970, as a result of the combined actions of the Pueblo of Taos and the AIPC, President Richard Nixon signed significant legislation returning 48,000 acres (Blue Lake) to the Pueblo. This event signaled the complete turnabout of assimilationist policies and served as a milestone for other federal agencies. The long-term objectives of this policy shift, as stated by the American Indian Policy Review Commission (AIPRC), were simple but politically and economically difficult to attain: adequate education for everyone; full employment; and a system of tribal taxation.

In its report to Congress the AIPRC had verified that "dependency on the federal government increased from 1968 to 1972" (AIPRC 1976: 18). In 1973, however, the tribes received their first opportunity to break this dependency. Indian control was given both an impetus and major sums of money under the auspices of the Indian Action Team and the Comprehensive Employment and Training Act (CETA). Under provisions of the Indian Manpower Programs (CETA Title III, sec. 302), classroom training, on-the-job training, work experience, and public service employment were provided to more than 50,000 qualifying Native Americans nationwide. It was estimated that expenditures of $985.58 per person were made through this program (AIPRC 1976: 116).

The Native American Programs Act of 1974 was specifically aimed at "increasing the capabilities of Native American groups to provide services for its members" (Jones 1982: 117). About $33 million were appropriated in 1978 and "average" awards of $125,000 were given. The changes wrought by such programs in the various Indian reservations were substantial. For example, the Pueblo of Zuni was the first Indian tribe to completely transform its tribal operations by assuming complete responsibility for the administration and supervision of all Bureau of Indian Affairs programs and personnel. The consequent onslaught of new programs and initiatives directed by the Zuni tribe was enormous. Between 1970 and 1981 the number of tribal employees increased 900 percent and its tribal operations expanded from three to seventy-one (Fergusson et al. 1989: 130). Similar situations were to follow among other tribes. Major tribal funding initiatives were undertaken by the following federal agencies, among others: Bureau of Sport Fisheries and Wildlife; Department of Labor; Economic Development Administration (EDA); Farmers Home Administration; Forest Service; Housing and Urban Development (HUD); Office of Economic Opportunity (OEO); Rural Electrification Administration; Small Business Administration; and the U.S. Geological Survey (AIPRC 1977: 1:88).

The capstone for solidifying this shift in policy was the passage of the Indian Self-Determination and Education Assistance Act in 1975. The legislation allowed tribes to contract services principally from the Bureau of Indian Affairs, Indian Health Service, and education offices. Programs were consequently decentralized, and infrastructure to support tribal operations on the reservations were significantly improved. Essentially, the tribal offices were taken out of the homes of tribal officials and placed in tribal building complexes. Programs were consolidated from remote sites and placed in areas that were easily accessible to the tribal residents. And for the first time in history federal/tribal operations were accessible to the general public.

Such was the case when the AIPC took its own initiative for consolidation of shared contracting among various tribal governments. AIPC established its own corporation and relocated its offices out of borrowed space and into a large new complex built specifically for its economic development and planning purposes. The All Indian Pueblo Cultural Center contained business offices but also included retail space for arts and crafts, a museum, and a restaurant.

But growth came at a cost. In 1989 the corporation was dissolved after it became insolvent. AIPC members had become dissatisfied with the business aspects of the corporation. "The corporate entity acquired so many social and economic development programs that it had detracted the council from its original role as coordinator and arbiter of tribal issues" (*Albuquerque Tribune*, August 21, 1989). This was the conclusion that was ultimately used to reorganize its business operations.

Today, the AIPC continues to arbitrate in many areas of concern to the Pueblos. It serves as a unique institution that advocates on behalf of Pueblo and other tribal nations. There continues to be an underlayer of more ancient traditions, but in its constitutional form the AIPC is also cognizant of modern institutional development. Also significant is that the AIPC has begun to fashion a strong role within the state of New Mexico as well. This is to say that its actions now affect non–Native Americans as well as Native Americans in areas specific to Indian gaming, touring, water management, and environmental regulation.

Planning continues to play an integral part in Pueblo affairs. Neither its own settlements nor those of its competing adversaries were random. Rather, the Southwest continues to be dominated in a structured fashion by many of the accords achieved by the Pueblo governments and their own planning initiatives. Unfortunately, even today, little credence is given to the power of the Pueblo people by outsiders. Instead, outsiders consider Pueblo affairs as inconsequential to the process of Westernization.

CONCLUSION

The All Indian Pueblo Council is indigenous to the Americas and existed at the time of European contact. Its purpose continues to be to solidify the alliance of tribal groups for purposes of establishing domestic peace, securing economic trade, and providing for the collective needs of its membership. The AIPC operates in a framework reminiscent of a regional planning model.

The existence of tribal confederations, particularly in light of the destabilization wrought on their communities, in many ways provides for the persistence of their collective identity. It provides for a larger regionally based political venue that allows the individual tribes to represent themselves as a collective body. Through this unity they have been able to negotiate larger concessions. At the same time they are able to protect elements of their own tribal autonomy.

As regional development becomes an increasingly important issue, the confederations will become dominant forces in this arena. Tribal confederations are now involved in matters of tremendous importance to their regions. AIPC is involved in national policy concerns pertaining to the repatriation of cultural artifacts, land claims, recreational and historic tourism, gaming, and environmental regulations.

More significant, such issues are no longer confined within the purview of the tribal nations per se. Rather, their outcomes will affect the surrounding region and will have direct impacts on the welfare and economies of non-native people. As reservations gain strength through such alliances, they will also seek to expand their presence throughout their regions.

Although AIPC is an example of a confederation that has survived, there is nothing to preclude other tribes from revitalizing their own regional confederations. Especially as many other confederations existed at the time of European contact, many tribes are still in the position to revive ancient institutions. They will fit these within a contemporary context and in a manner that befits their own styles of development.

The downside, however, is the creation of a distinct "managerial class" (Deloria 1986: 199). In 1989 it was estimated that the Bureau of Indian Affairs employed some fifteen thousand civil servants and, according to congressional sources, only twelve cents of every federal dollar designated for Indian programs had directly been received by a Native American. Nearly half of all Native American incomes were attributed to federal and tribal jobs (White 1990: 274). The situation inspired the infamous statement by then Secretary of Interior James Watt, "If you want an example of the failures of socialism, don't go to Russia. Come to America and go to the Indian reservations" (*New York Times,* January 19, 1983). But whereas the infrastructure necessary to manage tribal operations has become so large as to completely dominate the labor force on some reservations, it also revitalized a great number of tribal operations. The federal funds necessary to sustain such activity are tremendous but continue to fluctuate with the mood of Congress.

Watt's sentiment continues into the Republican-controlled federal regime of the second term of the Clinton administration. In spite of promises made to strengthen tribal sovereignty, the downsizing of the federal budget has also targeted programs and services that technically should be guaranteed under the provisos of federal/Indian treaty rights. Because of widespread successes among tribal governments in augmenting their local economies from windfall profits raised through Indian gaming, for example, both the Congress and state governments are poised to use such profits to terminate its financial obligations.

I have demonstrated that the planning resolve of tribal governments is not a concept that was imposed from the outside. Rather, tribes have continued to revitalize and strengthen what is an indigenous capacity to plan for their own communities, using their own internal resources and culturally appropriate solutions. In the end, dependency relationships between the tribes and the federal government will prove to be largely nonconstructive (New Mexico Advisory Committee to the U.S. Commission on Civil Rights 1982: 19).

Posturing before a group of Soviet students at Moscow State University in 1988, President Reagan declared, "Maybe we made a mistake. Maybe we should not have humored [Native Americans] in wanting to stay in that kind of primitive lifestyle [reservation life]. Maybe we should have said, 'No, come join us' " (*New York Times,* June 1, 1988). Political leaders like Reagan will doubtless continue to impose their own revisionist histories, overlooking the dynamic role of tribal nations in shaping America. As long as this persists, the history of tribal accomplishments will continue to be invisible.

REFERENCES

American Indian Policy Review Commission (AIPRC). 1976. *Task Force Seven: Reservation and Resource Development Protection.* Report on Reservation and Resource Development and Protection. Washington D.C.: Government Printing Office.

———. 1977. *Final Report.* Vol. 1. Washington, D.C.: Government Printing Office.

Boas, Franz. 1932. *Anthropology and Modern Life.* New York: Norton.

Bolton, Herbert E. 1949. *Coronado: Knight of Pueblos and Plains.* Albuquerque: University of New Mexico Press.

Collier, John. 1963. *From Every Zenith: A Memoir and Some Essays on Life and Thought.* Denver: Sage Books.

Deloria, Philip S. 1986. "The Era of Indian Self-Determination: An Overview." In *Indian Self-Rule: First Hand Accounts of Indian-White Relations from Roosevelt to Reagan,* ed. Kenneth R. Philp, 191–207. Chicago: Howe Brothers.

Engels, Friedrich. 1972. *The Origin of the Family, Private Property, and the State in the Light of the Researches of Lewis H. Morgan,* ed. Eleanor Burke Leacock. New York: International Publishers.

Fergusson, T. J., et al. 1988. "Twentieth-Century Zuni Political and Economic Development in Relation to Federal Indian Policy." In *Public Policy Impacts on American Indian Economic Development,* ed. C. Matthew Snipp. Development Series, no. 4. Albuquerque: Native American Studies, University of New Mexico.

Hewett, Edgar L. 1930. *Ancient Life in the American Southwest, with an Introduction on the General History of the American Race.* New York: Tudor.

Johnson v. M'Intosh. 1823. 21 U.S. (8 Wheat) 543.

Jones, Richard S. 1982. *Federal Programs of Assistance to American Indians: A Report Prepared for the Senate Select Committee on Indian Affairs of the United States Senate.* Congressional Research Service. Washington, D.C.: Government Printing Office.

Morgan, Lewis Henry. 1876. "Montezuma's Dinner." *North American Review* 212: 265–308.

New Mexico Advisory Committee to the United States Commission on Civil Rights. 1982. *Energy Development in Northwestern New Mexico: A Civil Rights Perspective.* Report. Santa Fe, January.

Philp, Kenneth R., ed. 1986. *Indian Self-Rule: First Hand Accounts of Indian-White Relations from Roosevelt to Reagan.* Chicago: Howe Brothers.

Prescott, William H. 1843. [1936] *History of the Conquest of Mexico, and History of the Conquest of Peru.* New York: Modern Library.

Roosevelt, Theodore. 1889. *The Winning of the West.* New York: Putnam's.

Stanislawski, Stan. 1947. "Early Spanish Town Planning in the New World." *Geographic Review* 37:95–105.

U.S. v. Lucero. 1869. 1 N.M. 422.

U.S. v. Sandoval. 1913. 231 U.S. 28.

White, Robert H. 1990. *Tribal Assets: The Rebirth of Native America.* New York: Holt.

Yava, Albert. 1978. *Big Falling Snow: A Tewa-Hopi Indian's Life and Times and the History and Traditions of His People.* New York: Crown.

FIVE

Remember, Stonewall Was a Riot

Understanding Gay and Lesbian Experience in the City

Moira Rachel Kenney

It is now more than twenty-five years since the gay liberation movement was sparked by three nights of street protest in Greenwich Village against police entrapment and harassment in a bar frequented by Puerto Rican and African American drag queens—the riots at Stonewall. In recent years a wealth of scholarship and political debate about the history and relevance of gay and lesbian experience in the city has revealed, on the one hand, extensive and systematic practices of oppression and discrimination targeting gays and lesbians as threats to the urban social order and, on the other, a century of resistance to this oppression, resistance that has been both overt (in the form of political and social activism) and covert (through the establishment of independent gay and lesbian enclaves and cultural forms hidden from mainstream urban society). Few urban theorists and historians (including planning academics) have dared to acknowledge the importance and relevance of this research. Take away, for the moment, the identifiable markers of the gay and lesbian experience, and imagine a social protest movement that, throughout the twentieth century, has created an independent urban culture, suffered police harassment, been legally subject to housing and employment discrimination, and, in response, waged a campaign for social justice that has intensified over the past fifty years. Then imagine that, as planning historians, we have overlooked these experiences. If nothing else, the implausibility of this occurrence marks the gay and lesbian experience as worthy of current attention.

The inclusion of gay and lesbian histories and viewpoints in planning history continues the recent shift of planning history and theory away from a focus on the institutional responses to urban inequalities toward the collective, street-level responses of those subject to this discrimination. More directly, however, the discussion of these particular histories reveals a set of cultures and communities for whom the city has been not only the location of struggle but the essence of that struggle as well. City life offers, as Iris Marion Young (1990: 238) has argued, both the cover of anonymity and the potential for social interaction, the creation of "a critical mass" that becomes the basis for political action and transformation. Planning has yet to fully conceptualize, on its own terms, the city as activator of social and political empowerment. The stories of those groups for whom this is the central tenet of urban experience force this shift.

What, then, is the process of integrating the experience of marginalization based on sexual difference? Despite the useful challenge offered by Leonie Sandercock in her introduction to this volume, opening up planning history to gay and lesbian experiences requires more than a new chapter; it demands a new vocabulary, a radical rethinking of sexuality, and an acknowledgment of the fluid boundaries we have drawn around other divisions in the city—class, race, gender, age. The gay and lesbian struggle crosses these other boundaries and compounds many of the difficult social and cultural questions we have only recently begun to consider. How can a history so poorly understood and skeptically approached be easily integrated into a field that, as Sandercock duly notes, has only recently begun to explore the experiences of African Americans, women, and other marginalized groups whose oppression is more universally acknowledged? What groundwork needs to be laid before mainstream planning history can begin to understand the nuances of this story? And what is the role of gay and lesbian planning academics in making the necessary connections? Embedded in these questions is a concern about the context of marginalized history and the complicity of the planning profession in keeping these experiences hidden.

As a first step, this chapter follows the framework Sandercock offers and reviews the three approaches to the diversification of planning history— the "great heroes" approach, the "effects of planning" approach, and a "reinterpretation of planning and the city." As Sandercock reveals, only a careful combination of each of these approaches will approximate the complexity of roles marginalized groups have played in the development of American landscapes—as both subjects and objects. I begin with an overview of the history of gay men and lesbians, which is probably unfamiliar to most planning professionals. Then I review these three approaches, pointing out some of the pitfalls in extending the methods of history recovery to the experiences of gays and lesbians.

Historians must first contend with the irrelevance of terms such as "gay" or "lesbian" (or "homosexual") to define the practices and lives of women and men prior to the early twentieth century. "Put bluntly, we lack any general agreement about what constitutes a lesbian" (Vicinus 1993: 433). In the past two decades lesbian theorists and historians have produced groundbreaking work tracing the development of lesbian identity, both as a group and as an individual process. Building on the work of feminist theorists on the meaning of the category "woman," lesbian theorists have called attention to the inadequacy of their own investigations, which may obscure the different constitution of same-sex relationships over time and across cultures. From Victorian era relationships between women friends to late-twentieth-century practices among Asian women, the specificity of lesbian desire and the cultural taboo cloud the connections between these experiences and prevent simple categorization. Lesbian historians, including Martha Vicinus (1993) and Lillian Faderman (1981, 1991), trace the development of modern lesbian identity, recognizing that the task of identifying behavior or cultural formation as distinctly "lesbian" has been in part a political choice by historians wishing to define, re-create, or recover a hidden history. In the process instances of lesbian group formation that do not coincide with contemporary visions of lesbian culture have been overlooked, while dominant images of the "presentable" lesbian—romantic friendships of the nineteenth century, Harlem Renaissance poets and blues singers, and "mannish" lesbians of the 1950s—have become the basis for a collective historical identity. These images are the result of a close interplay of cultural norms at work in the larger culture, the changing nature of discrimination and prohibition, and the independent development of lesbian iconography. What is less clear, however, is who remains outside these dominant images, leaving those who read lesbian history on shaky ground when it comes to transferring this research and theorizing to a wholly new endeavor, such as the rediscovery of great lesbians and gay men.

For gay men, the written record is more extensive, but perhaps less theorized concerning the omissions and prejudices of their writers. Historians focusing on the gay male experience have been more willing to identify in cultures far different from their own the existence of a premodern gay identity (Katz 1976; Halperin 1993; Duberman 1991). David Halperin's 1993 work traces same-sex male relationships back to ancient Greek and Roman societies, although he problematizes the meaning of sexuality as an indicator of identity, arguing that for men as well as for women it remains a modern conception.

The starting point for understanding this modern conception of sexual difference in a context recognizable to planning historians is John D'Emilio's *Sexual Politics/Sexual Communities* (1983). D'Emilio accepts the notion that erotic desire for persons of the same sex is a transhistorical fact, documented in cultures far different from the modern United States, but narrows his own research to the formation of group identity. For planning history, which seeks to understand the interaction among city, city politics, and specific groups of individuals, this is an important dividing line.

D'Emilio's work clearly traces not only the development of gay and lesbian culture in the United States but also, and more important, the visible signs of this culture that became the basis for systematic discrimination. To summarize D'Emilio's work, which could easily find its way into urban history and urban political economy courses, the gays and lesbians are "a product of history." He says, "It has been the historical development of capitalism— more specifically, its free labor system—that has allowed large numbers of men and women in the late twentieth century to call themselves gay, to see themselves as part of a community of similar men and women, and to organize politically on the basis of that identity" (1993: 468).

D'Emilio then connects capitalism to sexual identity formation in the following ways. First, capitalism allowed for the separation of sexuality from procreation through the creation of wage labor, which minimized the role of the family as the unit of production. Producing offspring was no longer necessary for survival, and sexual intimacy became a means of establishing closeness and experiencing pleasure. Some women and men, as exemplified in the case of lesbians and gay men, have been free to "organize a personal life" around their sexual desires. Ultimately, women and men were free to leave the family unit altogether and establish their own communities. Second, D'Emilio argues that the relationship between capitalism and the family is contradictory: capitalism pushes individuals out of families and into the workforce and at the same time requires the formation of families to produce "the next generation of workers" (1993: 476). The importance of the family in this respect, although substantially less than in precapitalist societies, "guarantees that capitalist society will reproduce not just children, but heterosexism and homophobia." Capitalism, then, becomes both the solution and the problem for lesbians and gay men.

With this barest of outlines of the development of gay and lesbian urban communities, we can return to the three approaches to history outlined above. Who are the women and men living in these urban communities whom we might identify as great planners? Conversely, which of our planning heroes have been gay or lesbian? Second, what is the nature of urban repression, especially that in which planners may have played a part, which has targeted gays and lesbians? And finally, how have lesbians and gay men resisted this oppression and created urban spaces for their own uses?

FINDING THE HEROES

The "great heroes" approach has been the subject of debate, not only from the traditional or feminist perspective Sandercock lays out but within the gay and lesbian communities of the United States as well. The corollary to the closet, which is the analogy for the process of maintaining privacy and secrecy about one's sexual identity (both as the result of personal and societal homophobia and oppression), is coming out, the process through which lesbians and gay men make public their identity. Throughout the history of the modern gay movement, this process has often been wrested from individuals by the state, employers, or the family as a way of punishing and ostracizing gay and lesbian individuals. As Eve Kosofsky Sedgewick has argued, "The closet is the defining structure for gay oppression in this century" (1993: 48). This imposition of a closet is obviously complicated by the promise of safety that the closet implies, particularly in the context of an American faith in the "right to privacy."

More recently the coming-out process has also been used by gay and lesbian activists, who declare that the closet is for some a luxury that keeps others oppressed. In the early 1990s, partly as a response to the AIDS epidemic that caused a resurgence of oppression by the American public against lesbians and gay men, many activists argued against the individuality of the choice to remain "closeted," choosing instead to emphasize the collectivity of gays and lesbians and the undue benefits some closeted lesbians and gay men were receiving while others suffered (Schulman 1990). As a result attempts to "out" public officials have been used for political purposes. It would be possible, with the slightest effort of digging through the more popular accounts of gay history and certain Internet mailing lists, to find a list of semifamous gay and lesbian planners and urban reformers. The usefulness of such an approach, however, is obviously limited. This controversy over outing, as well as the fluidity of definitions of identity, further complicates the notion of a history of planning centered on the great gay and lesbian planners of the past.

At the same time, however, the sexual identity of planners is not insignificant. While Roberta Achtenberg's appointment to the Clinton cabinet, as assistant secretary of Housing and Urban Development, was not a watershed issue for the history of planning, her presence in Washington—as an openly lesbian mother who has committed much of her professional career to combating discrimination against gay and lesbian families, gays and lesbians in the workplace, and a number of local policy issues—was important for gays and lesbians. Unfortunately, this example is unique. Most gay and lesbian planners are not open about their sexuality, let alone fighting for change as gays and lesbians. But across the country the presence of openly gay or lesbian planners has been instrumental in the recent attempts to counter local and nationally sanctioned discrimination against gays and lesbians. Cities where gays and lesbians have successfully created visible presences—in residential neighborhoods, small businesses, and local politics—are those where, in the last decade, gay rights ordinances have been passed.

BUILDING COMMUNITIES

The nature of this discrimination is central to the second approach to planning history—the institutionalized policies and practices that have shaped the development of gay and lesbian communities. As the idea of the closet suggests, this discrimination defined the existence of gays and lesbians in the city, through proscriptions against both public and private gatherings, their housing decisions, and their workplace decisions. While urban planning has not been the focus of any histories of gay and lesbian settlements, a number of broader cultural and social histories have begun to tell these stories. In particular, Lillian Faderman's *Odd Girls and Twilight Lovers* (1991), a study of lesbian life in the United States in the twentieth century, and George Chauncey's *Gay New York* (1994), trace the development of gay and lesbian enclaves in specific historical settings. For planning historians, Chauncey's book is particularly intriguing. In the following passage, Chauncey argues that the thinking about the city that ultimately coalesced into urban planning theory identified "sexual deviants" as one of the causes of social disorganization:

> Some theorists in the first generation of American urban sociologists, who echoed many of the concerns of the reformers with whom they often worked, expressed similar anxieties about the enhanced possibilities for the development of a secret homosexual life that urban conditions created. Urbanization, they warned, resulted in the breakdown of family and social ties that kept an individual's behavior under control in smaller, more tightly organized and regulated towns. The resulting "personal disorganization," the sociologist Walter Reckless wrote in 1926, led to the release of "impulses and desires ... from the socially approved channels," and could result "not merely in prostitution, but also in perversion." (1994: 132)

Sandercock quotes Elizabeth Wilson as an urban historian who has begun to probe the connections between urban thinking and discriminatory urban policies, uncovering the darker side of urban planning history. Chauncey's book widens that lens; it places gays and lesbians at the center of the debate over the meaning of urban disorder. Chauncey argues that the draw of the urban was not merely the anonymity that theorists feared and Wilson argues was central to the use of the city by women, but "an organized, multi-layered, and self-conscious gay subculture, with its own meeting places, language, folklore, and moral codes. What sociologists and reformers called the social disorganization of the city might more properly be regarded as a social reorganization" (1994: 133). *Gay New York* shows the geography of this reorganization: bars and clubs were but the tip of the island. Chauncey chronicles the few places gay men could meet and socialize without vice squad harassment: cafeterias; YMCAs, where many single men took rooms as an entry to gay culture; and the streets, parks, and riverfronts of New York City, which were the prime cruising spots in the early part of the century.

One of the aspects of planning history in which gays have been actors is the gentrification of a number of urban neighborhoods and the particular patterns of gay residential development. Although nongay and nonlesbian scholars have tended to overlook this literature, the debate about the participation of gay men in this redevelopment process is a fascinating and ongoing debate. A landmark article on gay community development by Mickey Lauria and Larry Knopp cited the development of gay neighborhoods as a primary spatial response to gay oppression made possible by the relative openness of urban dwellers to "interaction with 'alien groups' " (1985: 189).

The development of visible gay neighborhoods often begins in the context of the simultaneous process of gentrification and urban redevelopment that has been made possible by the expansion of service sector jobs in the central business districts of large cities. Lauria and Knopp make an important argument in tying the spatial processes of urban renaissance to the social dynamics of gay communities with access to the capital (through service sector employment) necessary to participate in this renaissance. They contend, "Gays have done more with space than simply use it as a base for political power. They continually transform and use it in such a way as to reflect gay cultural values and serve the special needs of individual gays vis-à-vis society at large. . . . In the context of a rapid commodification of space, the optimal strategy for gays with respect to the development of political and economic power is to participate in the revalorization of physical structures in a neighborhood—in other words, to emphasize exchange value" (1985: 159).

For gays who are able to participate in the process, residential neighborhoods serve as the ultimate safe space, particularly to the extent that visibility as home owners "committed to improving their neighborhoods" translates into political power. For planning historians, Lauria and Knopp's research should raise questions about the effect of gentrification on the displacement of other urban residents and the critical analysis of this transfer of neighborhood control relative to other instances of neighborhood turnover, including from one ethnic or racial minority to another.

Both Lauria and Knopp's research and the discussion of San Francisco's gay gentrification in Manuel Castells's *The City and the Grassroots* (1983) read the creation of enclaves as an almost exclusively gay male phenomenon. These authors argue that lesbians have less need for such places; or as Castells argues, lesbians lack the territorial imperative to form physically identifiable communities. This analysis has been well critiqued by Sy Adler and Johanna Brenner, who have found in San Francisco "a spatial concentration of lesbians, a neighborhood that many people know about and move into to be with other lesbians. But the neighborhood has a quasi-underground character; it is enfolded in a broader counter-cultural milieu and does not have its own public subculture and territory" (Adler and Brenner 1992: 31). Other factors, including economic disadvantage, greater fear of visibility, and lesser mobility, are crucial in understanding the residential choices of urban lesbians. However, none of this research has been compared across time in a way that would create a major chapter in urban history. Part of the problem is the marginalization of this litera-ture, but more research also needs to be done. Across the country there are examples of neighborhoods that have been transformed by gay and lesbian ownership. Planners need to understand this basic territorial shift.

The research by urban geographers like Lauria, Knopp, Adler, and Brenner focuses on gays and lesbians as actors, in spite of discrimination. One of the questions begged by this research is the specific features of the discrimination involved. For the most part such an investigation has not been undertaken. Below I look briefly at three aspects of systematic discrimination against gays and lesbians of specific interest to planning historians.

Harassment in Public Places

Discrimination against gays and lesbians gathering in public places—both on the streets and in commercial establishments—represents historically the clearest example of the systematic role of city officials (planners, po-lice, politicians) in regulating gay and lesbian desires in the city. According to Chauncey, police and Liquor Authority regulation of bars catering to gay men began with the end of Prohibition, as the city of New York deter-mined to make the newly reopened bars and saloons more orderly than the speakeasies of the 1920s. State courts gave the Liquor Authority full power to close down any bar that served homosexuals. "In the two and a half decades that followed [the repeal of Prohibition], it closed literally hundreds of bars that welcomed, tolerated, or simply failed to notice the patronage of gay men or lesbians. As a result, while the number of gay bars proliferated in the 1930s, '40s, and '50s, most of them lasted only a few months or years, and gay men were forced to move constantly from place to place, dependent on the grapevine to inform them of where the new meeting places were" (Chauncey 1994: 339).

Despite the prosecution, gay bars constituted for both lesbians and gay men the most important social institution prior to the liberation move-ments of the 1970s. For lesbians in particular, the gay bar as safe haven became an enduring aspect of lesbian culture, chronicled in numerous sources, from the pulp novels of the 1950s to important autobiographical works by Joan Nestle (1981), Audre Lorde (1982), and Leslie Feinberg (1994). As Faderman writes,

> Since the bars alone provided a home for them [lesbians], they had to risk whatever was necessary for the sake of being there. They tolerated the smallest crumbs and the shabbiest turf in their desperation for a "place." And even that was periodically taken away, whenever the majority community wanted to make a show of its high moral standards. But in their determination to establish some area, however minute, where they could be together as women and as lesbians, they were pioneers of a sort. They created a lesbian geography despite slim resources and particularly unsympathetic times. (1991: 167)

Evidence that police harassment of gay and lesbian bars was not merely a blanket condemnation but was also used strategically for urban improvement projects comes from New York, where research on the use of decency codes has shown that officials often stepped up harassment during major city events. One particularly obvious example is Mayor Robert Wagner's closing of nearly all the gay bars in New York "to make the city respectable for the World's Fair in 1964 and 1965" (Rosen 1980: 167).

Housing

To understand the nature of housing discrimination against gays and lesbians is to begin to glimpse the extent to which the entire bureaucracy of the urban areas had been mobilized, until only very recently, against the civil rights of gays and lesbians. According to a 1989 survey of sexual orientation discrimination and the law in the *Harvard Law Review,* "Unmarried homosexual and heterosexual couples are subject to substantial discrimination—both overt and covert—in their efforts to acquire housing. This discrimination is the product of a variety of factors, including exclusionary zoning laws, restrictive statutory provisions, discriminatory landlord practices, and narrow judicial constructions of the meaning of 'family' " (1989: 1612–1613).

Perhaps the most important aspect of this discrimination for planning historians is the prevalence of exclusionary zoning laws. These ordinances typically restrict both the sale and the rental of housing to a single nuclear family. The exclusivity of this definition of family is changing in some legal arenas (particularly child welfare law), but planning, for the most part, continues to rely on the stricter guidelines. Although housing statutes have been extended in some cases to include unmarried heterosexual families, the Missouri State Court of Appeals has ruled against extending housing rights to gay and lesbian family configurations (*Harvard Law Review* 1989: 1613). In New York City, where rent control has made the issue of successorship (who can legally stay in a rent-controlled unit after the death of the tenant of record) crucial, courts have usually held that this provision does not extend to gay and lesbian partners (*Harvard Law Review* 1989: 1614). Without equating the discrimination experienced by these other groups, this legally approved discrimination should make clear even to the most skeptical researchers the importance of including gays and lesbians in the list of minority groups marginalized through urban policies.

Public Accommodations

Public accommodation statutes, which seek to preserve access to the whole range of public space, from streets to commercial establishments, have not covered gays and lesbians and have, therefore, limited their public gatherings in nearly every corner of the city. One of the ways planning historians can uncover this history is again to look at legal cases that have challenged restrictions in states where public accommodation laws have been changed to cover gays and lesbians. Public accommodation statutes generally allow local governments to extend the limits of more general antidiscrimination laws to any place considered public by law. One of the first cases of extending public accommodation protections to gays and lesbians was a 1984 California law that required a restaurant to allow gay and lesbian couples to sit in private booths reserved for couples. More recently a 1992 Massachusetts case resulted in the judge ordering organizers of the Boston Saint Patrick's Day Parade to allow gays and lesbians to participate on the grounds that the parade, through its continual use of the same streets year after year, became in effect a public accommodation and thus subject to Massachusetts' sweeping antidiscrimination statute. In response the local organizers canceled the annual parade to avoid marching with gays and lesbians.

CLAIMING PLACE

The third stream of history directs attention away from the mechanics of discrimination to the subversive practices of gays and lesbians who have sought to make the city conform to their needs in spite of rampant discrimination. Throughout modern urban history, gay men and lesbians have appropriated spaces for their own use for both social gathering and political organizing. I have mapped the place-claiming strategies of gays and lesbians in Los Angeles—the appropriation of physical, social, and mental spaces that is the basis not only for community formation but for political organizing as well.

Politically, there are struggles for visibility on the streets, representation at city halls and in Washington, D.C., and recognition in the courts. Economically, entrepreneurs establish new strongholds, in the form of cooperatives, headquarters, office space, stores, or bars, as a way of "recycling dollars" within the community and proclaiming economic self-sufficiency. Socially, groups and individuals appropriate and establish churches, schools, or parks, using space in ways intended by society-at-large and in ways that reflect the community's marginalization. All of these practices constitute activist strategies that can be examined in the context of both political goals and cultural expression.

The importance of this approach to reclaiming history, through the study of activism, is that it starts from the recognition that sexual difference in the city is a collective endeavor, not an individual one. As individuals, gays and lesbians have the choice to be out or not, and the spatial decisions—where to live, work, or play—may result from a number of factors, many distinct from the implications of one's sexuality. However, when the city—rather than personal space—becomes the backdrop for the validation of one's self, one's identity, one's rights, and one's responsibilities, then visibility and risk are inevitable. Visibility, in the context of gay and lesbian activism has been at the center of collective attempts to confront these risks.

Planning has much to learn from histories that foreground political struggle, for it is through an examination of this resistance to discrimination and isolation that the process of cultural formation and the use of urban space become relevant to planning historians. The mapping of this activism reveals the connections between place and collective identity that are at the heart of the gay and lesbian experience in the city.

PLANNING IMPLICATIONS

Beyond the specific instances of discrimination and resistance I have outlined here, the recognition of gays and lesbians as actors in the city and the incorporation of their histories into a new planning history contribute to a re-visioning of planning theory as it relates to activism and activists. Despite the vital debate in planning theory about the meaning, object, and trajectory of radical planning, planning theory and practice has yet to comfortably expand to address many of the social and political movements that cannot traditionally be considered part of a planning agenda. Even where planning theory has begun to address activism, particularly as it relates to difference, the discussion has centered on questions of identity and ideology rather than the day-to-day practices of activists on the front lines of these debates as they are being conducted in the streets. Social theorists in many fields have begun to address the meaning of sexual difference and identity, using ideas from gay and lesbian theorists to extend their work on gender, class, and race. Planning historians need to trace these links between identity, difference, and discrimination through their own particular, place-centered frameworks.

Finally, however, as I have tried to emphasize here, there are practical reasons for looking at the gay and lesbian experience which go beyond the experiences of gays and lesbians and suggest new approaches to understanding general urban processes. The political victories gays and lesbians are now experiencing will no doubt change our cities in dramatic ways. One of the things gay and lesbian planners will be thinking about in the next decade is the continuing effect of the civil rights struggle on the characteristics of gay and lesbian communities. In the 1950s these neighborhoods served an important role in creating safe havens. As they were located on the edge of cities, in abandoned areas of downtown, they were easily ignored in the larger context of urban renewal efforts. In the 1970s these communities were the first open evidence that gay and lesbian culture existed. In the 1980s they became centers of urban growth and development. Cities like Los Angeles, San Francisco, New York, and Chicago became magnets for gay and lesbian refugees from other parts of the country. The establishment of gay and lesbian businesses, social services, and residential neighborhoods transformed parts of these cities by generating growth and displacing other marginalized groups. But in the 1990s it is as yet unclear what role these neighborhoods play. In an article in the *New York Times,* Karen DeWitt documents a new pattern of urban transformation, as gay and lesbian neighborhoods emerge in smaller cities, including St. Louis, Miami, Denver, Cincinnati, and Oklahoma City (1994: A14). As planners watch these contemporary trends, calculate the tax revenues generated by these new neighborhoods, and participate in the rewriting of local ordinances that a decade earlier would have inhibited such development, planning historians should be able to explain the struggles that have made these latest shifts possible. What does the current attitude of embracing these new business and residential neighborhoods tell us about the rules cities live by, the sources of urban growth, and the new constituencies of planning practice?

The title of this chapter comes from a New York City ACT UP march held on the twentieth anniversary of Stonewall to counter the celebratory atmosphere of gay pride events. For AIDS activists struggling against indifference to the AIDS epidemic, their chant—"Arrest us, just try it, remember Stonewall was a riot"—referred to the need for gays and lesbians to remember the radical beginnings of their movement, the struggles of earlier generations, and the battles yet to be fought. For planners and planning historians, the chant suggests something else as well. Social and political upheavals cannot be ignored or overlooked. What may well appear to us as insignificant or marginal activity today is more likely evidence of a transformation that will openly shape our cities tomorrow.

REFERENCES

Adler, Sy, and Johanna Brenner. 1992. "Gender and Space: Lesbians and Gay Men in the City." *International Journal of Urban and Regional Research* 16(1):24–34.

Castells, Manuel. 1983. *The City and the Grassroots.* Berkeley: University of California Press.

Chauncey, George. 1994. *Gay New York: Gender, Urban Culture, and the Making of the Gay Male World, 1890–1940.* New York: Basic Books.

D'Emilio, John. 1983. *Sexual Politics/Sexual Communities.* Chicago: University of Chicago Press.

DeWitt, Karen. 1994. "Gay Presence Leads Revival of Declining Neighborhoods." *New York Times,* September 6, A14.

Duberman, Martin. 1991. *About Time: Exploring the Gay Past.* 2d ed. New York: Penguin Books.

Faderman, Lillian. 1981. *Surpassing the Love of Men: Romantic Friendship and Love Between Women from the Renaissance to the Present.* New York: Morrow.

——. 1991. *Odd Girls and Twilight Lovers: A History of Lesbian Life in Twentieth-Century America.* New York: Penguin Books.

Feinberg, Leslie. 1994. *Stone Butch Blues.* Ithaca, N.Y.: Firebrand Books.

Halperin, David M. 1993. "Is There a History of Sexuality?" In *The Lesbian and Gay Studies Reader,* ed. Henry Abelove, Michele Aina Barale, and David M. Halperin, 416–431. New York: Routledge.

Harvard Law Review. 1989. "Developments in the Law: Sexual Orientation and the Law." *Harvard Law Review* 102(7):1508–1671.

Katz, Jonathan. 1976. *Gay American History.* New York: Crowell.

Lauria, Mickey, and Larry Knopp. 1985. "Towards an Analysis of the Role of Gay Communities in the Urban Renaissance." *Urban Geography* 6:651–669.

Lorde, Audre. 1982. *Zami: A New Spelling of My Name.* New York: Crossing Press.

Nestle, Joan. 1987. *A Restricted Country.* Ithaca, N.Y.: Firebrand Books.

Rosen, Steven. 1980. "Police Harassment of Homosexual Women and Men in New York City 1960–1980." *Columbia Law Review* 12(2):159–190.

Sedgewick, Eve Kosofsky. 1993. "Epistemology of the Closet." In *The Lesbian and Gay Studies Reader,* ed. Henry Abelove, Michele Aina Barale, and David M. Halperin, 45–61. New York: Routledge.

Vicinus, Martha. 1993. " 'They Wonder to Which Sex I Belong': The Historical Roots of the Modern Lesbian Identity." In *The Lesbian and Gay Studies Reader,* ed. Henry Abelove, Michele Aina Barale, and David M. Halperin, 432–452. New York: Routledge.

Weathers, Thomas. 1993. "Gay Civil Rights: Are Homosexuals Adequately Protected from Discrimination in Housing and Employment?" *Pacific Law Journal* 24(2):541–560.

Young, Iris Marion. 1990. *Justice and the Politics of Difference.* Princeton, N.J.: Princeton University Press.

PART II

Textual and Theoretical Practices

SIX

Knowing Different Cities

Reflections on Recent European Writings on Cities and Planning History

Iain Borden, Jane Rendell, and Helen Thomas

Some differences are playful: some are poles of world historical systems of domination. Epistemology is about knowing the difference.
DONNA HARAWAY (1990)

In any historical field—whether planning history, social history, art history, architectural history, or military history—there is a danger that the methodology of the investigating author will conflate or conspire with the ostensible objects of study. Rather than taking an independent critical line, the interpretation takes the form of an excavation that can repeat only what it unearths, say only what it is allowed to say.

Nowhere, perhaps, has this process been more readily apparent than in the field of city and planning history, where the perpetual trend among historians has been to conduct their lines of inquiry less on their own theoretical or political agendas and more on the internal concerns of the planning profession and the intricacies of its procedural practices. This much is, perhaps, not in itself a bad thing, for the recording and explanation of planning's own concerns is certainly of some historical worth. Nonetheless, these concerns should not be the only things addressed.

Resisting the gravitational pull of the object, however, is particularly difficult in the case of city and planning history. First, there is the perplexing nature of the objectival object—that is, of the material character of the city. A more complex, dynamic, and opaque entity than the (post)modern metropolis would be hard to imagine. Second, there is the problem of the inextricably implicated relation that planning holds with this city-entity, being both challenged and constrained by a set of institutional practices stemming from such diverse sources as capital and economies, national and municipal governments, dominant classes, smaller yet mobilized interest groups, territorialized zones, and cultural conventions.

The problem planning faces—that of the physical and social complexity of its arena of action, compounded by the multifaceted negotiations required to act at all—is then replicated in the representations made of it in history. Unable to see the forest for the trees, historians are constantly tempted to focus on the minutiae of city planning, on individual agents, individual projects, individual codes as the constituting elements of their histories. This process occurs in myriad ways: thematized historical overviews such as those by Theo Barker and Anthony Sutcliffe (1993) on the megalopolis, Deyan Sudjic (1992) on the "100 mile city," Emrys Jones (1990) on the metropolis, or G. J. Ashworth (1991) on war and the city; geographically defined studies such as those by T. Hall (1991) on planning in Nordic countries, Harold C. Carter and C. Roy Lewis (1990) on nineteenth-century England and Wales, Lila Leonitidou (1990) on Greece and the Mediterranean, Alan Balfour (1990) on Berlin, Brian Ladd (1990) on imperial Germany, or Louis Bergeron (1989) and Bruno Fortier (1990) on Paris; and single tradition-based histories such as the ones on the Garden City by Stanley Buder (1990), Walter Creese (1992), D. Deakin (1989), Mervyn Miller (1989), and Stephen V. Ward (1992). All these provide glimpses or partial views of cities and planning but ultimately do little more than record the general character of cities, yielding a textual photograph of particular objects and surfaces. Not so much hidden away as lost altogether are the forgotten peoples, the alternative practices, the imagined representations that fall outside of the hegemonic realm. Also struck from the political agenda are the wider concerns, the mobilizing forces that provide both the occasion and much of the substance for city development and planning activity. What these studies lack is an overall, explicit framework in which to situate both their choice of objects of study and the relation of these objects to the rest of the urban condition. As a result the apparent implication is too often that the given subject is, at best, an isolated arena of activity and, at worst, the only one really worth studying.

Alternatively, unable to see the trees for the forest, historians are tempted to throw what they intend to be a catch net over their objects, seeking to cover all peoples, all things, all activities under one banner. For example, Peter Hall's 1988 work is an encyclopedic historical survey of much of twentieth-century Western planning ideas, supplying what is perhaps one of the very best introductions to canonic individuals and projects. The same all-encompassing task has also been undertaken for a greater historical range (Benevolo 1993; Whitehand and Larkham 1992), and for a narrower contemporary one (Burtenshaw, Bateman, and Ashworth

1991). But in such projects, city and planning historians run the risk of simply replicating the original political role of their objects, providing not a critical interpretation but a reflection of their objects that is just as politically implicated in the dominant ideology as were the historical agents—the planners in history—they seek to represent. A rare exception is the work of Andy Thornley (1991), who gives over the first half of his book to the origins and underlying concepts of Thatcherism, the "new right," and the latter's influence on British planning in the 1980s, although his critique falls short of elucidating much by way of an alternative political agenda. Michael Keith and Alisdair Rogers (1991) are much better on the alternative politics, as their volume contains various essays on the "inner-city" issues of leverage, gentrification, and "alternative realities" which suggest ways in which the social conditions of capitalism might be resisted and challenged. Again, however, this is less of a history book and more an account of current practice. Nonetheless, it raises the question of how subjective experience and knowledge of the city might be represented in a text, a question to which we shall return.

If planning is the regulation of the physicality, sociality, and spatiality of the city, then it is important to realize that this regulatory system occurs neither solely at the material and ideological level that the great projects purport to operate on (i.e., planning activities have discursive content and meaning far beyond their surface appearance) nor indeed only through these great projects. There are not only hidden meanings but hidden practices to planning.

How, then, to cut through this dense swath of money, power, and ideology? How to make sense of its concomitant spatial existence, the city, and of its regulating practice of planning? The aim must be, first of all, to recognize the grounds on which the historical interpretation is being made—not so much the meanings that can be located within the historical object as the questions that may be asked of it according to an explicit historian-centered agenda. It is to this problematic that we now turn.

THE NECESSITY OF THEORY

The notion that history can or should be written "without theory" seems to us to be an absurdity; it is impossible to approach history using the old ideas and minds of those who have gone before. How else are we to construct history except through our own contemporary concerns? And how are we to translate those concerns into interpretive questions to be asked of the past? Conversely, how are we to use the past as the grounds on which to conduct our own interpretive inquiries? Any consideration of the past must then use some kind of mediating concept to negotiate between its specific substance and the present condition of the historian. On one level, then, theory is the making explicit of this negotiation, setting out the interpretive agenda not as an implicit, invisible subterfuge but as a necessarily implicated set of thought processes.

The question of whether to use theory or not is an irrelevance. Rather, the questions must be, first, which theory to use and second, how to relate it to the ostensible objects of study. We say "ostensible" here because it should be borne in mind that history is always a representation, always a textual reconstruction of the past, and never a direct reflection of it. In this light it may even be that history is only ever theory and nothing more.

The difficulty in choosing which theory to use is highlighted by the more or less conventional Marxist account of cities provided by Ira Katznelson (1992), who undertakes a historical review that seeks to relate the formation of the working classes to capitalist economics through the medium of the city. But Katznelson's book is also notable for its omissions, especially of more recent writers such as Michel Aglietta, Mike Davis, Doreen Massey and, even more important, of the whole range of postmodern concerns such as feminist theories and critiques and poststructuralism. Difference here is not a challenge but a problem to be eradicated by a totalizing hegemonic metatheory.

If planning is inextricably implicated in the material and ideological practices that conduct and control city affairs, then it makes sense that for any planning history to provide a critical interpretation of planning, its theoretical grounding *must not* come just from within the planning discourse. The master will not provide the rope to place around his own neck. Instead, it is necessary to look at other arenas, other theoretical territories. It is our contention, therefore, that some of the best works in planning history—best, that is, both for planning historians to consider in relation to their own research and for those who wish to understand and confront the received history in which we live each day—do not in fact necessarily have the label "planning history" on their back cover. They are, however, of direct relevance to planning and city history.

This occurs in two ways. First, these works tell us something different about the way people live their lives other than through the conventional planning history discourse. Second, they provide a theoretical outside from which to challenge conventional representations. It is this double challenge—to the objects of study and to the framing of interpretive questions—that we believe to be theory's most important potential contribution to planning history.

How does this work in practice? Some books simply provide a useful guide through theory. Anthony King (1989a, 1989b), for example, does this for the intersection of colonialism, postcolonialism, urbanism, and global capitalism, outlining both the historically derived nature of the contemporary condition of London and the various theorizations that make an understanding of this condition possible. Derek Gregory (1994) does a similar job for spatial and geographic theory. These authors, however, tend to fall short of developing their own agenda and consequently tend to provide a map without a set of directions. More significantly, they tend to signpost what is already there rather than point out new roads to travel, although Gregory is much better than most in this respect.

It is Henri Lefebvre who provides perhaps the most useful strategic overview of where to go, where to look, and what to ask. As has been pointed out, Lefebvre's "analysis of the spatial exercise of power as a construction and conquest of difference, although it is thoroughly grounded in Marxist thought, rejects economism and opens up possibilities for advancing analysis of spatial politics into realms of feminist and anti-colonial discourse" (Deutsche 1988: 29). This is not the place to enter into a lengthy explication of Lefebvre's ideas, and others have already undertaken that task, but we would like to highlight two points in relation to historical studies of the city. First, of Lefebvre's (1991a) conceptual triad, spatial practices, representations of space, and spaces of representation, it is typically only the first two that have been addressed in city and planning history. By contrast, the third level, that of lived experience whether as dominated condition or as imaginative rethinking, has tended to be ignored. Second, as Lefebvre himself makes clear, these levels should not be conceived of as autonomous zones of spatial activity but rather as possessing dialectical relationships between all three.

We would therefore like to propose two possible arenas where some attempts have already been made toward this kind of theoretically minded history. The attack on the conventional representations of planning history comes simultaneously from two directions. The first is by questioning the nature of the object. Here we suggest that work on liminal and "other" spatial zones and practices, and on reconceptualized experiences of the city, offers new suggestions as to what actually constitutes a city, its peoples, and its regulatory practices. And second, the attack comes by challenging the questions we might ask of cities and planning. Here we suggest that work in feminist philosophical theory, geography, visual theory, and histories of various kinds offers a challenge to historical studies at their core, seeking to redefine not just what the objects of study might be, or even just what the interpretive questions might be, but also the very epistemological and political grounds on which they are founded.

We do not mean to suggest that these are the only ways by which such challenges can be made—others include those concerned with, for example, matters of race, postcolonial identity, or, rather differently, different approaches to the written and graphic script—but simply that they do offer much of potential interest.

DIFFERENT PLACES

Much of the recent literature that intends to generate new understandings of our physical environment features the spatiality of identity as a predominant theme. Many of these books are interdisciplinary studies that variously integrate social theory, history, geography, psychoanalysis, and sociology. As they investigate ever deeper into the spatialization of social systems and their effects on the consciousness of the individual, they produce new theoretical categories from which to establish territories of thought and questioning.

In these theoretically informed histories the effects of artificial self-identity are explored through the concepts of space and place. For example, John Bale (1993) draws on Foucault, Eichberg, and Tuan in his consideration of the intraurban and intrastadium space of British football. More provocatively, Rob Shields (1991) inquires into the physical and psychological spatial nature of marginal places, those liminal zones existing outside and beyond the mundane experience of everyday life and which offer the potential for social and cultural experimentation. They are the sociospatial other—"a moment of discontinuity in the social fabric, a social space, or history, . . . a life-changing experience" (Shields 1991: 84). Theory derived from Foucault, Bourdieu, and Lefebvre is largely used here to set the framework for the history, rather than as a continual referent. Nonetheless, Shields's interpretations of his empirical evidence do much to counteract the notion that planning and city history should only consider the great projects of named (white male) planners and urban designers. For example, the English south coast seaside resort of Brighton emerges as successive historical zones of medicalized bathing, mass vacations, forbidden sexual liaisons, and gang violence. Other spaces include the northside divide in England, the spatiocultural myths of Canada, and a representation of Niagara Falls as the "honeymoon capital of the world."

J. Nicholas Entrikin (1991) explores similar territory. Like some other inquiries into the relationship between identity and space (Keith and Pile 1993; Werlen 1993), Entrikin moves beyond the confines of a dualistic perception, deploying the concept of betweenness relative to place as a fusion of space and experience. The argument oscillates between objective and subjective realities, the former being represented by "scientific" analyses of place and the latter by the notion of place as being defined by the particular meanings of individual people's lives. The gap between polarities (objectivity/subjectivity, existential/naturalistic, experiential/geometric) is identified as the crisis of modernity. By evading the concept of place as simply an elusive milieu, Entrikin suggests a compelling field of investigation.

The city as a place of experience is also explored by other authors in varying degrees of subjectivity and objectivity. The former is most notably represented by Elizabeth Wilson (1991), in whose work ideas, particularly in literature, are recontextualized as theoretical tools for the perception and location of experience, with important implications for identity and action. Conversely, D. J. Walmsley (1988) approaches the experience of the city from the more empirical and objective perspective of behavioral analysis. The categories of discussion here derive from a concern with the spatial organization of housing, residential segregation, travel patterns, territorial conceptualizations, political motives, and planning issues. Despite their disparate approaches, both Wilson and Wolmsley recognize that reality within the experiential realm is always a tenuous entity.

A different approach to recognizing the existence of other perceptions and other places has come from a theoretically derived postmodern interest in artifice, which is perhaps best understood as a continuation of one of the great modernist preoccupations—alienation and the loss of the natural and the unconscious. To resist the artificial has required the conceptualization of the place-without artifice, the historical nature of which can be approached by an appeal either to the purely natural or to a recovery of the natural within the artificial.

One of the most striking characteristics of those who have taken the latter approach, particularly Richard Sennett (1990), is their consideration of the dominance of the visual sense in defining the boundaries of experience and the parameters of historical understanding. Although experience, and consequently memory, cannot be described exclusively by the visual, this is nonetheless a pervasive phenomenon within the (post)-modernist landscape. John Urry (1990) shows exactly this in his Foucaldian exploration of the tourist gaze as being socially organized and systematized. Others (Borden, Kerr, Pivaro, and Rendell 1996; Watson and Gibson 1995) also offer a wide range of experiential explorations of urban space.

The former approach is alluded to, if not directly confronted, by Colin Ward (1990). In his book Ward provides an unusual insight into both children's perceptions and valuations of the city and ways in which the city fails the child (through the dominance of traffic and through the fear of attack and crime). The planner's usual conception of the city as a child-free zone is confronted by a desire to change not only the urban fabric but also our general attitudes to children and their participation in the city.

In a rather different vein, a recent English translation allows a wider audience to gain access to another seminal text by Lefebvre (1991b). Lefebvre conceives of everyday life as the tracts and memories of spatial practices left untouched by modernity, a life of innocence that has nonetheless been impoverished and humiliated by twentieth-century capitalism. This book, albeit nearly forty years after its original French publication, perhaps remains the best theoretical call for an artifice-free world. The opposite of the visualized realm is then the landscape perceived through all the senses. It would be a space inhabited by the cyclical memory of everyday life; the place untouched by images outside of the directly experienced.

THE THEORY DIFFERENCE MAKES

So far we have asserted the necessity of theory for knowing the city differently. We now look at the possibilities feminist theory offers for this task. For if feminism is defined by a common ideology, that of exposing and opposing the inequality of gender difference, integral to it is a commitment to difference reflected in its divergent theoretical and critical methodologies: there are, of course, differences among women. This divergence is also reflected in the feminist approaches taken toward urban history in the last few years. It is from this perspective that feminism's theoretical preoccupations suggest new ways of knowing the city.

Feminists involved directly with the production and analysis of the social space of the city, many of them in the disciplines of planning, architecture, or geography, have been concerned with women's occupation of social space and the gendering of this space through their activities. Parallel trends in the United States and Europe have focused on spatial practice and experience, on women as users of the city and on the man-made environment they occupy (Hayden 1981; Matrix 1984; Roberts 1991; Weisman 1992). The object of study here is the "real" city, the ideological assumptions made by men as the builders and planners of this environment, and the ways in which patriarchal ideology has taken physical form. Daphne Spain (1992) makes connections between the spaces occupied by women and their social status, but there is an urgent need to go beyond the conception of the transparent signifying value of this man-made environment, and to reflect on the role of representations in mediating between "reality" and "experience," to look at feminist analyses of textual and visual systems without losing touch with the political concern for material oppression.

If cities are complex systems of representation, then to study them historically is further complicated, as we have already noted, by the fact that history is itself a construct and that, historically, women have both been excluded from the dominant forms of representation and named as sign within them. This has obscured the lives of real women and an understanding of female subjectivity and identity. For this reason feminism has shifted from searching for the origin of oppression to addressing the interpretation of that oppression, decoding systems of representation in textual and signifying practices (Barrett and Phillips 1991). Poststructuralists such as Foucault have shifted the parameters of historical knowledge from reconstructing a "real" past and dealing with causation and determination to focusing instead on the discursive construction of power and knowledge and the political contestation of relations of domination and subordination. To consider gendered representations as constructed rather than natural implies that a feminist history is no longer simply about the categories of women and men and the things that have happened to them but about the construction of identity and the ways in which class, race, and sexuality as well as gender difference are organized within representational forms.

This kind of theoretical conception can be usefully applied to urban and planning history. Feminist historians Leonore Davidoff and Catherine Hall (1987) have documented the history of women's occupation of cities and the creation and contesting of their marginal role through patriarchal and capitalist ideological mechanisms. The history of women's role in the construction of the urban environment has so far concentrated only on gender difference and on the inclusion/exclusion of women in planning history (Greed 1994). Although they successfully reclaim the work of women, the "underside" of history, with the aim that a different female way of knowing might reformulate both the telling and the tale of urban history, studies like these would be enriched by theorizing difference among women as well as the construction of identity positioned only by gender difference.

The most pervasive of ideas about gender and space is the sociospatial paradigm, an ideological construct that prescribes a public sphere for men and a private sphere for women. The gendered representations embedded within this model are problematic for feminists, for not only are they contained within a binary hierarchy where the male-public assumes predominance over the female-private, relegating it to an inferior status, but they also work to deny women physical and psychological access to the public realm of the city, and to position the private at the margins of the urban center. The importance of representation in the difference between women's occupation of space and the coding of space as feminine has indeed been noted by Liz Bondi (1990) and Doreen Massey (1993).

The textual techniques of Jacques Derrida's deconstruction have been adopted by feminists as a way of deconstructing this sociospatial dichotomy through its representational forms. Art historians have dealt with representations of the feminine in connection with the imagery of the city. By strategically reversing terms of the binary, they show the feminine suburb, the nondominant category, as the site of a dominant quality, production, through looking at the Parisian suburb of Paissy as the site of production of the paintings of Mary Cassatt and Berthe Morrisot (Adler 1989; Pollock 1988). The deconstruction of the binary in this way allows us to see spaces inhabited differently and cities as gendered in an alternative way.

Architectural historians and critics such as Drone Agrest (1993) have looked at the signifying values of representations of the city in images and texts, while Marina Warner (1988) has analyzed the use of the female form as "other" in city statues to represent abstract values. Geographers such as Bondi (1992) have similarly started to deal with the interplay between gendered identity and the symbolism of the urban environment, noting that professionals and laypersons in the field have not gone beyond an essentialist and biological interpretation, but they have not yet commented on the sexual aspects of the visual and textual representations of the built environment. Beatriz Colomina (1992) marks the beginnings of research into the interactions between both architecture and sexuality as signifying systems in the city, here through the medium of photography and examined with reference to specific urban spaces as well as individual architectural pieces.

In order to look at the ways sexuality is constructed and represented in textual and, in particular, visual systems, feminist theory has used psychoanalytic as well as semiotic models. Issues of the anxieties of fetishism, voyeurism, and scopophilic pleasure that result from viewing the female body in representation are used to connect the fetishized body of the woman in psychoanalytic formulations to Marxist analyses of the fetishized commodity, where in capitalism under patriarchy the woman is sign in the patriarchal economy (Irigaray 1985a). The convergence of the social and psychic fetishism of the female body in the photograph has extended discussions of the fetishized nature of the photographic image. The dominance of the visual in the psychoanalytic construction of the male subject has ramifications for both the city and the female as objects of the male gaze, for it limits both the possibilities of self-representation for women in photographs and any glimpses of the experiential qualities of the city from photographic images. The city recorded through photographic images becomes a mask (Colomina 1994), and the feminine presence in the city is recorded by its absence (Nesbit 1992). There is work to be done here in uncovering the connections between the mask of the city and the surface construction of female spatiality through the masquerade of femininity and the possibilities of attaining identity through mimicry (Irigaray 1985b).

The representational form of written text has been used to reclaim the city as space for women by looking at descriptions written by women of their positive and exhilarating experience of the city (Wilson 1991). There has, however, been some argument over whether forms of male ideology in representational form, specifically the texts of modern writers, are able to deny women's experience of the city on a physical and psychological level (Wilson 1990; Wolff 1985). Certainly the fluid space of a narrative can represent the city of the female imagination, in diachronic as well as synchronic time (Winterson 1988). The text can operate as both a metaphoric site in which to explore potential experiences, dreams of possible urban places, and also as a space for sharing memories of the city (Heron 1993). Modes of writing, such as memoir, can express a different way of looking at the city through the intimate and personal rather than the objective, and through sensual rather than purely visual stimulation (Wolff 1993). To treat the text as a metaphoric city is one thing; but it is another, as Jennifer Bloomer (1993) undertakes, to analyze architectural representations as spatially structured by a narrative plot. Just how useful these textual strategies are for interpretive histories of the city remains to be seen.

While deconstruction has shown the limitations of binary constructions and revealed that the dominance of the masculine term is based on the repression of the feminine term, as some of the studies identified above show, certain issues still need to be raised concerning the validity of this technique for feminism. First, and critically, since the starting point of a feminist textual practice is not a theoretical interest in the nature of language but the painful and interested recognition of women's oppression, do we accept that a textual technique can radically alter an ideological system? Derrida's "feminine" must be understood to be a continuation of the philosophical condition of naming the indefinable "female," a label that, as Jane Flax (1991) and Andrea Nye (1989) show, has nothing to do with the reality of being a woman. Second, if we accept that feminism, motivated by the inequalities and constraints of the sex/gender dichotomy, desires to construct a position that differs from a representation of an "other," should it adopt strategies developed through the work of those with different intentions, and should it adapt methods that have evolved in a discipline, such as philosophy, that locates women as "other," both internally as sign and externally as women (Lloyd 1984)?

How, then, do we begin to address questions of female experience, knowledge, and identity in history? Who was the female subject who never existed? Where is she now? It is precisely this latter question of "where?" that is providing theoretical solutions to the problem of essentialism, for the opposition of essentialism and constructivism can be deconstructed by considering subject position or place instead of essence (Bondi 1993a). Feminist practice must be positioned as "standpoint theory" (Flax 1990) or placed in a "locality" (Probyn 1990) in order to open possibilities for a dialogue between feminism and postmodernism (Bondi and Domosh 1992). These spatial references are used to deal with knowledge through positionality (McDowell 1993; Rose 1993a, 1993b) and to deal with identity through a sense of place. They help to identify positively with a space on the "margin," and transform the place you occupy (hooks 1989). But to establish an identity beyond representational forms means also producing images that "displace the boundaries of space" (Braidotti 1994).

Yet the task remains as to how to use this conceptual work to illuminate our knowledge of the city. How do these real and metaphoric spaces interact? Spatial practices can be reformulated around the concepts of metaphorical space; likewise spatial concepts could be materially grounded by information on the gendered occupation of "real" social space (Bondi 1993b), Indeed, there have been positive responses from Australian geographers such as Louise C. Johnson (1994) to deconstructive theory, suggesting that it can add something new to the spatial practice of geography and planning, and from the English geographer Gillian Rose (1993b), who has commented on the relevance of Luce Irigaray's work for defining new fluid spatialities. Indeed, it is the work of feminist philosophers that is perhaps the most relevant for those looking for new conceptions of gendered space and time (Grosz 1994). For feminists writing the history of cities, while the object of the city may provide a unique site for exploring new theoretical approaches, new ways of thinking about sexuality and spatiality may equally suggest new parts of the city to explore. The role of females in producing the city may be reexamined without recourse to the "feminine" (Bergren 1994), for although this may sound reminiscent of "her story," a different subject knows a different city.

REFERENCES

Adler, Kathleen. 1989. "The Suburban, the Modern and une Dame de Paissy." *Oxford Art Journal* 12(1):3–13.

Agrest, Diane. 1993. *Architecture from Without: Theoretical Framings for a Critical Practice*. Cambridge, Mass. MIT Press.

Ashworth, G. J. 1991. *War and the City*. London: Routledge.

Bale, John. 1993. *Sport, Space and the City*. London: Routledge.

Balfour, Alan. 1990. *Berlin: The Politics of Order, 1737–1989*. New York: Rizzoli.

Barker, Theo, and Anthony Sutcliffe, eds. 1993. *Megalopolis: The Giant City in History*. Basingstoke, England: Macmillan.

Barrett, Michele, and Anne Phillips, eds. 1992. *Destabilising Theory: Contemporary Feminist Debates*. Cambridge: Polity Press.

Benevolo, Leonardo. 1993. *The European City*. Oxford: Oxford University Press.

Bergeron, Louis, ed. 1989. *Paris, genèse d'un paysage*. Paris: Picard.

Bergren, Ann. 1994. "Dear Jennifer." *ANY*, no. 4 (January–February): 12–5.

Bloomer, Jennifer. 1993. *Architecture and the Text: The (S)crypts of Joyce and Piranesi*. New Haven: Yale University Press.

Bondi, Liz. 1990. "Feminism, Postmodernism, and Geography: A Space for Women?" *Antipode* 22, no. 2 (August): 156–67.

———. 1992. "Gender Symbols and Urban Landscapes." *Progress in Human Geography* 16(2):157–70.

———. 1993a. "Locating Identity Politics." In *Place and the Politics of Identity*, ed. Michael Keith and Steve Pile. London: Routledge.

————. 1993b. "Gender and Geography: Crossing Boundaries." *Progress in Human Geography* 17(2):241–46.

Bondi, Liz, and M. Domosh. 1992. "Other Figures in the Other Places: On Feminism, Postmodernism and Geography." *Environment and Planning D: Space and Society* 10:199–213.

Borden, Iain, Joe Kerr, Alicia Pivaro, and Jane Rendell, eds. 1996. *Strangely Familiar: Narratives of Architecture in the City.* London: Routledge.

Braidotti, Rosa. 1994. "Body-Images and the Pornography of Representation." In *Knowing the Difference: Feminist Perspectives in Epistemology,* ed. Kathleen Lennon and Margaret Whitford, 17–30. London:Routledge.

Buder, Stanley. 1990. *Visionaries and Planners: The Garden City Movement and the Modern Community.* Oxford: Oxford University Press.

Burtenshaw, D., M. Bateman, and G. J. Ashworth. 1991. *The European City: A Western Perspective.* London: Fulton.

Carter, Harold C., and C. Roy Lewis. 1990. *An Urban Geography of England and Wales in the Nineteenth Century.* Sevenoak, England: Arnold.

Colomina, Beatriz, ed. 1992. *Sexuality and Space.* New York: Princeton Architectural Press.

————. 1994. *Privacy and Publicity: Modern Architecture as Mass Media.* Cambridge, Mass.: MIT Press.

Creese, Walter. 1992. *The Search for Environment: The Garden City, Before and After.* Expanded ed. Baltimore: Johns Hopkins University Press.

Davidoff, Leonore, and Catherine Hall. 1987. *Family Fortunes: Men and Women of the English Middle Class, 1750–1850.* Chicago: University of Chicago Press.

Davis, Mike. 1990. *City of Quartz: Excavating the Future of Los Angeles.* London: Verso.

Deakin, D., ed. 1989. *Wythenshawe: The Story of a Garden City.* Chichester, England: Phillimore.

Deutsche, Rosalyn. 1988. "Uneven Development: Public Art in New York City." *October,* no. 47:3–52.

Entrikin, J. Nicholas. 1991. *The Betweenness of Place.* Basingstoke, England: Macmillan.

Flax, Jane. 1990. "Postmodernism and Gender Relations in Feminist Theory." In *Feminism/Postmodernism,* ed. Linda Nicholson, 39–62. London: Routledge.

————. 1991. *Thinking Fragments: Psychoanalysis, Feminism and Postmodernism in the Contemporary West.* Berkeley: University of California Press.

Fortier, Bruno. 1989. *La métropole imaginaire: Un atlas de Paris.* Liège: Pierre Mardaga.

Greed, Clara H. 1994. *Women and Planning: Creating Gendered Realities.* London: Routledge.

Gregory, Derek. 1994. *Geographical Imaginations.* Oxford: Blackwell.

Grosz, Elizabeth. 1994. "Women, Chora, Dwelling." *ANY,* no. 4 (January–February): 22–27.

Hall, Peter. 1988. *Cities of Tomorrow: An Intellectual History of Urban Planning and Design in the Twentieth Century.* Oxford: Blackwell.

Hall, T., ed. 1991. *Planning and Urban Growth in Nordic Countries.* London: Spon.

Haraway, Donna. [1985] 1990. "A Manifesto for Cyborgs: Science, Technology, and

Socialist Feminism in the 1980s." In *Feminism/Postmodernism*, ed. Linda Nicholson, 190–233. London: Routledge.

Hayden, Dolores. 1981. *The Grand Domestic Revolution.* Cambridge, Mass.: MIT Press.

Heron, Liz, ed. 1993. *Streets of Desire: Women's Fiction of the Twentieth Century.* London: Virago.

hooks, bell, 1989. *Yearnings: Race, Gender, and Cultural Politics.* London: Turnaround Press.

Irigaray, Luce. 1985a. *This Sex Which Is Not One.* Ithaca, N.Y.: Cornell University Press.

———. 1985b. *The Speculum of the Other Woman.* Ithaca, N.Y.: Cornell University Press.

Johnson, Louise C. 1994. "What Future for Feminist Geography?" *Gender, Place and Culture.* 1(1).

Jones, Emrys. 1990. *Metropolis: The World's Great Cities.* Oxford: Oxford University Press.

Katznelson, Ira. 1992. *Marxism and the City.* Oxford: Oxford University Press.

Keith, Michael, and Steve Pile, eds. 1993. *Place and the Politics of Identity.* London: Routledge.

Keith, Michael, and Alisdair Rogers, eds. 1991. *Hollow Promises: Rhetoric and Reality in the Inner City.* London: Mansell.

King, Anthony. 1989a. *Urbanism, Colonialism, and the World-Economy: Cultural and Spatial Foundations of the World Urban System.* London: Routledge.

———. 1989b. *Global Cities: Post-Imperialism and the Internationalization of London.* London: Routledge.

Ladd, Brian. 1990. *Urban Planning and Civic Order in Germany, 1860–1914.* Cambridge, Mass.: Harvard University Press.

Lefebvre, Henri. 1991a. *The Production of Space.* Oxford: Blackwell.

———. 1991b. *Critique of Everyday Life.* Vol. 1: *Introduction.* London: Verso.

Leonitidou, Lila. 1990. *The Mediterranean City in Transition: Social Change and Urban Development.* Cambridge: Cambridge University Press.

Lloyd, Genevieve. 1984. *The Man of Reason: "Male" and "Female" in Western Philosophy.* London: Methuen.

McDowell, Linda. 1993. "Space, Place and Gender Relations, Parts 1 and 2." *Progress in Human Geography* 17(3):157–179, 305–318.

Massey, Doreen. 1993. "Politics and Space/Time." In *Place and the Politics of Identity*, ed. Michael Keith and Steve Pile, 141–146. London: Routledge. Reprinted in Massey, *Space, Place and Gender.* Cambridge: Polity Press, 1994.

———. 1994. *Space, Place and Gender.* Cambridge: Polity Press.

Matrix. 1984. *Making Space: Women and the Man-Made Environment.* London: Pluto Press.

Miller, Mervyn. 1989. *Letchworth: The First Garden City.* Chichester, England: Phillimore.

Nesbit, Molly. 1992. "In the Absence of the Parisienne." In *Sexuality and Space,* ed. Beatriz Colomina, 307–325. New York: Princeton Architectural Press.

Nye, Andrea. 1989. *Feminist Theory and the Philosophy of Man.* New York: Croom Helm.

Pollock, Griselda. 1988. *Vision and Difference: Femininity, Feminism and the Histories of Art*. London: Routledge.

Probyn, Elsbeth. 1990. "Travels in the Postmodern: Making Sense of the Local." In *Feminism/Postmodernism*, ed. Linda Nicholson, 176–189. London: Routledge.

Roberts, Marion. 1991. *Living in a Man-Made World: Gender Assumptions in Modern Housing Design*. London: Routledge.

Rose, Gillian. 1993a. *Feminism and Geography: The Limits of Geographical Knowledge*. Cambridge: Polity Press.

———. 1993b. "Progress in Geography and Gender: Or Something Else?" *Progress in Human Geography*. 17(4):531–537.

Sennett, Richard. 1990. *The Conscience of the Eye*. London: Faber and Faber.

Shields, Rob. 1991. *Places on the Margin*. London: Routledge.

Spain, Daphne. 1992. *Gendered Spaces*. Chapel Hill: University of North Carolina Press.

Sudjic, Deyan. 1992. *The 100 Mile City*. London: Deutsch.

Thornley, Andy. 1991. *Urban Planning under Thatcherism: The Challenge of the Market*. London: Routledge.

Urry, John. 1990. *The Tourist Gaze: Leisure and Travel in Contemporary Societies*. London: Sage.

Walmsley, D. J. 1988. *Urban Living: The Individual in the City*. London: Longman.

Ward, Colin. 1989. *Welcome, Thinner City: Urban Survival in the 1990s*. London: Bedford Square Press.

———. 1990. *The Child in the City*. London: Bedford Square Press.

Ward, Stephen V., ed. 1992. *The Garden City: Past, Present and Future*. London: Spon.

Warner, Marina. 1988. *Monuments and Maidens: The Allegory of the Female Form*. London: Picador.

Watson, Sophie, and Katherine Gibson, eds. 1995. *Postmodern Cities and Spaces*. Oxford: Blackwell.

Weisman, Leslie Kanes. 1992. *Discrimination by Design*. Urbana: University of Illinois Press.

Werlen, Benno. 1993. *Society, Action and Space*. London: Routledge.

Whitehand, J. W. R., and P. J. Larkham, eds. 1992. *Urban Landscapes. International Perspectives*. London: Routledge.

Wilson, Elizabeth. 1990. "The Invisible Flâneur." *New Left Review*. 191:90–110.

———. 1991. *The Sphinx in the City: Urban Life, the Control of Disorder, and Women*. London: Virago.

Winterson, Jeanette. 1988. *The Passion*. London: Penguin.

Wolff, Janet. 1985. "The Invisible Flâneuse: Women and the Literature of Modernity." *Theory, Culture and Society* 2(3):37–46.

———. 1993. "Memoirs and Micrologies: Walter Benjamin, Feminism and Cultural Analysis." *The Actuality of Walter Benjamin, New Formations*, no. 20 (Summer): 113–122.

SEVEN

City Planning for Girls

Exploring the Ambiguous Nature of Women's Planning History

Susan Marie Wirka

In 1928, less than a decade after city planning became a profession in the United States, the University of Chicago Press published *City Planning for Girls*, the fifth in its prestigious series of social service monographs. The modest volume, numbering exactly 150 pages, was subtitled "A Study of the Social Machinery for Case Work with Girls in Philadelphia, with Comments on Present Methods, Brief Histories of Past Experiments, and Recommended Plans for the Future." More precisely, it studied juvenile delinquency among girls in Philadelphia between 1923 and 1928. At the time of publication the author, Henrietta Additon, was executive secretary of Philadelphia's Big Sister Association; she also taught social economics at Bryn Mawr College. Additon's singular publication is a rich source for understanding the gendered nature of early-twentieth-century professionalization as well as the relationship among women, sexuality, and the city. For our purposes here, it is an ideal medium through which to explore the ambiguous nature of women's planning history.

Additon takes a critical view of early-twentieth-century social work on behalf of Philadelphia girls. She especially finds fault with the profession's lack of understanding about how such urban conditions as overcrowding, poverty, unsanitary housing, and the practice of child labor might affect a girl's early development. Other issues that Additon sees as influencing female juvenile delinquency include one or both parents' unemployment, alcoholism, or desertion. Throughout her meticulous analysis of social work case records, Additon repeatedly observes three things girls want to help get their lives "back on track": education, recreation, and a decent job. Girls also express a desire for sound and stable direction as they find a place for themselves in the city. These are the things Additon feels are poorly understood by social workers dealing with female juvenile delinquents.

As a partial remedy to the "girl problem," Additon proposes a fourteen-point *plan* for the care of Philadelphia girls.[1] Among other things, it involves the coordination of needed social resources like educational, recreational, and employment opportunities, the provision of child guidance and psychological facilities, and the continuation of state support for the safety of children in industry and the Mothers' Assistance Fund. It also includes recommendations for the provision of special scholarships for girls, an increase in the number of school counselors, and the establishment of a Policewoman's Bureau within the Philadelphia Police Department to better serve girls. Additon's text is as much a planning vision as it is a vision of social welfare. Yet, reflecting on the forward-looking picture then recently prepared by the chamber of commerce, she does not see her ideas articulated anywhere in the official view of Philadelphia's future.

Additon is also critical of early-twentieth-century city planning. Contemplating the Philadelphia Chamber of Commerce's "city of wide streets, beautiful parks, and magnificent business blocks" free of "bad housing conditions" and "wretched surroundings," she asks rhetorically: "But what of the men and women, the boys and girls to inhabit this beautiful city?" (Additon 1928: 138). Clearly challenging the City Beautiful orientation in planning, which did not necessarily focus on the social needs of girls in the city, Additon suggests: "They are after all an essential part of that picture and to be complete city planning must include those measures which help to keep its children as clean and beautiful in body and spirit as are the material symbols of human progress" (1928: 138). Here, Additon is essentially calling for cooperation between city planners and social workers in developing visions of the city that reflect human needs and in designing social welfare programs that work in the city. And yet her phrase "clean and beautiful in body and spirit" invokes another, very different undercurrent in planning thought—the stream of bodies, cities, and social order;

1. Additon's plan includes the following fourteen points: (1) a "girls-case-working agency with representatives on its board of directors of the Catholic, Jewish, and Protestant faiths"; (2) expansion of clinics for child guidance and psychological help; (3) a few "carefully selected supervised private homes where unadjusted girls . . . may board"; (4) an experimental boarding school; (5) better facilities for unmarried black mothers; (6) scholarships for advanced education; (7) more school counselors; (8) a policewoman's bureau to protect community girls; (9) employment safeguards to ensure a well-trained probation department; (10) substantial appropriations for the Mother's Assistance Fund; (11) adequate state facilities for the mentally ill; (12) enforcement of child labor laws; (13) provision of "wholesome" and "interesting" recreational opportunities; and (14) continued study of juvenile delinquency and its solution (1928: 137–138).

the stream that saw the morality of bodies and the morality of cities as intricately linked.[2]

At least two histories important to women, cities, and planning are thus embedded in the language of Additon's text. As a template for the control of female sexuality in the city, *City Planning for Girls* never attempts to redefine the notion of "public women" as the embodiment of urban immorality, a "disorder" in need of strict ordering through moral, educational, and recreational reform. In that way the text clearly reflects the lasting influence of City Beautiful ideas with their heavily laden sexual and moral subtexts (Boyer 1978; Hooper, this vol.). As an exercise in social planning, however, the book also defies another dimension of City Beautiful ideology by envisioning a planning process that responds to the everyday needs of, in this case, girls in the city. Exploring these apparently contradictory readings of Additon's text is my purpose here. Understanding and resolving this paradox requires us to sharpen our theoretical tools and to problematize the very notion of "women's planning history."

THE SUBSTANCE OF ADDITON'S ANALYSIS

City Planning for Girls is organized into seven distinct chapters, an index, and an appendix that reads much like the cultural and recreational resources element of a contemporary general plan. In chapter 1, Additon introduces the problem at hand, acknowledges the help of cooperating agencies, and describes her research objectives and methodology.[3] In true social science fashion, chapters 2 and 3 lay the necessary background work for the study by surveying the resources of existing social agencies, the

2. Barbara Hooper explores this link, specifically, how urban planning came to conceive of its project as "mastering" disorderly cities and bodies, in her essay "The Poem of Male Desires," which appears in this volume. See also Wilson 1991 for the relationship between planning and the control of female sexuality in the city.

3. Additon classifies the cooperating social service agencies as follows: (1) special agencies for girls, including the Girls' Aid, the Church Mission of Help, the Big Sister Association, and the Personal Service Bureau; (2) children's agencies, including the White-Williams Foundation, the Catholic Children's Bureau, the Children's Aid Society, the U.S. Children's Bureau, the Juvenile Aid Society, the Society to Protect Children from Cruelty, the Philadelphia Child Welfare, and the Lutheran Children's Bureau; (3) agencies that serve the black community, including the Philadelphia Association for the Protection of Colored Women and the Women's Christian Alliance; (4) family welfare agencies, including the Family Society, the Jewish Welfare Society, the Home Missionary Society, the Union Benevolent Society, and the American Red Cross (Home Service Section); and (5) miscellaneous service agencies, including the Traveler's Aid Society, Emergency Aid of Pennsylvania, the Social Service Department and the International Institute of the Young Women's Christian Association, the Philadelphia Federation of Churches, the Girl's Fellowship League of the Methodist Episcopal Church, and the Associated Committee on Policewomen (1928: 5–6).

courts, and correctional institutions dealing in any way with "wayward" girls. Chapters 4 through 6 form the bulk of Additon's analytical work; here she examines individual case records, identifies important causative factors, and evaluates the quality of casework (including investigation, diagnosis, and treatment) done in each instance. Additon's concluding chapter places her work in historical context, compares female juvenile delinquency in 1927 with the situation ten years earlier, and offers recommendations about social resources needed for effective work with girls.[4]

As a piece of social science research *City Planning for Girls* is a classic planning document in the finest tradition of social surveys. Additon's objectives were twofold: to understand what social agencies engaged in "work with girls" were actually doing in the 1920s and to propose a comprehensive plan that "might serve as a basis for future work" (1928: 5). Surveying numerous Philadelphia organizations, she asked two research questions: "What understanding of the reasons 'Why girls go wrong' have the staff members of these agencies? [and] . . . What do they know about the methods of helping girls who have already got into trouble and of keeping other girls out of trouble?" (1928: 1). Additon's method was simply a close reading of selected case records, through which she concluded that the complex causative factors, both hereditary and environmental, of such "girl problems" as prostitution, unmarried motherhood, incorrigibility, disorderly conduct, and running away from home were seldom fully understood by social workers. Even more rarely did the social work machinery successfully institute ameliorative measures with lasting impact. Thus, she argued, the need for a plan to address the multifaceted causes of female juvenile delinquency.

Although never explicitly stated, the control of female sexuality is the real subject of *City Planning for Girls*. Veiled behind such language as "vagrancy," "sex offense," "serious immorality," "waywardness," and "moral delinquency," premarital sex and prostitution are the ultimate "social evils" that lead young girls into a life of delinquency. While Additon defines "delinquency in a girl" as "behavior in conflict with the sex mores of the time and place," she also believes there is no single definition of "delinquency" since it depends on "such purely fortuitous circumstances as the protection offered by the family, the friends, and the standards of a particular community" (1928: 92, 93). This confusion is evident in her treatment of everything from simply walking the streets to genuine "streetwalking" as confirmation of delinquency. While the 1920s saw the emergence

4. Although *City Planning for Girls* was published in 1928, Additon uses the years 1917 and 1927 for comparative purposes here because her source for material on the earlier period was a study conducted by Miss Anna B. Pratt, director of the Magdalen Society, which was published in 1917 (see Additon 1928: 124).

of the image of the "sexually sophisticated" woman, most notably the flapper, as well as the proliferation of commercial forms of recreation, giving many women places to freely explore their sexuality, sex within marriage was still the social norm.[5] Indeed, the increased public presence of women likely fueled the continued efforts of reformers like Additon (see Wilson 1991).

Despite her reliance on the language of morality, Additon occasionally comes close to advancing a feminist argument. For example, quoting the municipal court report of 1924, she notes, with curiosity, that stealing is the most common offense among young boys while "either suspected sex immorality or the danger of its development" is the most common among young girls (1928: 24). Through statistical variations, Additon further illustrates the different community standards regarding the conduct of girls and boys and agrees with the charge made by women's organizations that in the case of sex crimes, "men and women do not receive the same treatment in many of our courts for similar or identical offenses." Later Additon remarks that she does not believe unmarried mothers should be classified "as 'criminals' at all" (1928: 29, 30). Nevertheless, her analysis goes no further than acknowledging the existence of both an unfair classification and a judicial double standard in the treatment of male and female juvenile delinquents.

Sometimes Additon explicitly discusses the sexuality of Philadelphia girls. While protection from sexual danger and the preservation of sexual morality were the underlying goals of social "work with girls," attempts to control female sexuality had very real, often dire, consequences. Nowhere is this more clear than in Additon's treatment of the individual case records. Here, she reports examples of young girls unsuccessfully inducing abortions, unwillingly placing newborns up for adoption, and reluctantly signing adoption papers (1928: 41, 65, 43). Clearly, these are examples of girls struggling to conform to the "sexual mores" of their "time and place." Masturbation repeatedly appears as a difficult issue for social workers; Additon cites numerous cases of a young girl's "habit of masturbation" being identified as a problem needing reform. While rape and incest do not explicitly appear in the case records, there are vague references to girls "witnessing rape" and refusing to talk about early "sex experiences" (1928: 84, 86, 24). Of course, social workers' obsession with the privacy of sleeping arrangements in the home is another indication of concern regarding

5. For examples of ways in which working-class women carved out corners of the city in which to become sexually and economically independent, see Meyerowitz 1988. For a fascinating treatment of the relationship between commercial entertainments and female sexuality, see Peiss 1986.

sex between girls and family members or boarding strangers.[6] Here, the social work machinery understandably tried to protect girls from unsavory sexual experiences.

INTERPRETING ADDITON FOR PLANNING HISTORY

Recent historical scholarship exploring the relationship among bodies, cities, and social order and between city planning and female sexuality suggests one possible approach to reading Additon's text. In her essay in this volume, Barbara Hooper argues that planning, at its inception in nineteenth-century Paris, was infused with ideas associating the "disorderly city" with the female body, specifically the prostitute's body. Thus planning concerned itself with controlling and cleansing, policing and pathologizing urban women. As policing the city became largely a project of policing female bodies, Hooper explains, planners joined forces with "gynecologists, social scientists, sanitation engineers, public hygienists, and other . . . disciplinary experts" to implement reason's order over the " 'disease and disorder' of the modern metropolis and its bodies." Elizabeth Wilson makes a similar argument in *The Sphinx in the City* (1991). Presenting the city as a place of sexual danger *and* sexual adventure for women, Wilson sees planning discourse as attempting to rein in the menace of female sexuality through the regulation of women's access to urban, public space.

City Planning for Girls seems to support the interpretations offered by Hooper and Wilson. This is most evident in Additon's uncritical dependence on the language of sexual immorality to explain female juvenile delinquency and in her plea that planning help keep children as "clean and beautiful in body and spirit" as the city itself. Such sentiments echo City Beautiful ideas that sought to bring order, harmony, and morality to the city through the creation of more beautiful and pristine, thus more livable, urban environments.[7] Since Additon was not trained in any of the technical professions that informed early-twentieth-century city planning, it is hard to determine how consciously she used the controlling rhetoric of planning. She was, however, familiar enough with the language of planning to make a strong connection between urban and moral reform. Following Hooper or Paul Rabinow (1989)—or Michel Foucault, who inspired them both—we might then argue that Additon's "girl problem" is best

6. See Gordon 1988: 204–249 especially, for a discussion of reformers and the issue of incest.

7. See Boyer 1978: 261–276 especially, for a discussion of the moral vision of City Beautiful planners. See also Foglesong 1986: 124–166, chapter entitled "Planning the City Beautiful."

understood within the Foucauldian frameworks of producing and disciplining "docile bodies" (1977) and "the deployment of sexuality" ([1978] 1990).[8]

But Additon certainly did not believe that designing more beautiful and pristine urban environments alone would solve the problem of female juvenile delinquency in the city. On the contrary, she wanted planners to address the social needs of girls so they might create cities that offered viable alternatives to the urban pressures that often led to delinquency in the first place. And even though Additon relied on the language of sexual immorality, she was nonetheless genuinely sympathetic to understanding the complex causes—beyond a crisis in morality—of juvenile delinquency among girls. Urban social issues such as education, recreation, employment, poverty, and health were as important to her analysis as issues of morality and sexuality.

Beyond its moralistic agenda, *City Planning for Girls* is also an attempt to infuse social and humanistic perspectives into the planning process. Evidence of the very real, human needs of Philadelphia girls is clearly present in the case records, and Additon draws on these to portray the everyday life struggles that she believed were important causative factors in female juvenile delinquency. Often, family issues were at the core of a young girl's troubles, as Additon reports examples of broken homes, separated parents, and spousal abuse (1928: 60, 45, 39). Education, recreation, and domestic work were significant points of contention for many girls. Additon tells of one girl who hated her grandmother for not giving her an education; of another girl who wanted more than anything the opportunity to go to school; of another who was obsessed with belonging to a gymnasium to learn to swim and dance; and of still another who resented spending all her free time doing housework and caring for children (1928: 39, 67, 38, 62). More than any other factors, education, recreation, and employment consistently appear in the case records as areas that, if improved, have the potential to help set delinquent girls straight.

The economic reality of many girls' lives meant that they left school to go to work as soon as their parents saw fit. While domestic work was often

8. In *Discipline and Punish*, Foucault (1977: 135–169) traces the ways in which, through an obsession with discipline and efficiency, the military, schools, and apprentice workshops created "docility" through subjecting, using, transforming, and improving bodies. In volume 1 of *The History of Sexuality*, Foucault ([1978] 1990: 103–114) explains what he regards as the modern obsession with "talking sex," in part by delineating four strategies that form the specific mechanisms of knowledge and power about sexuality: (1) the hysterization of women's bodies, (2) the pedagogization of children's sex, (3) the socialization of procreative behavior, and (4) the psychiatrization of perverse pleasure. These constitute the domain through which obsessive talk about sexuality has been deployed in modern society.

the only work available, some girls expressed a desire for more gainful employment only to find none. Additon stresses that often vocational training was completely uncoordinated with a girl's educational ability or her interests. In some cases the "nerve racking" stress of work led to ill health among girls. Furthermore, Additon notes that a lack of "wholesome" recreational opportunities only exacerbated the problem of health (1928: 56, 99). Impoverished, overcrowded, and unsanitary housing conditions were also important factors in understanding the plight of young girls. Throughout her analysis of the quality of social casework, Additon laments the lack of any "proper plan," "constructive plan," "planned program," or "co-ordinated plan" to deal with the problem at hand (1928: 106, 51, 54, 116). Clearly, this social worker had a planning mentality; a comprehensive plan providing girls with social resources for health, education, work, and recreation was at the core of her planning vision.

Additon was not the first or the last woman to question the lack of concern for social issues within the dominant planning traditions, which focused on aesthetic urban form (City Beautiful) and efficient city management (City Practical). When Jane Jacobs published *The Death and Life of Great American Cities* in 1961, she asked planners to think about cities in social, economic, and human terms. Long before either Jacobs or Additon, the settlement house leader Mary Kingsbury Simkhovitch (1867–1951) repeatedly challenged the emerging planning profession to see planning "not only from a civic, but also from a social point of view" (1949: 126). In previous work I have argued that, in addition to the City Beautiful and City Practical movements, there was a third movement in planning called the City Social, which was largely the province of women reformers, settlement workers, and social workers. The City Social movement sought to understand, grapple with, and respond to the social and economic injustices underlying urban problems (Wirka 1989, 1994, 1996). Additon's insistence on understanding and providing for the social needs of girls in Philadelphia clearly places her within the City Social tradition. The roots of the renewed emphasis on social planning during the 1960s and 1970s can be found in the earlier work of City Social planners like Additon and Simkhovitch.

Yet another way of reading *City Planning for Girls* is to view the text as sitting at the crossroads between the history of planning and the history of social work. In it we can see how early-twentieth-century professionalization was gendered. Because women like Additon and Simkhovitch did not have access to the technical expertise available to male architects and civil engineers, they were excluded from the "city-building" professions and looked to social work as an avenue through which to carry out their interest in and dedication to urban and social reform issues. Indeed, some scholars have argued that women created the profession of social work precisely because they wanted a professional outlet for their reform work when none was open to them.[9] Many female reformers who made an impact on ideas about social planning were trained through the hands-on experience provided by the settlement house movement, where social service was central to their work. During the early twentieth century settlement houses were urban institutions that were centrally involved in the coordination and delivery of the same services (education, recreation, employment, health) that Additon identified in her study. This history of women's marginalization raises a significant question. If women reformers, settlement workers, and social workers had not been marginalized outside of planning, might city planning have evolved as a more socially conscious profession and avoided the "identity crisis" that characterized planning during the 1960s and 1970s?

OUR CHALLENGE AS HISTORIANS

By now it should be clear why this social work text has relevance for new directions in planning historiography. With few exceptions planning historians have ignored the significant contributions women have made to the profession.[10] This is in part due to the dominant paradigm of historical inquiry in planning; more often than not planning historians have confined their analysis to one or another aspect of the City Beautiful and City Practical movements (Foglesong 1986; Hall 1988; Krueckeberg 1983; Schaffer 1988; Scott 1969). As Leonie Sandercock points out in her introduction to this volume, another problem is that planning historians have concentrated too much on documenting the rise of the profession. These biases necessarily exclude women, since women concentrated their urban reform efforts on social and economic issues; women were also more likely to receive an education in social work or social service administration than in the technical professions of architecture and engineering. A simple corrective to this "oversight" is to expand the definition of planning beyond the strict boundaries of male professional identity and the dominance of

9. In particular, see Fitzpatrick 1990 and Muncy 1991 for insights on the relationship among settlement work, women reformers, and the creation of social work. Women's involvement in social work was also fundamentally linked to the emergence of the welfare state, which was gaining strength by the time *City Planning for Girls* was published. Again, see Muncy 1991. For the relationship among the rise of the welfare state, social workers, and the specific case of single mothers, see Gordon 1994.

10. Birch's (1983a, 1983b) and Hayden's (1981, 1984) work is notable as an exception to traditional planning historiography.

City Beautiful and City Practical ideologies, thus including other professions and movements in which women were actively doing social planning work. Thus we can easily see how *City Planning for Girls* is as much a source for planning historians as it is for historians of social work.

But as a source for historians, *City Planning for Girls* is rife with ambiguities. The enigmatic nature of the text is perhaps most obviously stated in the title. It signals Additon's insistence that planning address the social needs of young girls in the city, but the words she chooses have meanings she may not have intended. On the one hand, *City Planning for Girls* can be read as "planning *of* girls," meaning the ways in which planning tries to control women (especially their sexuality) in the city. On the other hand, *City Planning for Girls* can also be read as "planning *by* girls," meaning how women reformers have addressed human needs in urban space, not through "traditional," physical planning, but through social work and ideas about social planning. Inherent in these various readings is Additon's demand that planners and social workers work together. However unsuspecting Additon may have been about the implications of the title of her work, it is incumbent on historians to appreciate the tensions and contradictions intrinsic to this or any source. This is especially important for understanding what it means to accurately portray the history of women in planning.

The readings of Additon's text suggested above come from different theoretical standpoints within feminist historiography. Different theoretical approaches will yield at least two—apparently opposed—readings of this text. One kind of feminist historiographical approach, influenced by the pioneering work of Dolores Hayden and Eugenie Ladnier Birch, wants to redeem women's place in planning history by showing that women were present in public life in the city as urban and social reformers. But because they were excluded from the city-building professions of planning and architecture, at least in the early twentieth century, women had to find other outlets for their reform work. Hence they gravitated to housing reform, social work, settlement work, parks and playgrounds, and community activism. A redemptive—or what the historian Joan Kelly ([1976] 1987) terms a "compensatory"—historiography makes visible the important contributions of these women. This is one way of reading Additon's text and arguing for her inclusion in the pantheon of women planners. And this was my initial theoretical framework for approaching *City Planning for Girls*.

However, more recent feminist work inspired in part by Foucault's analysis of knowledge and power suggests a very different interpretation. Additon's moralistic program places her squarely in the Foucauldian framework of the disciplining professional—patrolling behaviors, policing norms, establishing new forms for the regulation of women in the city. Thus it would seem that "the poem of male desires"—in which women's voracious sexuality must be controlled by elite professionals—can also be authored by women. Are these two readings mutually exclusive? Is this history really ambivalent? Are we at an unresolvable impasse here? In each case, I would answer "no" and argue that both readings of Additon's text are equally valid and not necessarily contradictory. But perhaps the Foucauldian reading points best to the limitations of the redemptive, compensatory approach to women's history. Simply retrieving the women who have been lost to planning's memory should not be our only historical project. We need to critically examine what women themselves had to say about gender and sexual relations in the city and about planning's role in reproducing them. Once that is done, Additon's apparently feminist text looks less transformative. And while Additon's work offers an important challenge to the City Beautiful paradigm, it nevertheless reinforces existing power relations by not also challenging patriarchal notions about the distinction between, and the place of, respectable women and whores in the city. Analyzing *City Planning for Girls* from both these perspectives makes it a far richer, and ultimately more useful, source for planning historians.

REFERENCES

Additon, Henrietta. 1928. *City Planning for Girls: A Study of the Social Machinery for Case Work with Girls in Philadelphia, with Comments on Present Methods, Brief Histories of Past Experiments, and Recommended Plans for the Future.* Chicago: University of Chicago Press.

Birch, Eugenie Ladner. 1983a. "From City Worker to City Planner: Women and Planning, 1890–1980." In *The American Planner: Biographies and Recollections,* ed. Donald A. Krueckeberg. New York: Methuen.

———. 1983b. "Woman-Made America: The Case of Early Public Housing Policy." In *The American Planner: Biographies and Recollections,* ed. Donald A. Krueckeberg. New York: Methuen.

Boyer, Christine M. 1983. *Dreaming the Rational City: The Myth of American City Planning.* Cambridge, Mass.: MIT Press.

Boyer, Paul. 1978. *Urban Masses and Moral Order in America, 1820–1920.* Cambridge, Mass.: Harvard University Press.

Cott, Nancy F. 1987. *The Grounding of Modern Feminism.* New Haven: Yale University Press.

Fitzpatrick, Ellen. 1990. *Endless Crusade: Women Social Scientists and Progressive Reform.* New York: Oxford University Press.

Foglesong, Richard E. 1986. *Planning the Capitalist City: The Colonial Era to the 1920s.* Princeton, N.J.: Princeton University Press.

Foucault, Michel. 1977. *Discipline and Punish: The Birth of the Prison.* New York: Pantheon Books.

————. [1978] 1990. *The History of Sexuality, Vol. 1: An Introduction.* New York: Vintage Books.

Gordon, Linda. 1988. *Heroes of Their Own Lives: The Politics and History of Family Violence, Boston 1880–1960.* New York: Penguin Books.

————. 1994. *Pitied but Not Entitled: Single Mothers and the History of Welfare.* New York: Free Press.

Guttenberg, Albert Z. 1993. *The Language of Planning: Essays on the Origins and Ends of American Planning Thought.* Urbana: University of Illinois Press.

Hall, Peter. 1988. *Cities of Tomorrow: An Intellectual History of Urban Planning and Design in the Twentieth Century.* New York: Blackwell.

Hayden, Dolores. 1981. *The Grand Domestic Revolution: A History of Feminist Designs for American Homes, Neighborhoods, and Cities.* Cambridge, Mass.: MIT Press.

————. 1984. *Redesigning the American Dream: The Future of Housing, Work and Family Life.* New York: Norton.

Jacobs, Jane. 1961. *The Death and Life of Great American Cities.* New York: Vintage Books.

Kelly-Gadol, Joan. [1976] 1987. "The Social Relation of the Sexes: Methodological Implications of Women's History." In *Feminism and Methodology: Social Science Issues*, ed. Sandra Harding. Bloomington: Indiana University Press.

Krueckeberg, Donald A., ed. 1983. *Introduction to Planning History in the United States.* New Brunswick, N.J.: Center for Urban Policy Research, Rutgers University.

Marcuse, Peter. 1980. "Housing in Early City Planning." *Journal of Urban History* 6, no. 2 (February): 153–176.

Meyerowitz, Joanne J. 1988. *Women Adrift: Independent Wage Earners in Chicago, 1880–1930.* Chicago: University of Chicago Press.

Muncy, Robyn. 1991. *Creating a Female Dominion in American Reform, 1890–1935.* New York: Oxford University Press.

Peiss, Kathy. 1986. *Cheap Amusements: Working Women and Leisure in Turn-of-the-Century New York.* Philadelphia: Temple University Press.

Rabinow, Paul. 1989. *French Modern: Norms and Forms of the Social Environment.* Cambridge, Mass.: MIT Press.

Schaffer, Daniel, ed. 1988. *Two Centuries of American Planning.* Baltimore: Johns Hopkins University Press.

Scott, Mel. 1969. *American City Planning Since 1890.* Berkeley: University of California Press.

Simkhovitch, Mary Kingsbury. 1949. *Here Is God's Plenty; Reflections on American Social Advance.* New York: Harper.

Ward, David, and Olivier Zunz, eds. 1992. *The Landscape of Modernity: Essays on New York City, 1900–1940.* New York: Russell Sage Foundation.

Wilson, Elizabeth. 1991. *The Sphinx in the City: Urban Life, the Control of Disorder, and Women.* Berkeley: University of California Press.

Wirka, Susan Marie. 1989. "Mary Kingsbury Simkhovitch and Neighborhood Planning in New York City, 1897–1909." Master's thesis, University of California, Los Angeles.

————. 1994. "Introduction to Mary Kingsbury Simkhovitch's Housing Chapter from *Here Is God's Plenty: Reflections on American Social Advance.*" In *The American Planner: Biographies and Recollections,* 2d ed., ed. Donald A. Krueckeberg. New Brunswick, N.J.: Center for Urban Policy Research, Rutgers University.

————. 1996. "The City Social Movement: Progressive Women Reformers and Early Social Planning." In *Planning the Twentieth-Century American City,* ed. Mary Corbin Sies and Christopher Silver. Baltimore: Johns Hopkins University Press.

EIGHT

Tropics of Planning Discourse

Stalking the "Constructive Imaginary" of Selected Urban Planning Histories

Olivier Kramsch

> *But in the diverse invitations to suspend artistic experimentation, there is an identical call for order, a desire for unity, for identity, for security, or popularity (in the sense of Offentlichkeit, of finding a public). Artists and writers must be brought back into the bosom of the community, or at least, if the latter is considered to be ill, they must be assigned the task of healing it.*
>
> JEAN-FRANÇOIS LYOTARD (1984)

INTRODUCTION

In his survey of the discipline of history that extended into the 1960s, Hayden White observed a generalized hostility to the field throughout the humanities. For White, this antagonism stemmed from a perception of historians' relationship to their subject matter as both a symptom and a cause of a "potentially fatal cultural illness," lending a moral dimension to the critique of history by "responsible social scientists" (1985: 30). Throughout the nineteenth and twentieth centuries, historians had claimed an epistemologically neutral middle ground for their craft that supposedly situated them in a privileged position between the arts and the sciences. In this view the historian's task was not only to mediate between past and present but also to join two modes of understanding the world that would normally remain cleanly separated. Historical discourse was seen as a "mirror image" of the set of events that it purported to describe (White 1987: 106). Unlike the fiction writer, the historian provided "rhetorical flourishes" or "poetic effects" to engage and sustain the reader's attention in an underlying "true story" (1987: x). Narrative was regarded as a form of discourse, "a form featuring the story as its content" (1987: 25).

For White, such a perception of the historical discipline's raison d'être and its methodological mandate proved increasingly untenable, serving only to thwart a serious consideration of important theoretical advances in literature, social science, and philosophy in the latter part of the twentieth century. Inspired by the writings of semiologically oriented literary theorists and poststructuralist philosophers of the postwar period,[1] historians began to question the supposed transparency of historical discourse based on an "illusion of a centered consciousness capable of looking out on the world" and grasping it objectively (White 1987: 36).

Following White, it may be useful to rethink and critique the idea of an "objective" history of urban planning practice, to challenge the very notion of a monolithic reading of urban planning history. One way of achieving this is to read what are regarded as mainstream texts by asking which voices or stories are included, which are marginalized or excluded. Another way of challenging the notion of an objective history is to deconstruct specific texts in the search for their underlying interpretation. These exercises can be useful in situating texts within specific theoretical traditions and in opening the planning historical discourse to broader theoretical debates.[2]

Yet after we have captured the interpretive underpinnings of various texts, what "sense" are we to make of the divergent perspectives on the field of urban planning history, perspectives that seem to multiply before our eyes? By what criteria are we to judge the "validity" of one theoretical approach over another once the "reality" of urban planning history is discarded? Are we to embrace one interpretive stance over another through a leap of faith? Or should we rely on our subjective affinities with the life and circumstance of an individual author as a guide to her or his truth claims? If theory construction does not follow the evolutionary paradigm of Darwinian natural selection—in the sense that theories do not "displace" one another along an ever-improving teleological trajectory—then we must confront the uneasy truth of distinct theoretical formulations standing in relation to each other in a perpetual state of "presence" (Derrida 1986: 85). Do we then risk standing at the juncture of a potentially reactionary postmodern relativism in the interpretation of urban planning

---

1. Hayden White cites Barthes, Foucault, Derrida, Todorov, Kristeva, Beneviste, Genette, and Eco as among those writers in the field of semiotic theory and philosophy who have most shaped his ideas on the role of narrativity in historical discourse.

2. Such a rethinking and critique of traditional urban planning historiographical discourse was the approach undertaken in a graduate seminar at UCLA's Graduate School of Architecture and Urban Planning in fall 1994. Methodologically, the course challenged the notion of a monolithic reading of urban planning history by providing a constellation of views and styles of writing on the subject, with special attention given to voices that have previously been marginalized from "telling their story," such as women, gays, and people of color.

histories, each paradigm—in that most American of postures—agreeing to disagree with its neighbor?

These questions acquire an increased urgency to the extent that—as my reference to Lyotard makes clear—the shift of "meaning" from an external referent to textual representations and positionings accompanying the "linguistic turn" in the humanities has produced a psychic anxiety in society at large. And this has resulted in a "call for order, a desire for unity, for identity, for security," with all the dark political undertones such demands entail.

In the context of a historical juncture marked by pleas to go "back to the basics" and maintain "disciplinary integrity," I explore the implications posed by Hayden White's writings as a way to transcend the impasse of theoretical relativism confronting the field of urban planning history. Specifically, I apply his notion of the poetic-mythical nature of historical discourse—posited as a third level of meaning situated at a deeper level of consciousness than that of either description or narrative interpretation—to a group of selected planning history texts as a way to explore the potential for not only establishing a different typology of urban planning historical discourses but also, and more critically, for translating *between* alternative modes of representation. Such an act of translation will make it possible for interpretations of urban planning history to "talk to one another" rather than stand rigidly in place, waiting for an appropriate suitor. But before we engage in acts of theoretical bridge building we must return to Hayden White's critique of traditional historiography and examine the construction of his tropological escape.

WHITE'S TROPICAL SAFARI

For White, historical narrative is always shaped through acts of interpretation, since historians must exclude certain facts from their accounts as irrelevant to their narrative purpose while including accounts of other events for which the necessary facts are missing. It is this act of "filling in the gaps" that is expressed in historical narrative, a discourse that is inherently mediative in operation, always "as much about the nature of interpretation as it is about the subject matter under elaboration" (White 1985: 4). Because it is "ironic" with respect to its own adequacy—"always slipping the grasp of logic, constantly asking if logic is adequate to capture the essence of its subject matter"—discourse is also innately prelogical, consistently leaning toward "metadiscursive reflexiveness" (1985: 4).

For White, master tropes are the literary device ideally suited for rendering familiar the realm of the historical past. They evoke a third level of meaning from the historical text, transcending mere description of data and interpretive argument to encompass "the very rules which determine the objects of discourse, the way in which description and argument are combined, the phases through which the discourse must pass in the process of earning its right of closure" (1985: 5). Such a synthesis of description and argument is essentially tropological in nature, involving the display of four master tropes: metaphor, metonymy, synecdoche, and irony. The interpretation of history entails the provision of a plot structure for sequences of events so that through the display of tropes their nature can be comprehended as "a story of a particular kind, such as comedy, satire, tragedy, romance, epic, etc." (1985: 6). It is this level of interpretation that operates on a level of mythic consciousness by means of tropological conventions. Finally, the level of interpretation marked by poetic-mythical elements is shaped in turn by moral-ideological commitments. Thus one can discern in every historical narrative a "constructive imagination" that is contained precisely in the myth the historian has chosen to identify a story of a particular kind. According to White, "Our interpretation of the work of historians would be to explain the tropological wager buried at the heart of their strategies of explanation, emplotment, and ideological implications" (1985: 73).

White associates various modes of emplotment, explanation, and ideological implications with the four master tropes (see table 8.1). Armed with these tropological insights, how is the historian to interrogate texts? For White, historical discourse must be subject to a rhetorical analysis "so as to disclose the poetic understructure" of what is normally passed off as a "modest prose representation of reality" (1985: 104). Beyond the facts and formal interpretation of the text—its literal "surface"—lies a "deep structural meaning," the generic story type expressed through figurative language. Recognition of the figurative dimension of historical discourse reveals the "equally relativistic nature of all discourse" (1985: 117).

Yet this observation does not imply a return to a nineteenth-century historical relativism—which attempted to ground points of view in particular epochs, places, or ideological allegiances—but does provide a space for translation *between* different language codes to break through the hardened encasements of rigid ideological shells.

> And if the tropes of language are limited, if the types of figuration are finite, then it is possible to imagine how our representations of the historical world aggregate into a comprehensive total vision of that world, and how progress in our understanding of it is possible. Each new representation of the past represents a further testing and refinement of our capacities to figure the world in language, so that each new generation is heir, not only to more information about the past, but also to more adequate knowledge of our capacities to comprehend it. (1985: 118)

TABLE 8.1   White's Tropological Interpretive Framework

Guiding Tropes	Mode of Emplotment	Mode of Explanation	Mode of Ideological Implication
Metaphor: attempt to catalog specific attributes by noting similarities to other, apparently different phenomena	Romance	Idiographic	Anarchist
Synecdoche: integration of all apparent phenomena into a whole; understanding the particular as the microcosm of a macrocosmic totality	Comedy	Organicist	Conservative
Metonymy: reductive in operation; apprehending historical field as a complex of part-part relationships and understanding it as a cause-effect relationship	Tragedy	Mechanistic	Radical
Irony: attitude toward knowledge that is critical of metaphorical identification, integration, or reduction; the linguistic strategy underlying skepticism as an explanatory tactic	Satire	Contextualist	Liberal

Source: Adapted from White 1985: 75.

To clarify his method, White engages in the rhetorical analysis of a passage of historical prose chosen at random. He reveals a description of events, explores its main interpretive argument, and probes the particular "kind of story" implicated through its tropical discourse, thereby drawing specific ideological conclusions about its author. I seek to attempt the same with a select group of texts recounting various histories of urban planning. I choose to denote these histories in the plural to draw attention to and justify the heterodox quality of my material. Some of my sources are firmly embedded within the "canon" of urban planning history; others are not. I include works located outside the traditional ken of urban planning historiography because I believe they have nevertheless had a critical impact on current debates related to the past, present, and future of the city in the industrialized West.

After depicting in broad brush strokes the "chronicle" and main interpretive thrust of each text, I seek out its "constructive imaginary." Though White does not provide examples of his ability to "translate" between alternative modes of representation, at the end of the chapter, I offer some personal insights and a critique on the basis of my forays.

MEL SCOTT'S *AMERICAN CITY PLANNING SINCE 1890*

In commemorating the fiftieth anniversary of the American Institute of Planners, Mel Scott offers "a personal view of the growth of a significant profession and the development of the planning function in modern government" (1969: xvii). At the outset of his work Scott has the clarity to proffer that no "one can liberate himself entirely from his biases, attachments, and limitations, no matter how earnestly he attempts to be thorough, dispassionate, and intellectually honest" (1969: xvii).

Following the themes of traditional U.S. planning historiography, Scott's work engages with the wide sweep of events beginning with attempts to grapple with issues of urban sanitation and population concentration on the part of late-nineteenth-century reformers and settlement house workers, followed by transformations of the city's built environment according to the standards of the City Beautiful campaign in the early part of the twentieth century, the development of a "scientific" foundation for the profession under the crusade of the City Functional movement, the emergence of planning at regional and national scales by midcentury, and finally a call for a renewed human-centered comprehensiveness in the field of urban planning.

In pursuing these grand topics, and keeping "attachments and limitations" at bay, Scott offers the history of urban planning practice as a seamless evolutionary continuum in which ideas take root in the substratum of preceding paradigms, only to be supplanted through some process of inexorable logic by subsequent intellectual developments. If metonymy is associated with the mechanistic appropriation of a historical field defined by causal relationships, I suggest that in relating the history of American city planning Scott deploys an overarching metonymic master trope grounded in a tragic mode of emplotment. I further argue that such a tragic emplotment is reinforced through a rich dialogue of competing minor tropes mixing metonymy illiberally with synecdoche in incestuous propinquity with irony, all reflecting a Babel of possible ideological configurations jostling for room in the space of the text and belying the author's claim to "dispassionate . . . intellectual honesty."

When describing the early obstacles confronting the application of a planning mentality in the United States, Scott writes,

> Another category of citizens bitterly resented any limitation on private initiative and displayed militant impatience with governmental restraint. The whole course of national development—a restless quest for new frontiers, greater opportunity, and sudden riches—reinforced this tendency to license when rules and regulations threatened to interfere with personal ambitions. Yet, paradoxically, Americans had an almost childlike reverence for law in the abstract—for principle rather than the whim of a tyrant or a latter-day political boss, for truth and justice as the ultimate refuge of the wronged and oppressed. (1961: 3)

Here Scott evokes the ironic trope of the "paradoxical" American character through his depiction of the "restless" search for gain and a "childlike" deference to the law, demonstrating a satirical plot structure.

The normative assumptions underlying Scott's vision of "good" city form are filtered indirectly through the successes of the early reformers and later reflected in the models of the City Beautiful movement. Despite the generalized "fear that planning would unduly curtail individual freedom . . . the ancient notions of property rights *which at times impeded better development of the peripheral areas of cities proved less troublesome* in the more popular struggle to regulate tenement houses and improve the living conditions of the urban poor" (1969: 6; emphasis mine).

Reflecting on the urban visions of the proponents of the City Beautiful, Scott evaluates the view of George Kriehn, who

> knew precisely the city for Americans to copy: of all modern cities, Paris, more than any other, deserves the title of "The City Beautiful." With its clean paved streets, with its public places surrounded by buildings in harmonious style and decorated with statuary which represents the highest development of modern art, with its river so beautifully bridged, with its old cathedral of immense proportions, it comes nearer than any other to reaching the ideal which is the object of this municipal art movement. (1969: 45)

The lines of authorship tied to the foregoing normative assertions—that "better" development implied development of "peripheral areas" and that Paris represented the apogee of urban aesthetics—are anchored in the author's voice, though in a fragile and tenuous way, never entirely separate from those actors he wishes to describe with utmost objectivity; his critical reflections on planning practice appear to surface through the sieve of a text acting as a ventriloquism. Scott's attempt to thus "hide" behind his prose produces the appearance of an integration of historical phenomena characteristic of synecdoche, belying a comedic mode of emplotment.

The synecdochic effect is reinforced in Scott's portrayal of paradigmatic shifts in planning practice. In describing the change from the City Beautiful to the City Efficient he writes,

> The emphasis on the City Efficient characterizing the city planning movement by 1912 was in some ways *a logical outgrowth* of the social impulses that had crept into the City Beautiful movement as it became concerned with playgrounds, transportation, and terminals. . . . City planning thus became a matter of altering spatial relationships to achieve the practical ends of efficiency and convenience. *In the evolution of the city planning movement the City Efficient was a logical phase.* Even so aesthetic a planner as Robinson kept in step with the times and was as eager as his fellows to stress practicality. (1969: 123; emphasis mine)

In this passage Scott relies on arguments of organicist causality that—by corraling the flow of history into an integrated flow of events—sustain the use of synecdoche as a strategy rooted in a comedic process of emplotment.

PETER HALL'S *CITIES OF TOMORROW*

Contra Scott, Peter Hall does not make any pretense to objectivity in recounting the history of Anglo-American urban and regional planning practice over the past one hundred years. Admitting to the "vastness" of his subject, he cautions his reader regarding the "highly selective" nature of his research: "The choice of major themes, each of which forms the subject matter of one chapter, is necessarily personal and judgmental. And I have deliberately made no attempt to conceal my prejudices" (1988: 5).

The main theme of Hall's book rests on the notion that the evolution of planning practice in the United States and Europe can be traced to the ideas of a few "visionaries" who lived and wrote in the decades straddling the turn of the century. Thus the birth of modern planning as a response to conditions of overcrowding and latent insurrectionary violence characteristic of the nineteenth-century Victorian city is traced to the garden city concept of Ebenezer Howard. Howard's idea of exporting urban populations and employment to self-contained new towns established in the countryside is then shown to influence the work of disciples in many other countries who would carve their own "niche in the pantheon of planning"; these would include Raymond Unwin, Barry Parker, and Frederic Osborn in Britain; Henri Sellier in France; Ernst May and Martin Wagner in Germany; and Clarence Stein and Henry Wright in the United States (1988: 8).

Parallel "strands" of planning history are similarly tied to key figures: the roots of regional planning are ascribed to the "vision" of Patrick Geddes, later to be interpreted by the founding members of the Regional Planning Association of America under the tutelage of Lewis Mumford, Clarence Stein, Stuart Chase, and Benton MacKaye and then filtered through the experience of the Southern Regionalists led by Howard Odum and the New Deal planner Rexford Tugwell; a monumental tradition of city planning expressed in the works of Georges-Eugene Haussmann in Paris and Ildefonso Cerda in Barcelona; the high-rise urban "solution" of Le Corbusier; and finally the fantasy of a "city of infinite mobility" that runs from the predictions of H. G. Wells to Melvin Webber's apocryphal nonplace urban realm and Frank Lloyd Wright's Broadacre City.

According to Hall, the ideas of these thinkers would often be ignored and rejected by their contemporaries, laying "fallow, because the time was not ripe. . . . When at last the visions were discovered and resuscitated, their implementation came often in very different places, in very different circumstances, and often through very different mechanisms, from those their inventors had originally envisaged" (1988: 2).

In setting himself the task of redeeming the ideas laid down by the "fathers" of modern city planning (there "were, alas, almost no founding mothers"), then, Hall is determined to permit the key figures to recount them in their own words (1988: 7). Through this rhetorical gesture Hall seeks to overcome Marxist economic reductionism by situating the explanatory "motor of history" in the acts of a few inspired individuals.

> Historical actors do perform in response to the world they find themselves in, and in particular to the problems that they confront in that world. . . .
> [I]deas do not suddenly emerge, by some kind of immaculate conception, without benefit of worldly agency. But equally, human beings—especially the most intelligent and most original among them—are almost infinitely quirky and creative and surprising; therefore, the real interest in history . . . lies in the complexity and variability of the human reaction. (1988: 4–5)

Accordingly, in exploring the contribution of Ebenezer Howard, Hall states that one must view him "against the background of his time," a London of the 1880s and 1890s in radical ferment (1988: 88).

> An eclectic thinker, he borrowed freely from the ideas that were circulating at the time. . . . [I]n the book [*Garden Cities of Tomorrow*] he was adamant that he had thought out the central ideas himself but that he had then found other writers who supplied the details. But there were certainly plenty of precursors. Edward Gibbon Wakefield, fifty years earlier, had developed the idea of planned colonization for the poor. The scheme he had promoted, Colonel Light's celebrated scheme for Adelaide in South Australia, provided the idea that once a city had reached a certain size, a second city separated from it by a green belt, should be started: the origin of the notion of Social City, as Howard acknowledged. . . . Every single one of his ideas can in fact be found earlier, often several times over. . . . The ingredients, then, were

far from original. What Howard could claim . . . was that his was a unique combination of proposals. (1988: 89–91)

Characteristic of the destiny of planning's foundational ideas as narrated by Hall, Howard's vision of the garden city is "diluted" as soon as it is translated to other geographic contexts (1988: 112).

> Before long, it was Howard's ideas which . . . were carried across the water to influence thinking on the European mainland; but there, almost immediately, they got misunderstood. One of the earliest foreign interpretations of Howard's ideas, Le Cité-Jardin by Georges Benoit-Lévy, managed to make an elementary confusion between garden city and garden suburb, from which French planners never afterwards extricated themselves. (1988: 114)

Hall apparently does not concede that the French have a right to weave Howard's ideas into the fabric of their own traditions, to adapt them to their own context. Moreover, despite acknowledging the influence of their own biographical trajectories on the development of planning ideas, Hall does not grant Howard's British disciples the freedom to modify their mentor's originary idea. In assessing Raymond Unwin's planning of Hampstead Garden Suburb, Hall writes: "But in the Central Town Square . . . Unwin defers completely to Lutyens, the designer of the two big churches and the adjacent Institute. The result is an anomalous, heavily formal exercise in the City Beautiful tradition" (1988: 104).

I argue that in writing a book about the impact of ideas on the history of planning practice yet considering these impacts as merely distorted expressions of the original ideas, Hall is guided by a metonymic drive to grasp the complex history of modern planning in terms of mechanistic cause-effect relationships. The narrative's mode of emplotment is tragic to the extent that the causal connections purported to underpin the evolution of ideas are continually disrupted and transmogrified as thought enters the domain of practice in space and time. In an elegiac passage, Hall sums up the legacy of this reality:

> After one hundred years of debate on how to plan the city, after repeated attempts . . . to put ideas into practice, we find we are almost back to where we started. The theorists have swung sharply back to planning's anarchist origins; the city itself is again seen as a place of decay, poverty, social malaise, civil unrest and possibly even insurrection. . . . [This] does mean that certain trends seem to reassert themselves; perhaps because, in truth, they never went away. (1988: 11)

ELIZABETH WILSON'S *THE SPHINX IN THE CITY*

The Sphinx in the City opens with a great and yawning Absence, the missing traces of Viennese cafés that sustained a vibrant intellectual and Bohemian

life, a nostalgia for "the very gloom and shabbiness now banished by gentrification, redevelopment, and the commercialization of leisure" (Wilson
1991: 5). Wilson links the origins of this quiet death to a town planning
movement that had systematically sought over the last one hundred fifty
years to domesticate the city, taming a growing disorder it had long associated with the ambiguous presence of females in the public realms of urban
life. For Wilson, the impulse to plan for the city was inextricably linked to
a patriarchal consciousness for whom the presence of women in the urban
realm was deemed problematical. In this arena women symbolized the
promise of extramarital sexual adventure, translated as a moral and political threat.

Through her case study of various "world capitals," the principal task
Wilson sets for herself is to examine how underlying assumptions—based
both on the unconscious division between male and female and on the
consciously expressed ideas about women's "rightful place"—have determined the shape of contemporary cities (1991: 8). She embeds this analysis within the larger project of reclaiming the space of cities for women as
a reaction to a perceived antiurban bias among contemporaneous feminist
theorizing, which, Wilson writes, "seemed like a betrayal, and made me
permanently disillusioned with utopianism" (1991: 9). Rather than reinforce the exclusion of women and minorities from the city, Wilson calls for
"a radically new approach," one that makes the urban order available to all
classes and groups (1991: 10).

Through her historical chronicles, Wilson demonstrates that although
women, members of minority groups, and children were still not considered full citizens of the city—never having been granted full access to the
streets—industrial life still drew them into public life and allowed them to
negotiate the contradictions of urban life in their own particular way.
Drawing heavily from fictional and biographical literary sources, her text
is rich with accounts of women who transgressed social conventions by
braving the city's streets alone; such heroines of urban life included Lucy
Snowe in Charlotte Brontë's *Villette,* the wives and lovers of the 1848 Pre-
Raphaelites, and Octavia Hill, who, as housing manager-philanthropist,
ventured unescorted into London's slums.

As her text unfolds, she presents such liberatory acts against the backdrop of a discourse on urbanism and the development of cities that
is uneasy about women "roaming the streets" (1991: 16). In Wilson's
view, the urban reformers' arguments against female working conditions
in the late nineteenth century were undergirded by the presumed harmful
effects of working women on the health of "traditional" family life. Moreover, the independence of the factory woman was perceived as "unnatural,"
yielding to insalubrious conditions and "disease" (1991: 32). The seclusion
of women from the active, bustling city would be completed in the City

Beautiful movement in the first decades of the twentieth century, characterized by Wilson as desiring "to eliminate all excess from city life" (1991: 69).

In seeking to trace every twist and turn of urban planning discourse to a subterranean patriarchal urge to banish women from the streets of the city, a latent overdeterminism creeps into Wilson's narrative. To ascribe to Lewis Mumford's distaste for the twentieth-century megalopolis the perception that large cities provided women with an escape from male-dominated social relations may be granted as true, but to attribute this logic as unitary is surely forced. To account for this rigid overdeterminism—surprising given the emancipatory intention of the text—Wilson's narrative is enacted through a romantic mode of emplotment guided in turn by the trope of metaphor. The overarching metaphor in Wilson's account is that of the Sphinx itself, that mythical creature—half-woman/half-monster—which stands for the chaos and instability of urban life: "Women have become an irruption in the city, a symptom of disorder, and a problem: the Sphinx in the city" (1991: 10). Relying on idiographic modes of explication, in this instance literary and cinematic sources, Wilson deploys a number of metaphoric tropes linking apparently disparate events in the lives of working women to the shadow of the Sphinx and its specifically urban habitat. The dress of the first salesgirls in nineteenth-century London is recounted by Wilson as being perceived as too elegant to fulfill the role of shopkeepers.

Conversely, the incidence of upper-class women "playing the peasant" represented a similar threat to law and order (1991: 50). Zola's literary figure, Nana, is the embodiment of female sexuality, uncontrolled disorder, "as threatening as it was desirable." Not even the staid French financial institutions of the late nineteenth century are immune to the Sphinx's gaze; the Parisian stock exchange is presented to the reader as a symbol for "the linked obsessions of frenzied speculation and sexual experience that gripped the Second Empire" (1991: 57). The simile linking "women," "sexuality," and "perceived threats" to the social order—circling in turn about the referent of the Sphinx—is invoked systematically as trope throughout the text. Correspondingly, the entire field of urban planning is viewed as the discursive and operational instrument embedded in a much larger network of oppressive patriarchal relations. Following White, I suggest that Wilson's deployment of these metaphoric tropological strategies betokens an anarchist ideological commitment.

CHRISTINE BOYER'S *DREAMING THE RATIONAL CITY*

Christine Boyer chronicles the rise of the institutional "planning mentality" in the United States, starting from its origins in the social reform movements of the mid-nineteenth century, extending through the City Beautiful and City Functional programs of the first half of the twentieth century, and embracing the planning of the American city and region in the postwar period. At the outset of her narrative Boyer states her intention to pass such a traditional urban planning historiography through the analytical prism of Michel Foucault's writings, deriving specific insight from his ideas on the articulation of power relations through language. By focusing on the manner in which shifting socioeconomic conditions gave rise to a discourse on urban planning practice that in turn provided the context for and legitimated an increased disciplinary control over society, Boyer hopes to shift attention away from a traditional search for cause-effect paradigms in urban historiography, as well as eliminate the figure of the ideational subject from the stage of planning history.

A close examination of Boyer's text reveals a number of rhetorical stratagems that ultimately serve to vitiate her claim to be following in Foucault's methodological footsteps. Contrary to her stated goals, I suggest that through the deployment of metonymic tropes Boyer reveals the underlying mythicopoetic nature of her text as one that in large measure succumbs to classic Marxist analysis, insinuating causal relationships into her account and resuscitating the figure of the "subject" as historic agent in the development of planning institutions in the United States. Boyer's metonymic tropological devices are enacted through a mechanistic mode of explanation belying a radical mode of ideological implication.

If metonymy is characterized by a reductive mode of analysis defined by a historical field constituted by cause-effect relationships, Boyer's narrative satisfies these conditions on both counts. Throughout her text Boyer relates the presence of Foucault's notion of "disciplinary order" to the evolutionary trajectory of urban planning efforts in an indiscriminate and reductive manner. The hegemonic strategy of "disciplinary order" is associated with professional charity societies' emergent control over volunteer activities in the post–Civil War period, with the settlement house movement as a whole, and subsequently with the creation of urban parks and garden suburbs (Boyer 1983: 24). Boyer writes, "Although their work never took a generalized approach, it began to seem as if a network of inspectors was subjecting the urban populace to an even more detailed surveillance" (1983: 40).

Boyer's rhetorically insistent use of the passive voice ("it began to seem"), though adhering to her stated goal of steering clear of the subject of traditional historiographic prose, serves only to doubly reinforce the reductive nature of her analysis by hiding from discourse the myriad actors involved in the creation of a disciplinary planning order. In another context she exclaims that "the discourse about cities . . . arose in order to articulate and transcend the contradictions embedded in the city" (1983: 7).

Who were the agents involved in raising such a discourse? On what basis were the "contradictions embedded in the city" grounded? In another account, she writes, "With the emergence of an American metropolis after the Civil War, two problems arose: how to discipline and regulate the urban masses and how to control and arrange spatial growth" (1983: 9). For whom was it incumbent to "discipline and regulate the urban masses"? For what segments of society was it necessary to "control and arrange spatial growth"? Boyer is silent.

At times Boyer's rhetorical reliance on the passive voice leads her into direct methodological contradictions, causing her to embrace momentarily those very ideational concepts of urban planning historiography that she is purporting to overthrow: "A change in orientation began to occur that eventually would bring a reevaluation of the potency of environmental reform *and the beginning of an idea* that the American city might be disciplined by the progressive development of human knowledge, state regulatory mechanisms, and public welfare provisions" (1983: 60; emphasis mine).

In those rare moments when Boyer embraces the active voice and glimmers of agency emerge in the text, the "subject" is none other than capital. In the accelerating movement to regulate the disciplinary order of the city, for instance, "the planners were to speak for the general interests of capital" (1983: 69). In a similar vein, as the debates raged over employment relief toward the end of the nineteenth century, "the capitalists were thrown into contradiction. . . . Here then we find the real roots of public relief" (1983: 13).

In one account Boyer momentarily relaxes her reductionistic impulse by illustrating the heterogeneous nature of capital in the urban development process:

> The diverse and opposing strategies of industrial and financial capital, small business and trade groups, professional concerns and middle-class outrages formed a network across which the power of capital was intricately webbed. Planning documents became the mode through which these contradictions found physical expression and idealistic resolution; they represented discourses of constraint that selected and organized the material according to implicit controls. (1983: 67)

But this ephemeral breathing space is quickly snuffed out; in the following footnote Boyer submerges the conflicting variety of interest groups underlying the production of planning discourse by invoking Foucault's definition of disciplinary order as being analogous to the planning profession, "an integrated system not meant to be seen but infused across an apparatus of observation, recording, and tracking" (1983: 67).

MIKE DAVIS'S *CITY OF QUARTZ*

In tracing the arc of Los Angeles's metamorphosis from the period of General Harrison Gray Otis's open shop at the turn of the century through the era of rampant real estate boosterism marking the city's phenomenal growth in the prewar years to the economic conditions leading to the Watts Riots in the mid-1960s and its late-twentieth-century festering malaise, Mike Davis explores the anguished historical political economy of the town of his youth. Here I center my attention on a contemporary moment in Davis's account, his description of "Fortress L.A.," as I believe it reveals with particular clarity the lineaments of the interpretive framework and tropological understructure guiding his oeuvre.

In "Fortress L.A." Davis demonstrates how Los Angeles's built environment has become a key factor in the spatial segregation and social polarization of the metropolis. For Davis, the resulting "spatial apartheid" made manifest in the urban landscape is interpreted as both a cause and a symptom of racial and class hostilities that have accompanied the growth of the city since its inception (1990: 230). Liberal architectural critics who ignore this immanent *intentionality* ascribed to the new urban space are blasted by Davis:

> [Sam Hall] Kaplan's vigorous defense of pedestrian democracy remains grounded in the hackneyed liberal complaints about the "bland response" and "elitist planning practices." Like most architectural critics, he rails against the oversights of urban design without recognizing the dimension of foresight, of explicit racial intention, which has its roots in Los Angeles' ancient history of class and race warfare. . . . [T]he "fortress effect" emerges, not as an inadvertent failure of design, but as deliberate sociospatial strategy.
> (1990: 229)

Davis thus grounds his interpretive analysis in an ostensibly neo-Marxist framework whose structural logic nevertheless floats in the undergrowth of his text, never fully articulated. What accounts for the subtle quality of this inchoate Marxist analysis? Would too great an emphasis on a fleshed-out Marxist paradigm have rendered him methodologically complicit with an academic world from which he strove so strenuously to disassociate himself in his acknowledging remarks? Would it lay his account open to charges of elitism and theoretical obscurantism? I suggest that Davis attempts to navigate between these dangers by employing a combination of powerful synecdochal and metaphoric tropes that impart to his narrative a tough, working-class "post-liberal"[3] critique of late-twentieth-century Los

3. In welcoming us to "post-liberal Los Angeles," it is presumed that Davis's post-liberal prose will guide us with the appropriate interpretive lenses through L.A.'s "badlands."

Angeles, one that nevertheless ultimately backfires by implicating him within a conservative ideological practice (1990: 223, inside back jacket).[4]

The grand synecdochic tropological gesture is inaugurated by Davis near the beginning of the book:

> Los Angeles in this instance is, of course, a stand-in for capitalism in general. The ultimate world-historical significance—and oddity—of Los Angeles is that it has come to play the double role of utopia *and* dystopia for advanced capitalism. The same place, as Brecht noted, symbolized both heaven and hell. Correspondingly, it is the essential destination on the itinerary of any late twentieth-century intellectual, who must eventually come to take a peek and render some opinion on whether "Los Angeles Brings It All Together" (official slogan), or is, rather, the nightmare at the terminus of American history (as depicted in *noir*). (1980: 20)

Through the synecdochic master trope, Los Angeles is hereby presented to the world as the embodiment of global economic forces in perfectly replicated iconic miniature. What greater inducement could be proffered through these rhetorical flourishes to a worldwide intelligentsia, those who would arrive all the better to salivate in voyeuristic glee at the underbelly of Western civilization? Moreover, emblazoned on the back of the city are the epiphany and the burden of utopian fulfillment *and* dystopian agony; both of these terms—freighted with centuries of Enlightenment-inspired meaning and desire—are cleverly deployed by Davis to illustrate the City of Angels as the crucible and battleground of world-historical tendencies as well as the prime stage of the international economy.

In his description of the semiotics of the downtown built environment, Davis's prose is redolent with metaphoric tropes:

> Downtown, a publicly-subsidized "urban renaissance," has raised the nation's largest corporate *citadel,* segregated from the poor neighborhoods around it by a *monumental architectural glacis.* (1990: 223; emphasis mine)

> In Watts, developer Alexander Haagen demonstrates his strategy for *recolonizing* inner-city retail markets: a *panopticon* shopping mall surrounded by staked metal fences and a substation of the LAPD in a central surveillance tower. (1990: 223; emphasis mine)

> Along the base of California Plaza, Hill Street *became a local Berlin Wall* separating the publicly subsidized luxury of Bunker Hill from the lifeworld of Broadway. (1990: 230; emphasis mine)

---

4. By using the expression "conservative" in this sense I obviously do not mean to associate Davis with a reactionary politics. However, I *do* think Hayden White's terminology can be applied in this case—though I realize that I may be unjustly trying to force Davis into an overly rigid typological matrix—to the extent that his use of the synecdochic and metaphoric obscures and mystifies relations of power that have created "Fortress L.A." and militates against a broader public access to his ideas beyond an anointed intellectual coterie.

The Downtown hyperstructure—*like some Buckminster Fuller post-Holocaust fantasy*—is programmed to ensure a seamless continuum of middle-class work, consumption and recreation, without unwonted exposure to Downtown's working-class street environments. Indeed, the totalitarian semiotics of ramparts and battlements, reflective glass and elevated pedways, rebukes any affinity or sympathy between different architectural or human orders. As in Otis's fortress *Times* building, *this is the archsemiotics of class war.* (1990: 231; emphasis mine)

Davis's synecdochic and metaphoric tropes are crafted by a "constructive imaginary" that seeks to avoid a nauseous pathos—of the liberal *and* Marxist variety—suffusing his more qualitative and overtly interpretive analysis with an aura of brash and gritty social realism that escapes the vice of a narrow academicism, on the one hand, while eluding charges of paternalistically emotive elitism, on the other. Such a tropological strategy is achieved through a romantic mode of emplotment whose passionate signifiers shine with the brilliance of insider cognoscenti, the reflections of which are captured far beyond the author's hometown across an archipelago of intellectual enclaves stretching from Los Angeles proper to New York to London to Frankfurt. In this sense Davis deploys what I would like to call a rhetoric of unfulfilled meaning; he employs a narrative structure in which metaphoric tropes operate on one level to stanch and muffle the liberal commiserative impulse or overdetermined Marxist narrative while at the same time igniting a range of meanings—"stand-in for capitalism," "utopia," "class war," "recolonizing," "Holocaust fantasy," "Berlin Wall"— laden with that very modernist perception of history from which he appears to want to distance himself.

CONCLUSION

In the preceding interpretations of selected urban planning histories I have attempted to excavate the deep "constructive imaginary," that mythic substratum cited by Claude Levi-Strauss which undergirds the description of historical facts and nurtures the surface layer of interpretation that runs alongside descriptive materials. I have sought to establish a typology of urban planning discourses derived from the enactment of four master tropes (metaphor, synecdoche, metonymy, irony) that in turn have determined the "type" of planning stories that get told (romance, comedy, tragedy, satire). Moreover, I have indicated through my revelations of tropological stratagems how the intentional interpretive frameworks erected by authors can often become subverted and even neutralized by their guiding master tropes, which in turn help illuminate their often unstated ideological commitments.

For instance, within the logic of White's typological framework I posit that in writing *The Sphinx in the City* Elizabeth Wilson deploys metaphoric tropes through a romantic mode of emplotment that belies an anarchist ideological perspective on planning history; that the ostensibly Foucauldian thematic of Christine Boyer's *Dreaming the Rational City* is subverted by her reliance on a mechanistic mode of explanation whose radical ideological implications are revealed through her enactment of metonymic master tropes and tragic mode of emplotment; and that Mel Scott, despite an expressed wish for textbook neutrality in writing *American City Planning Since 1890,* activates a range of tropological stratagems, thereby inserting elements of comedy, tragedy, and satire in rambunctious juxtaposition within the body of his work amid a multitude of possible ideological formations.

Yet having stepped back from the surface interpretation of various planning histories we are still stranded on the shore of relativism, this time not at the level of interpretation but on that of ideological implication. Wilson's purported anarchism, for instance, politely agrees to disagree with Boyer's radical reductivist perspective, and both would beg to differ with Scott's guarded ideological ecumenism. Meanwhile, Davis's conspiratorial organicism shakes its furrowed brow at Hall's radical voluntarism. In terms of our efforts at theory construction, are we to be content with this ideological stalemate? Are we left just to choose that conceptual framework with which we personally resonate the most? What implications does such a state of affairs have for knowledge building, if such an act is still possible? In other words, can we *transcend* the mythical imaginary constituting our subjective view of life?

White offers a potential road sign. In opposition to Karl Mannheim's conception of the ideological bases of historical consciousness, White claims that the historian's impulse to mythologize is not locatable in the real or imagined interests of the social groups for which different historiographies might be written but is situated at a yet deeper level, in the very nature of language itself. According to White, historical narrative is in a perpetual state of "saying one thing and meaning another" (1987: 45). The "truth" value of narrative form can therefore only be displayed indirectly, by means of allegory, and I presume that it is on this basis that he proposes the inherent translatability between alternative modes of representation. Yet by situating allegory in a position anterior to ideology, I believe White gives an inordinate primacy to language in the formation of consciousness, presenting language as standing alone and apart from subjectivity itself.

This edenic position—considered by White a prerequisite for establishing a consensual language that would rescue us from theoretical relativism—is itself problematic. For in my attempt to reveal an "objective" representation of various historiographical planning texts through an examination of their tropological "deep structures," I am acutely aware *of my own subjective implication* in the process of their rhetorical deconstruction and assignation within White's tropical framework. I cannot help recognize, for instance, that I was sensitized to the deployment of ironic tropes and satirical modes of emplotment in Mel Scott's narrative of the paradoxical American reaction to the idea of planning largely because the tension in the national culture between individual rights and broader social responsibilities that undergirds such a response speaks so strongly to my ongoing difficulty—as a foreign-born citizen raised in a European family in New England—in acculturating to the enervating individualistic milieu prevalent in Los Angeles as well as the broader U.S. society. Similarly, the ambiguous tropological strategies and ideological structure I chose to be emblematic of Mike Davis's work would not have presented themselves to me had I not—as a white Spanish-speaking male who has developed emotional attachments with the East Los Angeles barrio—identified myself personally to some extent with those very same ambiguities, resenting the voyeuristic intellectual class to whom *City of Quartz* caters but being one of "them," a perpetual outsider to the "real" city as well.

The irruption of the subjective presence in the interrogation of historical planning texts should stand as a salutary warning to those who would strive for the creation of a unitary or shared language of historical interpretation. For does not such an urge to "translate between" and ecumenically "select the best from" different theoretical constructs—albeit shaping the construction of knowledge at a "higher" level—replicate the need to fashion a sense of meaning in history grounded in that very notion of "reality" which we can only accept, at best, with nostalgia? Following Richard J. Bernstein, I assert that it is *precisely* through the incorporation of our own "historicity" in our understanding of texts that their meanings are revealed to us in "play, a to-and-fro movement, . . . in which both what we seek to understand and our prejudices are dynamically involved with each other" (1985: 276). Through a "dialogic encounter" we must interrogate texts from our own "historical horizon" (Bernstein 1985: 279).

Where does such a realization lead in the construction of a knowledge of planning history? As White observes, the stories we tell about our past are not infinite; they are limited by the cultural systems within which they are immersed. In a similar vein, we deform the very concept of historical understanding if we think of it as a self-contained entity, if we think that "we are prisoners enclosed within" it (Bernstein 1985: 279). "This appeal to truth—a truth that transcends our own historical horizon—is absolutely essential in order to distinguish philosophical hermeneutics from a historicist form of relativism" (1985: 282).

Citing the philosophical hermeneutics of Hans-Georg Gadamer, Bernstein elaborates: "I am suggesting . . . a concept of truth which comes down to what can be argumentatively *validated by the community of interpreters* who open themselves to what tradition says to us. . . . We judge and evaluate such claims by the standards and practices that have been hammered out in the course of history" (1985: 284; emphasis mine).

As urban planning historians, must we therefore humbly content ourselves to eternally circle the illusory autonomy of past "events"—that obscure object of historical desire—testing and pressing the inner contours of our culture's interpretive womb in our passionate debates with others, never alighting on a "truth" that transcends our own Western norms and values? Such a project appears less and less satisfying—not to mention tenable—in a culture whose monolithic facade is being eroded by the distensions and cracks of the postmodern condition and the parallel birth of (potentially emancipatory) oppositional practices centered on issues of radical otherness, identity, and difference. In such a world the cultural coherence on the basis of which White seeks to reconstruct a metalanguage for the Western "tropical imaginary" is in the process of disintegration.

Drawing a longer view from Bernstein, perhaps our ultimate task extends beyond the hermeneutical project altogether, involving instead a search for ways of "nurturing the type of dialogical communities" in which an ethically informed interpretation (phronesis) "becomes a living reality" (1985: 288). Of course, this would lead us directly onto the terrain of political action and practice, but then this is perhaps where White and Bernstein would have wanted us to be all along.

REFERENCES

Bernstein, Richard J. 1985. "From Hermeneutics to Praxis." In *Hermeneutics and Praxis*, ed. Robert Hollinger, 272–296. Notre Dame, Ind.: University of Notre Dame Press.

Boyer, Christine. 1983. *Dreaming the Rational City: The Myth of American City Planning.* Cambridge, Mass.: MIT Press.

Davis, Mike. 1990. *City of Quartz: Excavating the Future in Los Angeles.* New York: Verso.

Derrida, Jacques. 1986. "Structure, Sign, and Play in the Discourse of the Human Sciences" (1966). In *Critical Theory Since 1965*, ed. Hazard Adams and Leroy Searle, 80–93. Tallahassee: Florida State University Press.

Hall, Peter. 1988. *Cities of Tomorrow: An Intellectual History of Urban Planning and Design in the Twentieth Century.* New York: Blackwell.

Lyotard, Jean-François. 1984. "Answering the Question: What is Postmodernism?" In Lyotard, *The Postmodern Condition: A Report on Knowledge*, 71–82. Minneapolis: University of Minnesota Press.

Scott, Mel. 1969. *American City Planning Since 1890.* Berkeley: University of California Press.

White, Hayden. 1985. *Tropics of Discourse: Essays in Cultural Criticism.* Baltimore: Johns Hopkins University Press.

————. 1987. *The Content of the Form: Narrative Discourse and Historical Representation.* Baltimore: Johns Hopkins University Press.

Wilson, Elizabeth. 1991. *The Sphinx in the City: Urban Life, the Control of Disorder, and Women.* Berkeley: University of California Press.

NINE

Subversive Histories

Texts from South Africa

Robert A. Beauregard

The challenge is to set the reader beyond thinking that things had to be the way they turned out and to see the range of possibilities of how it could have been otherwise.

DAVID MCCULLOUGH, HISTORIAN

For the most part, planning history texts either celebrate planning or, through criticism, legitimize it. Even when lamenting planning's disasters (Hall 1982) or bemoaning the reluctance of otherwise enlightened individuals to embrace it, historians have found much of value. We read planning histories in order to swell with pride at our heritage, discover our identity, and draw analogies to present predicaments. Through history, we dedicate ourselves to making planning less inconsequential, less tied to property interests, more sensitive to race and gender, more technically sophisticated, or any of a number of tasks aimed at professional reform (Abbott and Adler 1989; Mandelbaum 1985; Sandercock 1990: 21–33).

As we begin the first stage of reflecting critically on planning history, we need to do more than question its purposes. It is not enough to ask *why* planning history is written, we should also ask *how*, thereby addressing not just the content of planning history but also its contribution to a planning practice that changes the world. The utility of history is more than its similarity or dissimilarity to the present—history as analogy. As important is its capacity to aid the reader in imagining effective action.

My intent is to discuss how planning histories might be written to empower or disempower their readers. Histories that undermine the possibility of effective action, that disempower, are subversive. They do not allow or enable us to imagine having a significant impact; they trivialize planning.

Two premises related to the writing of history and one pertinent to planning serve as the foundation for my argument. First, as writers of history we control how the past is represented, with and against the grain of the historical evidence (Johnson and Schaffer 1985; White 1978). Second, we write in and for the present. In doing so we explore both the justification for planning and the contemporary efficacy of planning practice. Finally, it is not enough to indicate what has been accomplished and suggest what might be done. Planners have to be empowered to act; good histories compel us to envision ourselves as people who make history (Flacks 1976).

As illustration for this argument, I use a recent collection of historical writings on South African planning (Planning History Study Group 1993). The planning profession in South Africa is at a crossroads. Those currently writing its history do so with the memory of almost fifty years of overt apartheid planning and decades of revolutionary struggle. The complicity of planners in producing the apartheid city and the contributions a number of planners have made to dismantling the apartheid regime set planning historians on a precarious perch between the past and the future. At such junctures we should find planning texts that empower.

WRITING HISTORY

Most historians view their primary task as explaining the past rather than solely describing it. One way to do this is to create "an achieved sense of dramatic inevitability" (Abrams 1980: 10) with a plot that accounts for past actions in the context in which they were taken. No unexplained events lie scattered about, and all contrary evidence is discredited. The story line is straight, the narrative neat (Hobsbawm 1973: 270–277; Scriven 1959).

Yet if we are concerned with the puzzle of human behavior and how the world is socially constructed, then we must write histories in ways that cast historical figures as responsible for their actions (Berlin 1959). Within the constraints of an institutionalized past, these actors create history by making choices and exercising free will. They could have made other decisions; the past could have turned out differently. Lurking threateningly behind our "straight" story is a "crooked" story, a counterfactual history (Kellner 1989).

Written in this way histories introduce us to the efficacy and contingency of human action and the constant social construction and reconstruction of enduring (that is, institutionalized) relations and behavior (Beauregard 1993: 39–49). The Chekhovian gun that appears on the wall in the first act of our historical play, inevitably to be used to resolve an unexpected turn of events, is transformed into a Brechtian instrument of emancipation.

Histories conceived in terms of imagined action can usefully, even if simplistically, be classified into one of two categories: deterministic or over-determined. In deterministic histories, all the causes are made clear, all outcomes can be traced to previously discussed causes, and all pasts are made to seem fixed and, most important, inevitable. Overdetermined histories (Althusser 1979: 87–128) have an overabundance of motivating factors, salient conditions, and significant actors. Whether powerful individuals, oppressed peasants, or mobs, these actors confront a dizzying array of possibilities, limited and distorted understandings of the world that they wish to change, and insights into their motives that are malleable and untrustworthy. There are many ways in which this history could have happened.

Both types of histories are subversive. Deterministic history suggests that if we can identify the forces that shape behavior, then we can manipulate them to produce the world that we desire. At the same time it implies that relatively stable social laws govern history and that they cannot be changed within our lifetimes. Often paradigmatic, determinative histories do not allow for revision; they are tragedies in which men and women are compelled to their fates.

Overdetermined histories offer us numerous opportunities but simultaneously inform us of the futility of taking up any one of them. We can never be sure that a specific action will lead to a particular outcome, and thus we can never expect that we can shape history. Such histories tend either to be intellectually eclectic (seemingly unfolding without theoretical intent) or they descend into discourse (Palmer 1990) so as to nimbly avoid evaluative judgments and thus the prescription that must follow. Life is not a tragedy but a Pirandellian comedy of missed opportunities, miscommunications, misinterpretations, fruitless actions, and frustrations. The odds are against purposive action.

My categorization scheme does not exhaust the range of subversive histories. As feminists have pointed out, histories that exclude women are also subversive (Scott 1988; Wilson 1991). Labeled subjugated histories, they disempower women by stripping them of historical relevance and conferring on men all power to change the world. Histories that ignore women dismiss their important contributions and devalue the essential spheres in which they labor, as well as deprive history of significant oppositional tendencies without which we cannot understand its contingent qualities (Hooper 1992). All exclusionary histories are disempowering for those who do not appear or who appear only as attendants to those who make history (Fitzgerald and Howard 1993; Spivak 1989).

Neither is this categorization reducible to the interplay of structure and agency. Structuralist arguments are often deterministic, but not always (Giddens 1979: 49–95). In them, the agents of history dance to the laws of history; they are swept forward—or aside—by institutions and events. By contrast, historical texts that stress agency, often of the "great man" variety, allow that people, rather than being its puppets, create history. Still, only certain types of people, a distinct minority, are eligible for these lofty positions, and history is reduced to a combination of psychology and family origins.

Deterministic and overdetermined histories and structure and agency intersect conceptually but represent different theoretical considerations. Deterministic histories can privilege either structure or agency. The inevitability of history might be anchored in a deep societal logic or rigid institutional framework, or historical actors might march to circumstances that allow only a narrow range of responses or embody within themselves the logic of unfolding events, bending history to their will. Overdetermined arguments, by contrast, deemphasize both structure and agency. The former is washed away by a tide of contingencies and the latter by unpredictable consequences. Clearly, too, making history more inclusive—writing history from below—adds agents without necessarily adding agency. The deterministic quality of a text is not contingent on who takes the role of the protagonist. Even if we resolve the dualism of structure and agency, deterministic and overdetermined texts will continue to exist and to disempower.

WRITING PLANNING HISTORIES

Why is the existence of subversive histories a problem for planning? How are these histories incompatible with, and thus detrimental to, the planning project?

The primary purpose of planning is to guide collective action by linking knowledge to action (Friedmann 1987). To be effective in this way, planners must be able to instill in other actors the confidence that (1) the future can be different and (2) proposed actions will bring about the predicted consequences. Planning is about purposive action, and the most desirable action is that which produces significant change and achieves worthwhile goals.

To engage in such action planners must imagine different futures and portray them to others. More specifically, they must imagine themselves taking action and achieving shared objectives within a changing and ever-negotiated social environment. If they cannot do this, they cannot plan.

To the degree that planning histories are simultaneously about the past and the present capacities of planners and to the degree that by reading planning histories planners are either empowered to imagine that they can act effectively or discouraged from doing so—disempowered—then subversive histories are antithetical to the planning project. Deterministic and overdetermined histories suggest that planned interventions will be successful only to the extent that they conform to historical laws or touch on, by chance, fleeting causal connections that are temporarily aligned with predicted consequences. The contributions of planners are either predetermined or serendipitous. Thus if planners are to think of themselves as doing more than serving pablum to power or "going with the flow," planning histories must be written so as to empower.

VIEW FROM SOUTH AFRICA

In late 1993 a group of South African planning academics met in Pietermaritzburg to reflect on the history of planning practice in their country. The published proceedings contain a mix of papers, many of which take the planning profession as the object of historical analysis. Others focus either on planning ideas (for example, the garden city) or on community development (for example, neighborhood transition). My focus is histories of the planning profession. Here is where the notion of empowerment needs to be planted.

The authors made their presentations knowing that in April 1994 the African National Congress, the leader of the revolutionary opposition to the apartheid regime, likely would ascend to national power. With this event the possibilities for transforming a racist, oppressive, exclusionary, unjust society into a nonracial, nonsexist, egalitarian one would be greatly strengthened. This profound transition would seem to compel both a rethinking of that past and a reformulation of the future, with the potential to produce startling innovations in planning practice. As the chairman of the Planning History Study Group remarked in his address to the symposium, "the planning profession remains entrapped in the reactionary mire of the divisive past. . . . [A] liberal, open-minded analysis of the history of planning could offer a cathartic release to the profession" (Muller 1993: 10).

My reliance on this collection of papers calls for a caveat. These writings do not "represent" the planning histories that have been written in South Africa. I do not view this as a problem, however. My intent is not to characterize all of South African planning history but to identify styles of presentation that subvert empowerment. Also, the reader should not conclude that South Africans write planning history differently from planning historians in other countries. The similarities between historical approaches in South Africa and the United States are striking.

South African Planning History

The outlines of South African apartheid are familiar (Lapping 1987). In 1948 the National party took power and declared its intent to institute "grand apartheid," a radical separation of the races. Using legislative decrees and police powers, blacks, coloreds, and Indians were denied access to certain areas, segregated within others, and relocated, not without resistance, to townships and "homelands" far removed from the centers of commerce and industry. Factories were also decentralized to reinforce racial segregation and governmental funds used to subsidize the commuting costs of nonwhite workers as well as dual public services such as schools. Built on a legacy of colonial segregation, the apartheid city required the expertise of planners to maintain separate and unequal environments (Smith 1992; Swilling, Humphries, and Shubane 1991; Western 1981: 59–124).

In the early 1990s the potential for the collapse of this edifice of oppression was recognized by a significant number of white politicians and businessmen. Their perception was strengthened by an anemic economy and by the success of the resistance movement in breaking down white dominance. Reforms were instituted, but they were too little and too late. Subsequently, resistance organizations such as the African National Congress (ANC) were unbanned and open elections were held. In April 1994 blacks, coloreds, Indians, and whites went to the polls and Nelson Mandela, head of the ANC, was elected to national office as president of the country.

It is against this turbulent and momentous background that planning histories are being written. Yet recognition of this historic transformation is absent, for the most part, from the histories published in the Pietermaritzburg proceedings. At the same time, and with a few significant exceptions, the authors fail to tell history in a way that reveals options for efficacious action. The dominant style is deterministic.

The deterministic histories take a quite familiar form; almost all of them posit a world in which the government and its legislation determine what planners do. In looking back at what planners have done and what their history has consisted of, the authors emphasize the sequence of planning laws from the Natives Land Act of 1913 and the Townships and Town Planning Ordinance in 1931 to the removal of the Group Areas Act in 1991. L. J. Oakenfull's portrayal of fifty years of planning practice is constructed around legislative events. For example, he writes that "the responsibility for town planning being at the provincial governmental level originates with the Financial Relations Act of 1913" (1993: 60). Phekane Ramarumo periodizes the evolution of black township planning in legislative terms: Phase 1 stemming from the Natives (Urban Areas) Act of 1923, Phase 2 from the Native Laws Amendment Act (1937), and Phase 3 from the Group Areas Act of 1950 and its 1957 amendments. B. M. Mohtle and T. N. J. Wanklin discuss planning in the Transkei homeland in similar terms. Not only did the homeland's existence depend on the South African state but its planning activities did so also: "Administration of urban locations/villages began to receive general and systematic attention only in

1923 with the passing of the first Native (Urban Areas) Act of 1923" (1993: 189).

The passage of legislation is mostly taken for granted, as if it were inevitable. Susan Parnell, in an interesting paper on the intersection of public health reform, Establishment worries about the white working class, and segregationist policies, makes it clear that legislation has to be proposed before it can be adopted and implemented but does not consider that it might be contested either from within or outside the government. She draws a direct line from legislative intent to social consequences: "South African adoption of international planning principles on overcrowding, housing funding, and slum removals were [*sic*] a deliberate endeavor to forge segregationist urban policies by enhancing the urban conditions of whites" (1993: 113).

Planners are portrayed as having had little influence over the content and form of the laws under which they toiled. All of this is reinforced by a tendency of many of those who write on planning legislation to marginalize the actors who turn interests and ideas into laws.

Planners in these histories thus appear as passive. They accept without question and operate under legislation set by the state. They have not influenced planning legislation to any great extent, although exceptions exist, and do not resist or change it in practice. Instead, planners exercise discretion within narrow legal bounds. In these deterministic histories planners function to identify socioeconomic and demographic trends calling for particular responses or heed cultural differences and then plan accordingly (Laburn-Pert 1993). Planners' history is one of dutifully implementing planning legislation and rationally reacting to environmental conditions.

More sophisticated versions of legislative determinism are also present. These recognize that individuals, some of whom could be characterized as planners, often play a key role in shaping legislation and assuring its passage. In Parnell's review of the influence on planning of early-twentieth-century concerns with public health and the white working class, she elevates Charles Porter, Johannesburg's first full-time medical officer of health, to a central role. His knowledge of planning in other countries, particularly England, and his ability to engage in discussions with legislators (and their reliance on him) shaped the early laws on public health and planning.

L. J. Oakenfull and F. J. Potgieter hint at the connection between individuals and key legislation but back away from serious consideration of this issue. Oakenfull (1993: 61) briefly mentions the contribution made by Colonel P. J. Bowling and the planners involved in the Witwatersrand Joint Town Planning Committee to the town planning schemes developed in the late 1940s in the Johannesburg region. In Potgieter's history of planning practice since World War II, T. B. Floyd, South Africa's first full-time planner, makes a cameo appearance (1993: 144) and Dr. H. J. van Eck is recognized as the chair of the influential Social and Economic Planning Council in 1942, but we never read about how these men might have shaped practice or legislation.

Although it is important to identify key actors, it is not sufficient if one wishes to write a nonsubversive history. A focus on individuals easily turns into a portrayal of elite individuals crafting legislation within a noncontested political realm. It might well be that the history of planning legislation in South Africa has not been contested either from within or outside "the white establishment." It might also be that these individuals knew exactly what they wanted to achieve and how and thus acted with certainty. Moreover, the legislation could have been implemented as written or without resistance, but all of this is doubtful. None of the planning histories I have mentioned raises such theoretical possibilities.

Two of the papers are sensitive to these issues and break from a determinative history grounded in irresistible legislation and an all-powerful state. Peter Wilkinson, in his discussion of a 1944 report on regional and town planning, not only admits to disagreement and conflict within an ostensibly monolithic state but also accepts the possibility that things might have turned out differently. He writes of "the hostility of provincial administrations" to central government regional planning proposals (1993: 273) and rivalry and competition within the bureaucracy (1993: 258). He points to uncertainty when he describes the vague brief given to the Social and Economic Planning Council (SEPC) that would eventually write the report (1993: 253). Wilkinson even confesses to authorial fallibility when, in reference to the divergence of the SEPC model of regional development planning from that proposed by the National Resources Development Act, he writes, "This is an hypothesis that I have not yet been able to explore in any depth" (1993: 275). His paper, moreover, is replete with cautionary phrases about the validity of his assertions.

Alan Mabin's interest is the surge of public housing provision in the 1950s and the transition from "locations" to townships. He comments on disagreements and conflicts within the state and divisions within the African population. He notes the contingency of implementation and the presence of resistance (1993: 326). Moreover, Mabin recognizes the uncertainty that pervades historical explanation when he writes that "such motives *probably encouraged* some employers and their representatives to express a desire for increased state involvement in housing workers" (1993: 309; emphasis added).

In addition, he accepts the possibility of a different history when he asks why the minister of Native Affairs, H. F. Verwoerd, changed his mind on a key commission recommendation (1993: 322). The recommendation in

October 1951 was to prepare legislation that would require that planning for locations be carried out regionally rather than nationally. "The ability of the Department of Native Affairs, and its minister and secretary in particular, to gain its own way in the siting of new, large townships" led to Verwoerd's about-face (1993: 326). Verwoerd's legal stature was not enough to override the political power of the department. Finally, Mabin is sensitive to the subjugated nature of these planning histories. He concludes by noting that "planning accorded no voice to the people who would live in the townships" (1993: 337).

As a generalization, then, the South African planning academics who participated in the Planning History Study Group symposium understand planning history to be mainly a consequence of planning legislation set by the state and implemented faithfully by planners. Capital, either independently or through the state, is absent. Instead, planners are portrayed as the receivers of laws that were politically motivated, with a few powerful individuals instrumental in shaping legislation. In sum, planners are presented as having been wholly reactive.

Equally as interesting is how planning histories are not written. Overdetermined histories, histories "from below," or histories that are sensitive (and this is quite shocking) to the startling differences among racial groups within the country do not appear in these proceedings.

The writing of overdetermined histories is likely a function of the extent to which a postmodern understanding of narrative has penetrated a discipline (Krieger 1994). South African writings on planning and urban development display little interest in the kind of poststructuralist experimentation one finds in Western Europe and the United States (e.g., Beauregard 1991; Sandercock 1994). South African urban analysis is deeply grounded in Eurocentric mainstream or Marxist perspectives or exhibits a pragmatic bias that is anchored to pressing issues on the ground that need to be addressed. As the chairman notes in his introductory remarks, "The history of planning cannot but be the history of the circumstances within which planning has developed" (Muller 1993: 2). Engaging in a postmodern playfulness seems frivolous in the South African context.

The one exception is Wilkinson's (1993) paper on the Social and Economic Planning Council's *Fifth Report on Regional and Town Planning*, released in 1944. Wilkinson grounds the council's report in the discourse of modernity and sets as his goal the unpacking of the material and ideological processes that shaped it: a belief in modernization theory, a commitment to the state as regulator of capitalist development, and an absorption in rationalist procedures. His argument suggests a postmodern alternative, an alternative that is never articulated.

Although histories from below do exist, and the history profession in South African has a radical element, planning histories written from the perspective of peoples planned for, as in the United States, are rare. These histories would have to consider issues of resistance, political strategy, and the hopefulness of alternative outcomes. Implementation of planning legislation would be problematic and planners viewed less as neutral technicians than as tools of dominant powers who are susceptible to reformist— and even revolutionary?—appeal.

Also revealing, and empowering, would be planning histories that take the perspective of various groups within South African society. Apartheid planning, I am sure, looked quite different from the vantage point of blacks or Indians than it did from that of whites, as it likely did also from the different positions of men and women as these categories crossed racial divisions. Yet most South African planning histories and all (except one) that came out of this symposium are oblivious to issues of gender (but see Pauline Morris's [1993] paper on Soweto) and make only passing reference to racial divisions, although this is unavoidable when discussing planning legislation or housing. Even Morris's paper only briefly touches on the role of African women as housing contractors and as the target of regulations that prevented them from being placed on the waiting lists for family housing (1993: 348–349).

Writing histories that account for and better define these differences would compel historians to confront oppositional and alternative goals and procedures. Planning would become less monolithic and unyielding, less a determined matter than one of negotiation and contingency.

I cannot help but suspect that the passivity that permeates many of the planning histories from this symposium is related to the complicity of governmental planners in the apartheid regime. Not one of the papers addresses this issue, though a number allude to the ethics of planning, the fact that planners worked primarily for white governments, or the planned dimensions of apartheid. Mark Oranje (1993), for example, historicizes recent planning history by dividing planners into a client-driven group who worked slavishly—my term—for the government and a context-driven group who, he implies, condemned apartheid planning and those involved in it. He is not forthcoming with criticism of apartheid planners, though, and his planners, once categorized, seem destined to behave in ways compatible with the "paradigm" that they adopted. A choice was made, for reasons that are not investigated, and subsequently planners become puppets of either legislation or "context."

The tendency of the symposium's authors is to avoid responsibility for apartheid. One would think that the startling transition from a white to an "African" government, and the success of the revolutionary movement (in which a number of planners participated), would lead the planning profession to reflect seriously and publicly on its former complicity. Although a time for healing, it would also seem an opportune time for confession and reconciliation. With the exception of Pauline Morris, who writes of the need to "unravel the complex legacy with which we have been left" (1993: 361), and the call by John Muller to search out "a cathartic release" for the profession, the written record of the symposium displays none of these tendencies.

Such reflection would have to confront how planners could have behaved differently and what they should have done. These queries are in themselves empowering, for they force us to imagine how history could have been different and thus to imagine the potential we have for bringing about the change we collectively desire.

HISTORY THAT EMPOWERS

To end without considering, even though briefly, how one might write non-subversive histories would be an embarrassing contradiction. Histories that empower have to portray a world that is complex, thus offering numerous opportunities for action, and contingent, thus allowing the less powerful to have influence. Moreover, the historian must convey a sense that actions do have more or less predictable consequences, even if those consequences are mediated by the resistances and assistance of others, have to be aggressively pursued rather than predicted and awaited, or are contingent on a variety of related events and conditions. The actual complexity of society must be made comprehensible (that is, emplotted) rather than simplified to the point of caricature (Weinstein 1990; White 1987). Because the world is neither determined nor random, it can be changed.

Within this world, planning must appear as a human activity that enables collective mobilization and action and that is proactive rather than reactive. All action must be cast in its real social context in real time rather than isolated in individuals who appear as mythical agents of history. Planners can be historical figures, but only when acting collectively, and given the resources they command in most societies, particularly South Africa and the United States, acting collectively means joining forces with others. In this way influence is created and enhanced rather than presented as a "right" enjoyed by those of a particular family background, skin color, or gender.

Historians must further search out the ways in which planners can either empower themselves or empower others who are like-minded. Where in specific situations and times do pressure points for social change intersect with the causal powers and liabilities attendant to planners and their constituents? How does planning empower planners, or disempower them when planning is trivialized? What bases of legitimacy enable planners to "sit at the table"? The answers to these and other questions can be used to make planning history.

Finally, the potential for empowerment is also a part of the language of historians. Straight stories and grand theories disempower; crooked stories suggest opportunities. Attesting to the ambiguity of historical evidence builds uncertainty into both the historical story and present interpretations (Hirschmann 1970). Speculation and discussions of counterfactual possibilities deepen the understanding that history might have turned out differently. Surfacing the author, confessing to fallibility and bounded rationality, and writing history with humility further empower a text. Last, one should write in the active voice and make use of conditional sentences, stylistic elements that reinforce a sense of possibilities.

To produce planning texts that empower, we must do more than recognize voices that have been suppressed and do more than approach history from below. Even these histories can be debilitating. Nonsubversive histories, by contrast, require a commitment to a contingent ontological viewpoint, an epistemology that recognizes the malleability and uncertainty that surround knowledge, and a writing style that reveals the indeterminacy of history. Planning histories written against this grain might well find interested readers, but those readers will remain passive subjects of history.

REFERENCES

Abbott, Carl, and Sy Adler. 1989. "Historical Analysis as a Planning Tool." *Journal of the American Planning Association* 55:467–473.

Abrams, Phillip. 1980. "History, Sociology, Historical Sociology." *Past and Present* 87:3–16.

Althusser, Louis. 1979. *For Marx*. London: Verso.

Beauregard, Robert A. 1991. "Without a Net: Modernist Planning and the Postmodern Abyss." *Journal of Planning Education and Research* 10:189–194.

———. 1993. *Voices of Decline: The Postwar Fate of U. S. Cities*. Oxford: Blackwell.

Berlin, Issiah. 1959. "Determinism, Relativism, and Historical Judgments." In *Theories of History*, ed. P. Gardiner, 320–329. New York: Free Press.

Fitzgerald, Joan, and William Howard. 1993. "Discovering an African American Planning History." Paper presented to the American Collegiate Schools of Planning Conference, Philadelphia.

Flacks, Richard. 1976. "Making History vs. Making Life: The Dilemmas of an American Left." *Sociological Inquiry* 46:263–280.

Friedmann, John. 1987. *Planning in the Public Domain*. Princeton, N.J.: Princeton University Press.

Giddens, Anthony. 1979. *Central Problems in Social Theory*. Berkeley: University of California Press.

Hall, Peter. 1982. *Great Planning Disasters*. Berkeley: University of California Press.

Hirschmann, Albert O. 1970. "The Search for Paradigms as a Hindrance to Understanding." *World Politics* 22:329–343.

Hobsbawm, Eric J. 1973. "Karl Marx's Contribution to Historiography." In *Ideology in Social Science*, ed. R. Blackburn, 262–283. New York: Vintage.

Hooper, Barbara. 1992. " 'Split at the Roots': A Critique of the Philosophical and Political Sources of Modern Planning Doctrine." *Frontiers* 13:45–80.

Johnson, David A. and Daniel Schaffer. 1985. "Learning from the Past: The History of Planning." *Journal of the American Planning Association* 51:131–133.

Kellner, Hans. 1989. *Language and Historical Representation.* Madison: University of Wisconsin Press.

Krieger, Martin. 1994. *The Institution of Theory.* Baltimore: Johns Hopkins University Press.

Laburn-Pert, Catherine. 1993. "Pre-Colonial Towns of Southern Africa: Integrating the Teaching of Planning History and Urban Morphology." In Planning History Study Group, *Proceedings of the Symposium on South African Planning History.* N.p. 227–237.

Lapping, Brian. 1987. *Apartheid: A History.* London: Palladin.

Mabin, Alan. 1993. "Conflict, Continuity and Change: Locating the 'Properly Planned Native Townships' in the Forties and the Fifties." In Planning History Study Group, *Proceedings of the Symposium on South African Planning History.* N.p. 305–337.

Mahotle, Manako, and Tom Wanklin. 1993. "Planning Approaches in the Transkei: Historical Overview." In Planning History Study Group, *Proceedings of the Symposium on South African Planning History.* N.p. 183–195.

Mandelbaum, Seymour. 1985. "Historians and Planners: The Construction of Pasts and Futures." *Journal of the American Planning Association* 51:185–188.

Morris, Pauline. 1993. "Soweto: Implications of the Historical Planning Process." In Planning History Study Group, *Proceedings of the Symposium on South African Planning History.* N.p. 339–373.

Muller, John. 1993. "The Past: Parent of the Present." In Planning History Study Group, *Proceedings of the Symposium on South African Planning History.* N.p. 1–13.

Oakenfull, Les. 1993. "Fifty Years of Planning Practice: Missing the Link." In Planning History Study Group, *Proceedings of the Symposium on South African Planning History.* N.p. 59–71.

Oranje, Mark C. 1993. "South African Planning History: The Big Bang Theory." In Planning History Study Group, *Proceedings of the Symposium on South African Planning History.* N.p. 281–303.

Palmer, Bryan D. 1990. *Descent into Discourse.* Philadelphia: Temple University Press.

Parnell, Susan. 1993. "Creating Racial Privilege: Public Health and Town Planning Legislation, 1910–1920." In Planning History Study Group, *Proceedings of the Symposium on South African Planning History.* N.p. 97–120.

Planning History Study Group. 1993. *Proceedings of the Symposium on South African Planning History.* N.p.

Potgieter, Fritz J. 1993. "Major Shifts in Planning Practice in South Africa since World War II." In Planning History Study Group, *Proceedings of the Symposium on South African Planning History.* N.p. 143–156.

Ramarumo, Phekene. 1993. "Social Marginalization through Zoning: A Historical Review." In Planning History Study Group, *Proceedings of the Symposium on South African Planning History.* N.p. 121–128.

Sandercock, Leonie. 1990. *Property, Politics and Urban Planning.* New Brunswick, N.J.: Transaction.

————. 1994. "Framing a New Historiography of City Planning." Paper presented at annual meetings of the Association of the Collegiate Schools of Planning, Tempe, Ariz.

Scott, Joan W. 1988. *Gender and the Politics of History*. New York: Columbia University Press.

Scriven, Michael. 1959. "Truisms as the Grounds for Historical Explanations." In *Theories of History*, ed. P. Gardiner, 443–475. New York: Free Press.

Smith, David M., ed. 1992. *The Apartheid City and Beyond*. London: Routledge.

Spivak, Gayatri C. 1989. "Who Claims Alterity?" In *Remaking History*, ed. B. Kruger and P. Mariani, 269–292. Seattle: Bay Press.

Swilling, Mark, Richard Humphries, and Khehla Shubane, eds. 1991. *Apartheid City in Transition*. Cape Town: Oxford University Press.

Weinstein, Fred. 1990. *History and Theory after the Fall*. Chicago: University of Chicago Press.

Western, John. 1981. *Outcast Cape Town*. Minneapolis: University of Minnesota Press.

White, Hayden. 1978. "Interpretation in History." In *Tropics of Discourse*, 51–80. Baltimore: Johns Hopkins University Press.

————. 1987. "The Question of Narrative in Contemporary Historical Theory." In *The Content of the Form*, 26–57. Baltimore: Johns Hopkins University Press.

Wilkinson, Peter. 1993. "A Discourse of Modernity: The Social and Economic Planning Council's Fifth Report on *Regional and Town Planning*, 1944." In Planning History Study Group, *Proceedings of the Symposium on South African Planning History*. N.p. 239–279.

Wilson, Elizabeth. 1991. *The Sphinx in the City: Urban Life, the Control of Disorder, and Women*. Berkeley: University of California Press.

TEN

Racial Inequality and Empowerment

Necessary Theoretical Constructs for Understanding U.S. Planning History

June Manning Thomas

If Leonie Sandercock is right in her assertion that no monolithic theory of planning history is possible, but rather a collection of theories appropriate to particular times and circumstances is necessary, then the search for an appropriate planning theory should include the search for appropriate theoretical constructs, or building blocks. While the concept of class and class oppression was a fairly common construct in previous theoretical work, perspectives related to gender or race were not (Sandercock 1990).

It is increasingly necessary to build historical approaches based on inclusive perspectives regarding race, gender, and class. And it is in the best interests of planning historians and the profession to do so. This is true even though complete exploration of urban planning's past, which includes a legacy of oppression of the "have-nots," may appear to tarnish the image of the planning profession. Those intent on documenting the contributions of the profession may find planners' record concerning minorities, women, and poor people embarrassing. Yet full inclusion and consideration of such concepts is in the best interest of the field, the profession, and the urban regions planners are trying to serve.

Racial inequality, for example, is inextricably linked with the development of twentieth-century U.S. cities and urban regions. Including racial inequality as a theoretical construct in planning history has certain decided advantages:

1. To do so avoids the appearance of naïveté, at best, or deliberate ethnocentrism, at worst. Given the general sophistication and extensiveness of the literature concerning the connections between racial inequality and policy making in cities and suburbs in the United States (and in other countries such as Great Britain and South Africa), planning histories that ignore the connections, or treat them superficially, raise questions of historical competence.

2. Full consideration of the role of racial inequality in planning contemporary cities heightens the value of history as a process of learning about the past so as to improve the present and the future. Without acknowledging and fully exploring the linkages, such lessons are not possible.

3. Examining the linkage between racial inequality and planning from the perspective of planning history allows for the correction of erroneous perceptions concerning the extent to which planners were to blame for the racism of policy makers and society in general and simultaneously highlights the importance of overcoming such racism if urban society is to progress.

4. As with the inclusion of gender issues, viewing planning from the perspective of racial minorities facilitates the discovery of surprisingly fresh insights and perspectives. From the vantage point of African American community history, for example, one can see the persistent determination of an oppressed group to fight the tide of oppression and to become empowered.

This essay briefly considers each of these four key points and offers evidence of their veracity.

CITIES AND RACE

The first point is that historians of urban planning ignore vast regions of the truth if they try to explain the evolution of urban planning divorced from the context of racial change and racial oppression, particularly in U.S. cities and regions.

The absurdity of ignoring race emerges most clearly from an extreme example: what opinion would we form of historians of urban planning in South Africa who chose to write about the origins and evolution of the work of their profession *without* addressing the implications of apartheid? Clearly racial politics shaped both historical and contemporary policy and planning decisions for that country's cities and urban regions. A creditable historian of urban South Africa and of urban planning in South Africa should be compelled to consider such issues in his or her work (Lemon 1991; Mandy 1984).

Observers have also noted a connection between race and planning in other less obvious cases, such as Great Britain. Although of a different nature than the connection in the United States—in Great Britain, for example, the people indigenous to the former British colonies are society's "blacks"—race still offers an important perspective for analyzing patterns of urban policy decisions (Blair 1988).

The state of race relations in U.S. cities similarly begs consideration by all who would purport to write modern urban history or urban planning history. Evidence suggests that metropolitan areas remain severely segregated by race and class and that in some regions such segregation is worsening (Massey 1993). While racial separation is not as rigid in the United States as it is in a country such as South Africa, it is still entrenched enough to cause major social and economic problems. To explain how metropolitan areas became so segregated, it is necessary to understand the evolution of urban policies that urban planners often helped to implement (Thomas 1994). Yet most major works on U.S. planning history have mentioned little or nothing about the relationship between racial change and urban planning. When they have done so, the subject has sometimes been treated incompletely or inappropriately, briefly mentioning African Americans only as victims of urban policies (Boyer 1983; Krueckeberg 1983; Schaffer 1988) or focusing exclusively on their alleged social pathologies (Hall 1989).

This is strange, especially considering that the literature documenting the importance of race in shaping U.S. urban areas and in influencing their planning policies is extensive and well established (Bauman 1987; Gans 1991; Hirsch 1983; Kusmer 1991; Schnore 1972; Thomas and Ritzdorf 1997). The question could easily arise: are twentieth-century American planning historians who ignore such considerations, or treat them incompletely, incompetent? Are they, perhaps, ethnocentric? Or are they simply unaware of their omissions, thinking that race is a "fringe" topic of little importance?

The best way to avoid such negative judgments is to become more inclusive. When modern authors conceptualize, research, and write about urban planning history, full inclusion of the role of race relations and racial oppression should become a sign of professional competence.

RACE AND PLANNING HISTORY

A second reason to consider the linkages between race and planning history is to offer planning students, scholars, and practitioners the opportunity to learn from past mistakes. From that perspective, past experiences become not so much an unpleasant memory to be avoided as a set of cautionary lessons to be embraced.

Consider, for example, the period of potentially greatest sensitivity for U.S. planning historians intent on documenting a nonracial past: the urban renewal era. Planners received such overwhelmingly negative press about that era that the natural tendency is to avoid it, or at least to avoid dwelling on the racial effects of urban renewal policies.

Yet the truth is that planners and redevelopment specialists learned a lot from urban renewal experiences, and those lessons continue to hold power today. They learned that planners were often held responsible for the racial effects of their actions even though the decision makers often were not planners. They learned that their actions had racial implications, even if these were at times unconscious. And they learned—or they should have learned—that city improvement efforts, in a context of racial oppression, can be racially oppressive (Gans 1991; Goodman 1971; Perloff 1965).

One of the major purposes of remembering this history must be to ensure that it is not repeated. The situation is far less extreme but somewhat comparable to that facing modern Germans: to ignore Hitler is to risk seeing him rise again. As contemporary planners attempt to move closer to positions governed by principles of justice, equity, and fair play, knowing how planning can be misused to subvert these principles is essential (Keating and Krumholz 1991). For this reason it is important to read sagas such as Robert Caro's (1975) account of power broker Robert Moses, America's quintessential nonplanner/planner. Understanding how power can be corrupted is important training for preventing future corruption.

The same general principle holds for other racially sensitive areas of planning and public policy, such as exclusionary zoning, expulsive zoning, segregation of assisted housing, public transportation policy, subdivision regulation, and environmental racism. The only hope for improving the record of the profession and the society in these areas is first to acknowledge that problems related to racial oppression existed in the past and continue to affect the present, and then to act to rectify them (Thomas and Ritzdorf 1997).

PLANNERS AND RACISM IN SOCIETY

Examining the actual role of urban planners in the history of urban development may clarify that the problem of racial prejudice and oppression originated not so much from bureaucratic planners as from the larger society. Inclusive historiography may reveal, more completely than nonracially sensitive analysis, the role of society's racism in hindering planners' ability to carry out their work effectively. This could allow for a more holistic explanation of the actual causes of urban deterioration.

One of the first examples of such work was Martin Meyerson and Edward Banfield's (1955) classic case study of public housing in Chicago. Although that book focused not so much on urban planners as on public housing professionals, it treated them as planners, and its lessons transcended job categories. In Meyerson and Banfield's case study, some urban professionals tried to carry out policies characterized by enlightened racial views but were prevented from doing so by the racism that pervaded the general society. Other authors have found similar examples of this gap between intention and outcome as municipalities wrestled with the issue of where to place subsidized housing that was open to all races (Bauman 1987; Hirsch 1983).

Although the issue of public housing has been perhaps the most easily documented historically, it usually affected only a few thousand families per metropolitan area. A larger, less easily documented problem is the ongoing difficulty of conserving urban residential neighborhoods in the context of residential racial segregation and turnover. Without understanding the racial context of U.S. urban cities and metropolitan areas, observers receive only a partial answer to the question, why have planners had such limited success historically in their efforts to conserve, rehabilitate, salvage, or upgrade inner-city residential neighborhoods?

There are several answers to this question, and many of them relate to racism. One quick but obvious answer, for example, is that many of these neighborhoods became holding pens for society's dispossessed, among whom racial minorities figured prominently. The collective burden of prejudice and discrimination left vast segments of the population with no other option than to remain in neighborhoods that offered little social and economic opportunity. Hence upgrading activities had little chance for success.

Another, longer answer to the same question relates to the problem of racial turnover. The difficulties facing urban neighborhoods that have undergone or are undergoing racial change, from dominant to subject race, are well documented (Goering 1978; Saltman 1990). It has proven difficult to maintain socioeconomic status and viability when neighborhoods have become all-black, or all-Latino. White flight and racial turnover have had debilitating effects on neighborhood stability.

Yet if one were to undertake a content analysis of what kinds of activities occupied U.S. central city planning staff during the historical period after World War II, surely neighborhood revitalization would emerge as a major initiative. First the federal public housing program, which purported to improve "slum" neighborhoods; then the conservation component of urban renewal, implemented in 1954; the short-lived Model Cities program, product of the 1960s; and most recently, the federal Community Development Block Grants and several smaller federal and state neighborhood preservation initiatives—all compelled planners to take deliberate steps to upgrade residential neighborhoods (Kaplan 1990).

Planners often undertook neighborhood revitalization activities in the decidedly unfriendly context of white flight. Under the conservation program in the 1950s, for example, deliberate attempts to get white and black citizens to work together and commit to neighborhood improvement failed when the program could not stop whites from leaving target areas. Similar problems occurred in neighborhoods that planners attempted to improve using Community Development Block Grants during the 1970s and 1980s. Even in those areas that stabilized somewhat when the neighborhood became all-black, the effects of racism lingered. This sometimes took the form of redlining, defined as systematic discrimination by lending institutions, or of income turnover, defined as transition from middle-class black owners to lower-class black renters (Darden et al. 1987; Thomas 1997b).

The problem of neighborhood stabilization illustrates why historians should be careful to examine a broad range of planning activities. Although they might be tempted to focus on the megaprojects that planners helped to create—riverfronts, downtowns, urban renewal projects (Hall 1989; Scott 1969)—scholars could learn just as much by examining smaller situations, such as neighborhood planning, where planners worked but had little impact. In those situations, societal racism may have been an important explanatory variable. Through their efforts to document the negative effects of racial injustice on urban revitalization initiatives, planning historians can educate the public and the profession about the need to overcome individual and institutional racial prejudice and to rectify past wrongs.

THE STRUGGLE FOR EMPOWERMENT

A final reason for linking planning history and sensitivity to racial inequality analysis is that scholars may thereby gain access to rich and varied new perspectives. This is what happened, for example, to those scholars who began to write planning history from the perspective of women. They found that women played an extensive role in remaking home, workplace, and city. Particularly valuable insights emerged when historians' focus shifted from the contributions women made to the urban planning profession to the planning activities that women carried out independent of professional sanctions (Hayden 1981, 1984; Sandercock and Forsyth 1992).

Similarly, viewing planning history from the perspective of oppressed racial minorities opens up enormous historical possibilities. One large and obvious example is the extensive community-building activities that African American and other minority communities undertook from the beginning of the century, through organizations such as the Urban League and other civil rights groups, various housewives' associations, and religious organizations (Fitzgerald and Howard 1993; McDougall 1993; Thomas 1992). One simple manifestation of such community building was the effort to develop suburban subdivisions targeted to African Americans (Taylor 1993). Studies that illuminate these activities throw a whole new light on urban improvement. Those historians who focus on the relationship between urban planning and minority communities can help clarify how

these communities fought, with greater or lesser success, for empowerment.

The concept of empowerment is, in itself, a theoretical construct. This
concept suggests that the disenfranchised will seek to gain control over
their life circumstances, whether through community development, politics, or other means. This struggle for control will take place in spite of (or
because of) the tendency of societies to bow to the stronger influence of
economic and political elites and to impose social controls on those who
have little power (Freire 1981; Friedmann 1992; McClendon 1993).

Empowerment as a concept is particularly applicable to poor people,
both in more and in less developed countries. In some countries, however,
few groups have remained consistently poor, since various ethnic and na-
tionality groups tend to shift in social status. Examples from North
America: although new Irish, Eastern European, and Chinese immigrants
tended to start at the bottom of society, they gradually moved out of poverty
through political or economic ascendancy; so have members of other ethnic groups, such as some Latinos, especially Cubans, and some African
Americans.

In spite of this, looking at planning history from the perspective of racial
inequality is one of the surest ways of tracking the struggle for empowerment in American cities. Such tracking cannot be done by examining
the experiences of the white working class, who ceased to struggle once
the suburbs and white-collar employment opened up. A high enough per-
centage of African Americans and Latinos have remained oppressed to
make their community histories a source of real insight into the movement
for empowerment in the context of urban planning.

Although the persistent movement for black community self-sufficiency
and self-determination during the early part of the century illustrates this
point, I will here briefly describe more recent events. Beginning with the
urban renewal era and continuing to the present, African American communities have consistently fought for the power to plan their own communities. This is particularly evident during the urban renewal era, when African American communities rose up to demand the right to determine
their communities' destinies, and the Model Cities era, a major federal
program dedicated to financing efforts by distressed communities to control their own planning. And in the present, community development in
largely African American or Latino areas has emerged yet again as a force
for empowerment in the inner cities of America.

The struggle for empowerment in the face of urban renewal was a widespread phenomenon. In large cities and in small, minority neighborhoods
were the most likely to be cleared, even though their residents had the least
mobility in racially restricted housing markets. Although for a number of

years these communities did not oppose the clearance, eventually they mobilized and succeeded in reshaping the planning and development
agenda. Their consistent efforts to counter the growth agenda's vision of
urban improvement is an important story of courage in the face of repression (Davis 1991; King 1981). Planning historians would do well to acknowledge that the conflict-ridden process of urban renewal gave birth to
community organizations and natural leaders who often went on to accom-
plish positive things for their communities, including the construction of
low-income housing.

During the Model Cities era, that struggle continued, under the spon-
sorship of the federal government. Although its critics maintain that this
much-maligned program accomplished little, it in fact allowed a continuation of the process of resident empowerment. From the perspective of the
African American community, the program was a respite from the unmiti-
gating pressures of top-down decision making. In many cities resident government boards were able to hire their own planning staff, facilitating the
rise of what planners might call the era of advocacy planners and what
community activists might call the era of citizen-directed planning. For all
of its difficulties, Model Cities allowed, for the space of a few short years, a
community to plan for itself (Thomas 1997a).

Finally, the current resurgence of community-based development, particularly by faith-based inner-city groups, surely qualifies as a continuation
of the struggle for community empowerment. Although this movement is
still in process, it suggests that stalwart inner-city communities are actively
engaged in efforts to empower the disenfranchised.

ILLUMINATING PLANNING HISTORY

Thus we have seen that racially sensitive planning history opens up great
opportunities for historical insight. First, such a perspective brings planning historians more in line with contemporary analysts and urban historians who have long realized the inseparability of race and urban studies.
This would help to remedy the sense that planning historians shy away
from critical analysis, particularly when it involves difficult subjects such as
racial inequality or racial oppression.

Second, exploring the role of race in planning history allows historians
to help to clarify past mistakes and prepare for a more equitable future. I
have used the example of U.S. urban renewal, but the principle holds for
other policies as well. If indeed urban planners and decision makers made
racially oppressive decisions in the past, we need to know this to avoid
similar situations in the present and the future.

Third, such explorations can also clarify the problem of racism within the broader society, balancing the tendency to blame planners and other bureaucrats for decisions that in fact came from politicians or individual decision makers. Particularly with such policies as neighborhood redevelopment, society's racism has consistently stymied some of the best efforts of society's urban planners. Full knowledge of this fact should help to enlist planners in the battle for racial equality within the larger society.

Finally, empowerment is an important construct to link with race and planning history. This is true in part because it offers new insights into history, but also because it offers a way of explaining how the human spirit can triumph in the face of oppression.

Without such a perspective, urban policy decisions become a double-edged sword: not only do they oppress in the first instance, when events take place, they oppress in hindsight, when historians recall events. If descendants of the oppressed class receive the message from historians that their communities really had very little role to play in historical events *other than to serve as victims,* what does this say about their power to make positive changes in the present? Rather than foster an attitude of helplessness, historians of social conscience can foster a sense of constructive self-initiative, a sense of human nobility. Acknowledging that self-initiative existed in the past is one way to do so, and this does no more than acknowledge the truth.

REFERENCES

Bauman, John. 1987. *Public Housing, Race, and Renewal: Urban Planning in Philadelphia, 1920–1974.* Philadelphia: Temple University Press.

Blair, Tom. 1988. "Building an Urban Future: Race and Planning in London." *Cities* (February): 41–56.

Boyer, Christine. 1983. *Dreaming the Rational City: The Myth of American City Planning.* Cambridge, Mass.: MIT Press.

Caro, Robert. 1975. *The Power Broker: Robert Moses and the Fall of New York.* New York: Vintage Books.

Cloward, Richard, and Frances Fox Piven. 1974. *The Politics of Turmoil: Essays on Poverty, Race, and the Urban Crisis.* New York: Pantheon Books.

Darden, Joe, Richard Hill, June Thomas, and Richard Thomas. 1987. *Detroit: Race and Uneven Development.* Philadelphia: Temple University Press.

Davis, John. 1991. *Contested Ground: Collective Action and the Urban Neighborhood.* Ithaca, N.Y.: Cornell University Press.

Fitzgerald, Joan, and William Howard. 1993. "African-American Contributions to the Emergence of Urban Planning in the United States." Paper presented at the annual meeting of the Society for American City and Regional Planning History, Chicago, November.

Freire, Paul. 1981. *Pedagogy of the Oppressed.* New York: Continuum.

Friedmann, John. 1992. *Empowerment: The Politics of Alternative Development.* Cambridge: Blackwell.

Gans, Herbert J. 1991. *People, Plans, and Policies: Essays on Poverty, Racism, and Other National Urban Problems.* New York: Columbia University Press.

Goering, John M. 1978. "Neighborhood Tipping and Racial Transition: A Review of the Social Science Literature." *Journal of the American Institute of Planners* 44:68–78.

Goodman, Robert. 1971. *After the Planners.* New York: Touchstone Books.

Hall, Peter. 1989. *Cities of Tomorrow: An Intellectual History of Urban Planning and Design in the Twentieth Century.* Oxford: Blackwell.

Hayden, Delores. 1981. *The Grand Domestic Revolution: A History of Feminist Designs for American Homes, Neighborhoods, and Cities.* Cambridge, Mass.: MIT Press.

———. 1984. *Redesigning the American Dream: The Future of Housing, Work, and Family Life.* New York: Norton.

Hirsch, Arnold. 1983. *Making the Second Ghetto.* Cambridge: Cambridge University Press.

Kaplan, Marshall. 1990. "American Neighborhood Policies: Mixed Results and Uneven Evaluations." In *The Future of National Urban Policy,* ed. M. Kaplan and F. James, 210–224. Durham, N.C.: Duke University Press.

Keating, Dennis, and Norman Krumholz. 1991. "Downtown Plans of the 1980s: The Case for More Equity in the 1990s." *Journal of the American Planning Association* 57(2):136–152.

King, Mel. 1981. *Chain of Change: Struggles for Black Community Development.* Boston: South End Press.

Krueckeberg, Donald, ed. 1983. *Introduction to Planning History in the United States.* New Brunswick, N.J.: Center for Urban Policy Research, Rutgers University.

Kusmer, Kenneth L., ed. 1991. *Black Communities and Urban Development in America, 1720–1990.* New York: Garland.

Lemon, Anthony, ed. 1991. *Homes Apart: South Africa's Segregated Cities.* Bloomington: Indiana University Press.

McClendon, Bruce. 1993. "The Paradigm of Empowerment." *Journal of the American Planning Association* 59(2):145–147.

McDougall, Harold A. 1993. *Black Baltimore: A New Theory of Community.* Philadelphia: Temple University Press.

Mandy, Nigel. 1984. *A City Divided: Johannesburg and Soweto.* New York: St. Martin's Press.

Massey, Douglas S. 1993. *American Apartheid: Segregation and the Making of the Underclass.* Cambridge, Mass.: Harvard University Press.

Meyerson, Martin, and Edward C. Banfield. 1955. *Politics, Planning and the Public Interest: The Case of Public Housing in Chicago.* Glencoe, Ill.: Free Press.

Perloff, Harvey. 1965. "Common Goals and the Linking of Physical and Social Planning." In *Planning 1965,* 170–184. Chicago: American Society of Planning Officals.

Saltman, Juliet. 1990. *A Fragile Movement: The Struggle for Neighborhood Stabilization.* Westport, Conn.: Greenwood.

Sandercock, Leonie. 1990. *Property, Politics, and Urban Planning: A History of Australian City Planning, 1890–1990.* 2d ed. New Brunswick, N.J.: Transaction.

Sandercock, Leonie, and Ann Forsyth. 1992. "A Gender Agenda: New Directions for Planning Theory." *Journal of the American Planning Association* 58:49–59.

Schaffer, Daniel. 1988. *Two Centuries of American Planning.* Baltimore: Johns Hopkins University Press.

Schnore, Leo F. 1972. *Class and Race in Cities and Suburbs.* Chicago: Markham.

Scott, Mel. 1969. *American City Planning Since 1890.* Berkeley: University of California Press.

Taylor, Henry. 1993. "Menace to the City: Black Suburbanization and the City Planning Movement in Cincinnati, 1870–1950." Paper presented at the annual meeting of the Society for American City and Regional Planning History, Chicago, November.

Thomas, June. 1994. "Planning History and the Black Urban Experience: Linkages and Contemporary Implications." *Journal of Planning Education and Research* 14(1):1–11.

———. 1997a. "Model Cities Revisited: Issues of Race and Empowerment." In *Urban Planning and the African American Community: In the Shadows,* ed. June Thomas and Marsha Ritzdorf. Thousand Oaks, Calif.: Sage Publications.

———. 1997b. *Redevelopment and Race: Planning a Finer City in Postwar Detroit.* Baltimore: Johns Hopkins University Press.

Thomas, June, and Marsha Ritzdorf, eds. 1997. *Urban Planning and the African American Community: In the Shadows.* Thousand Oaks, Calif.: Sage Publications.

Thomas, Richard. 1992. *Life for Us Is What We Make It: Building Black Community in Detroit, 1915–1945.* Bloomington: Indiana University Press.

ELEVEN

Afraid/Not

Psychoanalytic Directions for an Insurgent Planning Historiography

Dora Epstein

Psychoanalysis and historiography have two different ways of distributing the space of memory. *Psychoanalysis recognizes the past in the present; historiography places them one beside the other. . . . Two strategies of* time *thus confront one another. They do, however, develop in the context of analogous problems: to find principles and criteria to serve as guides to follow in attempting to understand the differences, or guarantee the continuities, between the organization of the actual and the formations of the past; to relate the representations of the past or present to the conditions which determined their production; to elaborate different ways of thinking, and to define and construct a narrative, which is for both disciplines the favored form of elucidating discourse.*

MICHEL DE CERTEAU (1986)

I often find myself making choices about my explorations of the city based on my ideas of what is safe or unsafe. I avoid certain routes because they are unlit at night, certain buses because they take me too far from areas I know, or certain places because of stories of danger from media and friends. As I sit at my apartment window and watch the city unfold and change, I am reminded of my childhood days, my earnest desires to experience the carnival of the city, and the boundaries imposed by my mother and father. But I am also reminded of the dangers I have encountered as a young adult—the time when a man spat at me on the street, the night I was followed by a stranger. I remember the city as a chain of places—*a topography of memories*—some exhilarating, some boring, and still others fraught with fear. Feeling much as my mother did when she raked up a snake in our front yard and ran screaming into the house vowing never to return to the leaves and the rake, there are places I will not return. There are places that I, having become a woman, will not go.

This story begins on ground level. Not in my apartment, practicing avoidance, but on the street. Not simply in locations and places but also in the kind of sensibility that constitutes me as a sentient being, a citizen of the urban environment (Benjamin 1979). Like so many women in the city, I fear rape. Like so many gays and lesbians in the city, I fear bashing. Like so many middle-class citizens, I fear assault and robbery. I fear bodily harm—from the rough grabbing of my wrist to the gunshot wound to my head. I fear mental and emotional harm—from the epithet *dyke* to the trauma of bodily victimization. I fear violation—of my materiality, of my un/conscious, of my self.

This fearing is a learning. It is an association of certain dangers with places over time—a cartography constructed within an identity (such as sexual/ethnic Other) and then repeated and reiterated by certain norms (such as the force of the law of the patriarchy): the topography of memories mentioned earlier (Butler 1993). It is the unconscious that continuously informs conscious choices about how and when we move through the city and how and in what ways we negotiate the many power relations implied by the setting *metropole*. It is mythologized as densely urban criminal activities. It is in the women who desire to "take back the night." It is in the communities who desire to "take back the streets." Indeed, it is in the very strategies that we employ on a daily basis, so routine that we do not always acknowledge them—the purposeful stride, the keys in our hand, the seat on the bus, the mace in our purse. It is taken as a part of the negotiation of everyday life in a city, which has been constructed and defined as a place (or set of certain places) for fearing.

THE FAILURE OF SAFE SPACES

If it were possible to write a totalizing history of planning activities and interventions from the Enlightenment (the "root" of the discipline) to the present day, a familiar strain, an ivy, would emerge, push through the many cracks—that ivy being the so-called promise of planning for the betterment of physical and social conditions. From the widened highway to the poverty of the inner city, the planning intervention is always aimed at an end point in which some people gain some advantage—an easier commute, residential security, job training, environmental soundness, and so on. Thus, as we begin to write insurgent planning histories, our focus remains on the subjective nature of this "betterment"—whether it succeeded in alleviating the malcondition, whether the transformative intervention was actually initiated by the actions of a heretofore "invisible" agency, or, and this is the crux of many critiques, whether the advantage gained by some was to the detriment of others.

Thus, while we may use planning histories to discuss racist, sexist, or homophobic consequences, and as one method of envisioning and elucidating new modes of insurgent planning activities, I speak of the rather ahistorical concept of fear to examine, not the outcomes, but the bases of planning interventions. There has been in planning a kind of pathology of solutions—an implicit belief that built environments and social interactions can be "made right," resolved, through "correct" actions. And this pathology of solutions has resulted in a type of erasure, through which the *topography of (planning's) memories,* reduced to a chain of causalities—actions and reactions, reverberations, means and ends—has undermined the significations and constructions that engendered the solution-oriented drive in the first place, the *topography of (citizen) memories.* In other words, a modern planning sensibility would dictate that fear is a problem to be resolved and that, more important, this resolution does not depend on an understanding of the ways in which fear has been socially constructed and signified. It is, to planning, an escapable and definitive peril of life in the city.

Thus, throughout the history of modern city planning, there have been attempts to create "safe spaces"—specific places where certain social groups can "escape" the pressures of the industrialized terrain, find communion with other members of difference, or create an ideology of community resistance and individual emancipation. Physically, there are barred entrances, fenced enclosures, lighted doorways, locks and bolts, entire neighborhoods practicing both insulation from the perceived dangers of outside forces and inclusion among its "members." Socially, there are community watch groups, sexual and ethnic collectives, even something as seemingly innocuous as a sticker naming a space as safe—for women, ethnic minorities, queers.

What is at issue here, however, is that these safe spaces, as effective as they may seem, do not actually serve to decrease or limit the *perpetuation* of fear. In fact, they may serve to reinforce it.

First, the belief that the community, or the construction of the community, perceived and enacted as the best means of allaying fear, may instead *increase* the alienation that lies at the heart of the fear engendered by the self/other encounter. In other words, the overriding belief that community associations will mediate the crises of living in the city undermines the exclusions entailed by its processes, or

[t]he ideal of community fails to offer an appropriate alternative vision of a democratic polity. This ideal expresses a desire for the fusion of subjects with one another which in practice operates to exclude those with whom the group does not identify. The ideal of community denies and represses social difference. . . . In its privileging of face-to-face relations, moreover, the ideal of community denies difference in the form of the temporal and spatial distancing that characterizes social process. (Young 1990: 75)

Second, the creation of a "safe space," the act of naming it as such, absolutely reinforces the notion that the rest of the city is inherently unsafe. Moreover, by initiating and "claiming space," the underlying statement is not only one of this "incremental resistance" but also a much wider acknowledgment, and thus legitimization, of the (much more magnificent) power that is being resisted. Thus when one adds in the recognition that these "safe spaces" are at best transitory—remaining at the most for a few years in a single location, or replete with the possibility of a new leadership that may be unsafe for many of its members—the intended safety unfortunately pales before the complex, varied, relative unsafety of the city in general. Thus:

> The question is not simply how to distinguish conducive from unconducive environments, but to examine how different cities, different sociocultural environments actively produce the bodies of their inhabitants as particular and distinctive types of bodies, as bodies with particular physiologies, affective lives, and concrete behaviors. . . . It is a question of negotiation of urban spaces by individuals/groups more or less densely packed, who inhabit or traverse them: each environment or context contains its own powers, perils, dangers, and advantages. (Grosz 1992: 250)

In the following, I examine some of the reasons why the planning tradition of fear resolution through safety measures has failed. I begin by describing the types of fearing that modern city planning has attempted to resolve as I illuminate the signification of what I call "city-fear": the type of fearing that is learned as one inhabits a city in which planning interventions have defined what to fear and then sought to allay. Through the lens of psychoanalytic theory, namely Jacques Lacan, I describe how the construction of fear is much more complex and deep-seated than has been formulated in planning, and then, using the work of Elizabeth Wilson, I show how city-fear has been repeated and reiterated through the norms of (patriarchal) power on the urban terrain. Further, it is my contention that without such analysis and interrogation, the historiographical project, of learning from the past and making the invisible visible, remains incomplete.

CITY-FEAR

To take up and critically examine the fearing I am describing—the ways in which we operate and negotiate our daily lives, the coping strategies we employ against fear, danger, and risk, and the Otherness implied by the urban environment, it is first important to emphasize that city inhabitants are actively and continually produced (and reproduced) by the form of the city and that the form of the city is actively and continually constructed (and de/reconstructed) by its *city-zens*.

Indeed, this is not a new formulation. It reaches into the surfaces of modern city structures where Cartesian cogitos found their reflections with delight and disgust. And it has resonated through to the postmodern subject aesthetically reading and writing an imaginary city of the eye/I.

In 1938 Lewis Mumford wrote,

> Mind takes form in the city; and in turn, urban forms condition mind. For space, no less than time, is artfully reorganized in cities: in boundless lines and silhouettes, in the fixing of horizontal planes and vertical peaks, in utilizing or denying the natural site, the city records the attitude of a culture and an epoch to the fundamental facts of its existence.

And in 1992 we have,

> The body and its environment produce each other as forms of the hyperreal, as modes of simulation which have overtaken and transformed whatever reality each may have had into the image of the other: the city is made and made over into the simulacrum of the body, and the body, in its turn, is transformed, "citified," urbanized as a distinctively metropolitan body. (Grosz 1992: 249)

What is crucial about this understanding of a constituting city (whether it is mind, or body, or both) is that real and perceived dangers, the fears and risks associated with liminal and subliminal places and spaces, do not occur merely because the city—as a set of places densely populated—lends itself to a "natural" sense of fear, as it has been treated historically by planning theories.[1] In fact, there is something quite unnatural about the way fear controls and precipitates our movements across cities and points quite clearly to our status as members of difference. It is, in a sense, a particular construction, city-fear, and one that is manifested, linguistically and materially, within the modern discourse on the metropolis and the metropolitan mind-body. Again, this fearing is a learning.

This city-fear, this peculiar modality of daily city life, of course has many shapes, many operations, many productions—for it is at once the sensibilities of the urban inhabitant as a social being (as in, "I don't go there") and the inner processes of psychic development and projection ("because I fear X"). It is both a conscious practice and a set of perceptions regarding the topographies of memory and power. It is mythic (because I live in a

---

1. I am referring here to the ways in which the city has been termed a disorderly (and thus evil) place in the "traditional" or "classic" planning literature, e.g., Fourier, Mumford, Simmel.

city, I fear the crimes associated with cities) and particular (because I was attacked in a dark alley, I do not go into dark alleys). It can be invoked by a smell (urine under the bridge), a stain (graffiti tags), or a sound (the hollow echo of footsteps). It can rise quickly with an adrenaline rush, dissipate slowly, be conquered with behavioral modification or pushed aside into a sea of denial. City-fear is rapid, dynamic, lingering, passionate, deadening, and always contingent on the ways in which planning interventions have described and informed the ways in which we *should* fear the city.

It is my contention that although city-fear inhabits the daily life of inhabitants, it is also a phenomenon constructed in part and then mistreated by the social sciences—planning, sociology, psychology, criminology, and so on. In the modernist academic formulations of the ways in which fear is expressed on the urban terrain, the focus has generally shifted away from the facets of the construction of fear (registered as *merely* an emotional *response*) and toward the resolution of fear through physical and mental coping strategies. In doing so, these same social sciences have seemingly absolved themselves from contributing to the ways in which the fear has been defined and delineated along such binaries as male/female, public/private, and reason/emotion. As in the case of city-fear, fear in the city has been reduced to the fear of strangers.

> The absence of specific correlations between actual victimization and fear has been noted by numerous researchers. . . . Furthermore, the fear of specific victimizations is far different from the most likely victimization. Most assaults, murders, and rapes occur in the home to victims who know their assailant; and yet, most fear is expressed in settings and situations where the crime is committed by a stranger in public places. Biderman et al. have summarized these findings most succinctly, "fear of crime is the fear of the stranger." (Hunter 1985: 17)

I do not wish to exacerbate the rather tired binary of public/private, but it should be noted that throughout the literature on fear—from psychology to criminology to planning—city-fear has historically been associated with the private and personal reactions to the real and perceived menacing deeds and misintentions of strangers in public places. In *The Death and Life of Great American Cities* (1961), Jane Jacobs proposed to make the sidewalks safe by eliminating the presence of strangers. More than ten years later, in 1973, Oscar Newman argued that the only way to "make people feel safe" was to create "defensible spaces," effectively insulating oneself from the possibilities of entry or violence by strangers. And even fifteen years after Newman, social psychologists continue to analyze fear according to one's "attractivity" to strangers (Van de Wurff, Van Staalduinen, and Stringer 1988: 141). To this day, as citizens, we are continually being warned about the dangers of certain urban situations, and we are urged to employ various methods of personal safety, from locks on doors to car alarms to handguns, in the (rare) case of a stranger attack.

I do not wish to labor this point, for a public/private discussion is not at issue here. For people faced with the violences of racism, sexism, and homophobia, the possibility of the amorphous and menacing stranger is but one of many difficulties in negotiating a city that may in some measure support crimes of hate. However, for many others (and especially women) the construction of fear, or at least inhibition, begins far earlier than one's encounter with the urban terrain. Thus, because the planning debate about the resolution of fear has been associated with the fear of strangers *in public places* and because this definition of fear has undermined a much deeper understanding of the bases, modes, and daily operations of fear, not as a concept, but as an everyday reality, an overwhelming and compelling *social construction,* we not only devalue our status as "urban researchers," but, perhaps more important, we also risk the annihilation of many possibilities for other voices to speak about the totality of their fear experiences. Or "the public debate about crime, in too many respects, wrongly silences our private understandings about personal danger. For despite the clear evidence that the risk of interpersonal violence is overwhelmingly from those near and dear to us, we all seem to worry more about threats from strangers" (Stanko 1990: 112).

Is the city itself a fearful place? Can fear be resolved through changing the city? Or is the "interpersonal" more provocative, more relevant, to the fact of our fears? Because the object of urban planning practices, and thus also of theories and histories, has been "the City," the treatment of the city has been one in which the city has been posed as the mutable Other. Thus when I refer to stranger-fear as associated with city-fear, I am recognizing that to a certain extent the geography/cartography of fears has been reduced to a "fear of the City."[2] And, in so doing, it has bounded the debate on fear to only those fears that are expressed, usually as crime, in the public realm of this Other. Is it any wonder, then, that active and insulating "crime prevention" has not been proven to resolve our fears?

Thus I ask that we go beyond this rather limited debate. What types of urban-based interactions reinforce the dynamism of our lived fears? To what extent does the diffuse nature of power and oppression play on the development of city-fears? And, finally, how do the historic

---

2. This phenomenon of the City as fearful Other has been best described by Davis (1992): "The city bristles with malice."

co-constructions of cities, norms, bodies, and subjects perpetuate city-fears as they have been constructed and defined as fear of the City?

LOCUS

I do not wish to stray from my original question—the perpetuation of city-fears despite the efforts of planning interventions—but I want to underscore the point that fear is not a cause unto itself,[3] nor is it merely a phobic reaction out of social ignorance. It may not be possible to actually reduce fear, or to fully emancipate the thinking subject from the fears that the city engenders.

Consider the city in this manner: "The city's form and structure provide the context in which social rules and expectations are internalized or habituated in order to ensure social conformity, or position marginality at a safe or insulated or bounded distance (ghettoization). This means that the city must be seen as the most immediately concrete locus for the production and circulation of power" (Grosz 1992: 250).

In the introduction to *Bodies That Matter*, Judith Butler reminds her readers that bodies are the result of a continual process of materialization and reiteration of social norms and that "sex" is a normative category in which the sexed subject (i.e., the sexed identification) is constituted only by its outside exclusions and abjections (1993: 10). Although she reinforces her argument with linguistic examples, there is a point to be taken up here—namely, that fear, and especially those fears shared among members of a social group/identity, does not exist in a vacuum. We may feel it strongly and highly personally, as a spaceless abstraction of the "mind," and we may as individuals seek to "conquer our fears," but the kinds of fears associated with city life are constituted as spaces and places (loci) for the constitution of the subject itself, and as I have discussed previously, the subject cannot occur in isolation. Nor—and this is the crucial point—can the subject's identity be constructed, materialized, or repeated without, at the very least, a psychical and spatial acknowledgment of an Other whose relationship to the subject will always be imbued with the power dynamic implied by the simple statement "You and I." In essence, then, fear is an effect of certain relations of power, a spatialized signification of power relations. Thus to interrogate the question of fear any further, we must first establish the psychical and spatial processes that produce fear and then investigate the relations of power that perpetuate it.

3. I contended earlier that most attention to fear in the social sciences has historically been focused on the resolution of fear, as if fear were a problem to be solved or an irrational emotion to be cured by rational actions.

THE ENCOUNTER

The other day, I was sitting on the bus, mute like the rest of the passengers, sitting alone yet pressed to the window. The bus stopped at one of those places where the whole city seems to converge at once, and quickly filled with people looking for their appropriate seats. The young men pushed toward the rear; the older women with their bags and bundles plopped themselves in the front. And I was thinking as each new person eyed the seat next to mine, "Don't sit here, please don't sit here, oh you look OK, you can sit here, no, no you go away, mmm, I hope they sit here"—as if I really had a choice.

It was merely the practice of a regular routine, one I am quite accustomed to as a city dweller. I was simply trying to separate out the possible "good" encounter from the possible "bad" encounter from the possible mundane and uneventful encounter, entirely based on the external appearances of the oncoming passengers—their look, their smell, their clothing. And although I wished for the ultimate "good" encounter (and this depends on what one may feel is "good" at that particular moment), I kept reminding myself that the ultimate "bad" encounter could also occur (e.g., I am followed off the bus, stalked, and killed).

However, in the midst of this monologic fantasy, I realized that everyone had sat down, the bus had moved on, and no one had chosen the seat next to me. The seat next to mine was not broken, nor did my bag crowd it. There was good air circulation, and it was close, but not too close, to the rear exit door. I thought that it was an ideal seat, until it occurred to me that the very same passengers I sorted through had also sorted through those who were already on the bus. They had chosen not to sit with me.

Although I was dismayed by the idea that these passengers had ruled me out as a possible "bad" encounter, I was also excited by this moment. What had they read in me, or on my body, that caused them to veer away? What marker of difference did they use to consciously choose not-me? Like so many other moments in the city, we had exchanged a meaningful, albeit silent, dialogue that had brought us close against other bodies, other lives, stories, and voices we may never know; and we had made conscious choices based on our appraisal of what those bodies, stories, voices might be. The encounter—which in so many ways can be said to define and distinguish city life—is at once exciting and stimulating, apprehensive and fearful. For while the variety and novelty of linking otherwise unrelated lives and bodies may not exist as intensely elsewhere but the urban terrain, the encounter always carries with it the possibility of pleasure (the good encounter) and the possibility of violence (the bad encounter).

City life also instantiates difference as the erotic, in the wide sense of an attraction to the other, the pleasure and excitement of being drawn out of one's secure routine to encounter the novel, strange, and surprising. The erotic dimension of the city has always been an aspect of its fearfulness, for it holds out the possibility that one will lose one's identity, will fall. But we also take pleasure in being open to and interested in people we experience as different. (Young 1990: 72)

What I must take up here, to explicate the encounter more fully and to critique the historic dogma of planning interventions, is not the conscious experience of difference (which can be novel, exciting, dangerous, boring, etc.) but the belief that the encounter contains within it an unconscious trauma. Indeed, what is provocative about the preceding quote is that the "erotic dimension . . . holds out the possibility that one will lose one's identity, will fall," as if that which is erotic (the fantasy of the violent/pleasurable act?) is ultimately a threat to our very being. This, in essence, serves to invoke some kind of New Testament morality, that the erotic is evil; but it also suggests that the kinds of social interactions that take place on the urban terrain have been constructed as a reason for fearing—that we must "sort" or else we risk the loss of our identities.

Consider the ways in which the subject is constituted. From squalling infancy to shallow grave, the subject's identity is constructed in oppositional terms to an other. From the first trauma of the mirror stage, our first recognition is that one is not "completely one" (i.e., whole) but a fragmented self and a (m)other. And, moreover, the imprint from this recognition is that the imagined wholeness of the body must continually be reiterated and symbolically repeated in order for the subject to retain a unified identity and not "dissolve into fragments."[4] Thus what remains is that one's imagined bodily wholeness can and will be taken away, can and will be revealed for the fragmented thing that it is, can and will lose its structure through the threat of an other. The anxiety that is produced is that in the face of (and through the actions of) another, the possibility remains that one's identity, marked as such and repeated over time, will change, will *morph,* "will fall."

Therefore, in order for the self to retain a somewhat constant subjectivity or identity, the subject must also retain both a psychic and a spatial distance, an "alienation," from not only the truths of one's incompleteness, but from the other—who, as the (m)other, continually threatens to reveal

4. This is a basic outline of what occurs in the "mirror stage," the point in infancy when the child comes into self-consciousness and thus may enter into the realm of language (the Symbolic) as an "I." Following from Freudian psychoanalysis, this stage was originally described by Lacan but has since become the basis for many feminist, cultural, social, and political theorists, for at its heart is an acknowledgment that we are all "speaking subjects." This is not to say that it is without contestation, but for a much richer and clearer description of the mirror stage, see Wright 1992.

the truth of the image. Like the crack of the bat that is both a constitution of the bat and its opposition to the ball and a struggle to inhabit the same space that resounds throughout the stadium, so it is also that the anxiety inspired by the encounter is exactly the threat that the other, who actively constitutes the subject in opposition and in language, could eclipse the subject's existence—by revealing the subject for what it truly is not (i.e., "whole").

Lacan spoke of this phenomenon as such:

> Does the subject not become engaged in an ever-growing dispossession of that being of his, concerning which . . . he ends up by recognizing that this being has never been anything more than his construct in the imaginary and that this construct disappoints all certainties? For in this labour which he undertakes to reconstruct *for another,* he rediscovers the fundamental alienation that made him construct it *like another,* and which has always destined it to be taken from him *by another.* (1977: 61)

Thus it is with the very constitution of the subject that the constitution of fear is engendered. The imprint (or the stain) remains that the very other that defines and constitutes the subject will so desire the subject's objectification that it will dispossess the subject of its subjectivity. The space maintained by symbolic interactions will collapse and thus reintroduce the initial subject, if just for a fleeting moment, to the trauma of the Real. And while this may sound absolutely horrific, I maintain that fear is the stain of that first unconscious (m)othering, that first memory of one's terrible recognition of one's own fragmentation, being played out on the field of desire.

This desire of which I speak is the fantasy of violence and pleasure as described in the encounter. The beauty of the urban encounter is that it could go either way, and by the mingling of bodies on the urban terrain, it reinforces the fantasy of both violence and pleasure, which is in essence desire, or better, the desire for the desire of the other. In other words, it is not that one actually desires victimization but that the "ever-wanting" implied by the desire for the desire of the other establishes a continual series of fantasies through which the possibilities of pleasure/violence (introduced by the encounter) are enacted physiologically through fear. It is my contention that modernist urban planning interventions, meaning those activities corresponding to post-Enlightenment planning discourse, have focused far more on the violent fantasy (i.e., focus on crime prevention) and have thus elided the possibilities contained within the enactment of pleasurable fantasy on the urban terrain.

Through the readings of planning doctrines over time, the aim of "betterment" implies that planners have rarely *liked* the city. In fact, the goal of our discipline has always been to change it—to treat it, the City, as the threatening Other. What this entails is that the construct of fear rendered resolvable by planning (city-fear) signals an attachment, or view, toward the city in which the violent fantasy is privileged. In essence, it thus represses the possibilities for the emergence of a discourse on fear in which the pleasurable fantasy is also invoked. Thus, through planning's reverberations in daily social life, the violent fantasy, registered as a *rational* response to city life, overrides the facet of desire that the city also yields pleasure. This fearing is a learning.

LOOKING BACK

In *The Sphinx in the City,* Elizabeth Wilson poses essentially the same critique I am posing here—that planning's historic role in the city has been one in which the City has been treated as a threatening, infested, and disorderly Other. She examines the development of industrial cities (such as London, Paris, and New York) within their specific cultural and geographic contexts and demonstrates how patriarchal societies have attempted to use the degradation of the urban terrain as a reason to both protect and denigrate women—in essence to blame women for all that is "ill" and disorderly at the core of the city. She writes,

> The city offers untrammelled sexual experience; in the city the forbidden— what is most feared and desired—becomes possible. Woman is present in cities as temptress, as whore, as fallen woman, as lesbian, but also as virtuous womanhood in danger, as heroic womanhood who triumphs over temptation and tribulation. Writers . . . clearly posed the presence of women as a problem of order, partly *because* their presence symbolized the promise of sexual adventure. This promise was converted into a general moral and political threat. (1991: 6)

Certainly, Wilson's historical critique has her readers nodding heads in agreement, for that which is Victorian is also here today. The modus operandi of patriarchies (or better, brotherhood of man) is precisely one of both blame and protection. Like the daughter who is filled with both shame and love by her father's look—the "double bind" of the Sphinx (the woman) in the city resonates. "Bad" women inhabit the core of the city and thus make it a fearful place; "good" women avoid it and thus learn to seek out men to protect them from the threat en-gendered by the city.

Certainly, also, we can enjoy the positive possibilities of Wilson's conclusions—that the industrialized city, while limiting women's movement (out of benevolent protection and absolute and uncanny terror), is also the place where, ironically, women have found the most freedoms, in various forms of employment, in chances to leave the domestic sphere, and through daily communion with other women. Thus, unlike many of Wilson's feminist contemporaries,[5] she asserts that the emancipatory desires of women are best served and best upheld by the very urban environment they have been warned against. Indeed, Wilson insists that planning movements (especially Utopian) have failed, not because of the direness of the city, but because of the direness of their outlook. She contends that to find liberation, we must first *like* the city.[6]

I do agree with Wilson's emancipatory project: "Women's experience of urban life is even more ambiguous than that of men, and safety is a crucial issue. Yet it is also necessary to emphasize the other side of city life and to insist on women's right to carnival, intensity, and even risks of the city" (1991: 10).[7] But I want to expand on her views on the way women experience the urban terrain—that the apprehensions of fear, danger, threat, and risk are somehow dissolved (or made less immediate) by the practice of an emancipatory sexual-social city life. Wilson, in fact, seems to contradict herself in her conclusion:

> Women have fared especially badly in western visions of the metropolis because they have seemed to represent disorder. There is fear of the city as a realm of uncontrolled and chaotic social sexual licence, and the rigid control of women in cities has been felt necessary to avert this danger. Urban civilisation has come, in fact, to mean an authoritarian control of the wayward spontaneity of all human desires and aspirations. Women without men in the city symbolise the menace of disorder in all spheres once rigid patriarchal control is weakened. That is why women—perhaps unexpectedly—have represented the mob, the "alien," the revolutionary.
>
> It is therefore rather ironic that women have often appeared less daunted by city life than men. (1991: 157)

Thus, although Wilson has made a very bold statement about the workings of patriarchal power, she does not seem to acknowledge that a woman's practice of liberation or resistance within a patriarchal society does not eclipse the fact of her fears. In fact, it would seem that those women who do take advantage of the urban terrain to experience the carnival may actually have, in their conscious choices to resist, an *increased* fear of reprisal—that such a woman is a much likelier target for victimization, not because she simply makes herself "available" in public places, but because

---

5. I am suggesting that Wilson's argument was also directed at the so-called antiurban feminists such as Susan Brownmiller, Alison Ravetz, and Andrea Dworkin, among others (especially in feminist science fiction), who seem to espouse that women are best emancipated by, or that it is "more natural" for women to live in, the small village or enclosed community structure.

6. "I am arguing that we will never solve the problems of cities unless we *like* the urbanness of urban life" (Wilson 1991: 158).

7. This quote reminds me of my struggles with my parents.

the disorderliness of her presence, her threat, must be tempered so as to continue to legitimate patriarchal powers. And while she may appear less daunted, perhaps it is also true that she has learned to live with the threat on a much more routine basis.

Thus I argue that city-fear is much more likely among the temptress, the whore, and the lesbian, the *flâneuse,* simply because it is they who are more likely to threaten the social and sexual contract. It is they who through their "uncanny" control of the city street or corner symptomize the most extreme anxieties expressed by males: they are the phallus who refuses possession, they are the hint of a castrated form of power. Indeed, I do not wish to distance myself from Wilson but rather to expand on the risks involved with the Sphinx in the city. Perhaps, following Wilson, city-fear is but one of the truly ingenious and insidious effects of a patriarchal power—that woman must either "disappear" (avoid the city) or "protect herself" in the (likely) event that victimization would occur.

STOP LOOKING AT ME

Our social life is structured by vast networks of temporal and spatial mediation among persons, so that nearly everyone depends on the activities of seen and unseen strangers who mediate between oneself and one's associates, between oneself and one's objects of desire.

YOUNG (1990: 74)

With footsteps now, allow me to return to the urban terrain. While I have already discussed how it may be that city-fear is constructed as the privileging of the violent fantasy implied by the self-other encounter, constructions must hold repetitions over time to hold meaning in the field of language and law. And, more important, these repetitions must be maintained and materialized by some regulatory agency, such as the institution of planning, which demands compulsory and normative identification and signification (Butler 1993: 12). To explicate this, I again take up city-fear as it is experienced by that social group whose identity is constructed as "woman."

I have noted previously that women restrict their movements within the city according to the perceived dangers of spaces, places, and times; and I have noted that the city is the most immediate locus for the "production and circulation of power"—which has been connected (obliquely) to the construct of the patriarchy. Now that the fantasy of the encounter has been introduced, we must reapproach these workings of power.

Space and place are important in the construction of gender relations and in the struggles to change them. From the symbolic meaning of spaces/ places and the clearly gendered messages which they transmit, to straightforward exclusion by violence, spaces and places are not themselves gendered but, in their being so, they both reflect and affect the ways in which gender is constructed and understood. The limitation of women's mobility, in terms both of identity and space, has been in some cultural contexts a crucial means of subordination. (Massey 1994: 179)

Often, when we speak of the fear that is en-gendered by city spaces, and especially public places, as Doreen Massey does, the clear association is made that women's fear is the direct result of the power of the patriarchy— a power that seeks to subordinate women through actual violence (rape) or, more likely, the threat of violence. I do not wish to refute this claim, but I do wish to emphasize that the mechanism through which the threat of violence is perceived—*the gaze*—is neither masculine nor feminine. Thus, although the disruption that entails threat is embedded entirely within the subject, not "I am watched" but vacillating between consciousness (I know that) and perception (you are watching me), the power of the gaze is that it is employed as a method of social control (for example, in surveillance tactics).

What this entails is what has been mentioned before: (1) that the presence of the (female) subject renders her a seeable member of sexual and threatening (castrating) difference; and (2) that the power of the gaze is only legitimated insofar as the subject's presence involves and acknowledges the subject's fantasy of the voyeuristic or scopophilic other, which in the case of the planning tradition can be the very same methods used to prevent the violent act. Indeed, urban surveillance tactics have often backfired, making those who are watched feel not only as if they will be threatened but also as if they may be the threat. "The subject is seeable, capable of being shown without being able to see the observer or itself— the gaze objectifies not because of the power of the other, but because the other's look is justified, legitimized by the Other. It is the result of being placed in the field of the Other" (Wright 1992: 449).

Thus it is within the performativity of gender, regulated by a normative value known as "sex," that it is possible for fear, which is constituted as the (female) subject is constituted, to find repetition within a patriarchal society. In other words, every time her presence is made known to the other as the other (the encounter), she not only becomes the object of the gaze but she also acknowledges, consciously or not, that the gaze contains for her a possible threat. By doing so, she not only legitimizes the power implied by the gaze but also legitimizes the reproduction of her violent fantasy, her city-fear.

This is not "blaming the victim." To reconceptualize city-fear as part of the normative categories materialized by relations of power[8] radically

---

8. And yes, I am implicating the security interventions of urban planning in these relations.

challenges not only the ways in which fear and safety have been usually ascribed but also the way of envisioning serious resistances to the modes of power. In other words, if we cannot or *will not* acknowledge the gaze, and thus legitimate its power, does its power cease to exist? Does its power cease to act on our bodies, our psyches, and thus cease to perpetuate our fears?

FEAR NOT

Taking into account that "safe spaces" fail by their very definition, that the tradition of city planning has been aimed at the resolution of a self-defined form of fear obliquely referenced as the fear of strangers (city-fear), that as the object of planning interventions the city has been treated as the mutable Other, that the violent fantasy has been privileged by planning discourse, and that this violent fantasy has been maintained in the circulations and operations of (patriarchal) power, our study of planning histories must begin to take up the complexities of these issues.

If the purpose behind insurgent planning historiography is to reconstruct the past to reimagine the future, then we must understand the construct itself, meaning that we must pay attention to microdetails and signifying effects of the construction, especially if the planning discourse has been at least partially responsible for its outcomes. And, perhaps more important, we must be careful in our historiography that we do not reify the immanence of the historic as Authority. History is indeed always a representation, and in order for that representation to be radically critical, it must by its presence actively interrogate the very discourse that has produced it. In the case of planning, then, insurgent planning histories should critically examine the discourse, not only of the city, but of planning itself.

Thus, while the specificity that has marked the most recent writings of multiple and varied histories has certainly lent itself to an emancipatory project of visibility, we must also acknowledge that this specificity has also led us to a type of essentialism, an exclusion based on sameness, that may indeed eclipse the possibilities of understanding the insidious, capillary levels at which power produces and reproduces obedient bodies. In fact, such historic specificity may serve to further ghettoize the subjects of their histories; their very distinctiveness as a community of difference may insinuate a type of homogenization among those members of difference and within the eyes of power. In other words, to write the history of the Other from the Other may not be enough to defeat the encumbrances of patriarchy, racism, or homophobia. It is with a certain insistence that I therefore ask that we begin to reconceptualize the writings of planning histories, not as a set of social group histories that have yet to be written, but as an encompassing view of the outcomes of planning's practices and theories as a heterogeneous discourse between subjects, bodies, cities, and the diverse intensity of power and repression.

I admit that I have used the psychoanalytic lens to illuminate the complexities of the urban social terrain. Psychoanalytic theory may be more involved with inner processes than it is with social processes, but it also has a certain use value in understanding the often-spatialized constructions and repetitions over time. Indeed, while historiography and psychoanalysis may seem to be opposed, the specific versus the universal, they may in fact, by the merging of disciplines, produce a far more radical theoretical praxis than either in isolation. As bell hooks writes, "Our living depends on our ability to conceptualize alternatives, often impoverished. Theorizing about [the marginal] experience aesthetically, critically is an agenda for radical cultural practice" (1990: 149).

Thus, through the crossing of disciplines, I urge us at this time to reexamine the visibilities implied by Other histories as but one method of deciphering the immense discourse of modern planning. This does not mean that I wish for planning to stop its practice of fear resolution, for that may be impossible considering the nature of the metanarratives. Rather, I wish to emancipate us from the particularities of historiography into the space of a much wider critique of power and repression, to relate the representations of the past or present to the conditions that determined their production, and to eventually learn to reproduce new and liberating conditions.

If we understand that fear is an effect of relations of power, that it is a signification, or *symptom,* then we must also understand that it is open to resignification and that it does contain, by its very nature, a possibility for transformation on a much larger social scale. Perhaps the fallacy of modernist thinking has been the belief that emancipation can be achieved fully and completely, that oppression can just be thrown off like a mantle, and that "freedom" will necessarily ensue. I contend, however, that power is not so monolithic and that each small resistance—from the drag performance to the rewriting of a history—establishes a continual process of transformative reinvention, reproduction, and repetition. Thus, by viewing something as seemingly insurmountable as fear as a learned signification, fearing becomes capable of being radically transformed—*not resolved but transformed.*

We as planners (theorists and practitioners) cannot continue to turn our backs to these constructions *formulated over time* if we are to truly act to eradicate the effects of our own practices, interventions, ignorances, or "detrimental betterments."

Fear not the snakes we may find in the yard.

REFERENCES

Benjamin, Walter. 1979. *One Way Street.* London: New Left Books.

Butler, Judith. 1993. *Bodies That Matter: On the Discursive Limits of Sex.* London: Routledge.

Davis, Mike. 1992. "Fortress Los Angeles: The Militarization of Urban Space." In *Variations on a Theme Park: The New American City and the End of Public Space,* ed. M. Sorkin. New York: Noonday Press.

de Certeau, Michel. 1984. "Walking in the City." In *The Cultural Studies Reader,* ed. S. During. London: Routledge.

————. 1986. *Heterologies: Discourse on the Other.* Trans. Brian Massumi. Minneapolis: University of Minnesota Press.

Forrester, John. 1986. "Rape, Seduction, and Psychoanalysis." In *Rape,* ed. S. Tomaselli and R. Porter. Oxford: Blackwell.

Grosz, Elizabeth. 1992. "Bodies—Cities." In *Sexuality and Space,* ed. B. Colomina. Princeton, N.J.: Princeton University Press.

hooks, bell. 1990. *Yearning: Race, Gender, and Cultural Politics.* Boston: South End Press.

Hunter, Albert. 1985. "Private, Parochial, and Public Orders." In *The Challenge of Social Control,* ed. G. Suttles and M. Zald. Norwood, N.J.: Ablex.

Jacobs, Jane. 1961. *The Death and Life of the Great American Cities.* New York: Random House.

Kaplan, E. Ann. 1984. "Is the Gaze Male?" In *Desire: The Politics of Sexuality,* ed. A. Snitow, C. Stansell, and S. Thompson. London: Routledge.

Kasinitz, Philip. 1995. "Social Relations and Public Places: Introduction." In *Metropolis: Center and Symbol of Our Times,* ed. P. Kasinitz. New York: New York University Press.

Lacan, Jacques. 1977. "The Function and Field of Speech and Language in Psychoanalysis." In *Ecrits: A Selection,* trans. A. Sheridan. New York: Norton.

Massey, Doreen. 1994. *Space, Place, and Gender.* Minneapolis: University of Minnesota Press.

Mumford, Lewis. 1938. *The Culture of Cities.* New York: Harcourt Brace.

Newman, Oscar. 1973. *Defensible Space.* London: Architectural Press.

Stanko, Elizabeth. 1990. *Everyday Violence: How Women and Men Experience Sexual and Physical Danger.* London: Pandora Press.

Van de Wurff, Adri, Leedert Van Staalduinen, and Peter Stringer. 1988. "Fear of Crime in Residential Environments: Testing a Social Psychological Model." *Journal of Social Psychology* 129(2).

Wilson, Elizabeth. 1991. *The Sphinx in the City: Urban Life, the Control of Disorder, and Women.* Berkeley: University of California Press.

Wright, Elizabeth, ed. 1992. *Feminism and Psychoanalysis: A Critical Dictionary.* Oxford: Blackwell.

Young, Iris Marion. 1990. *Justice and the Politics of Difference.* Princeton, N.J.: Princeton University Press.

TWELVE

The Poem of Male Desires

Female Bodies, Modernity, and "Paris, Capital of the Nineteenth Century"

Barbara Hooper

A city! It is the grip of man upon nature.
LE CORBUSIER (1987)

The politics of space are always sexual even if space is central to the mechanisms of the erasure of sexuality.
BEATRIZ COLOMINA (1992)

THE POEM OF MALE DESIRES, PART I

In the summer of 1878, seven years after the Paris Commune, Emile Zola sat down to write a preliminary outline for his new novel, *Nana,* the story of a "high-class cocotte" (1972: 8). *Nana,* like *L'Assommoir,* the novel in which Nana had first appeared as the child of slum dwellers, was to be another in the series of Rougon-Macquart novels. Written over a period of twenty years, these novels tell the story of Paris of the Second Empire: the contrasts between its ostentatious wealth and squalor, its spectacles, its rapid transformations and upheavals, the demolition of its old areas and the rapid construction of Haussmann's boulevards and apartment blocks, and finally of that Empire's end. More specifically, the story is one of body, city, and social order, a theme Zola states when setting out the novel's "philosophical subject" as the story of a "whole society hurling itself at the cunt. A pack of hounds after a bitch, who is not even on heat and makes fun of the hounds following her. *The poem of male desires,* the great lever which moves the world" (1972: 11; original emphasis).

When the novel is written, Zola's outline holds. Nana becomes an actress/prostitute, a sensation, a performer, a visual spectacle of sexualized flesh who thrills the male flaneurs and theatergoers of Paris: "a disturbing woman with all the impulsive madness of her sex, opening the gates of the unknown world of desire" (1972: 44–45). The novel narrates the story of Nana's rise and fall, her "labor of ruin and death," the destruction she engenders and leaves in her wake (1972: 453). Nana, "smiling the deadly smile of a man-eater" (1972: 45), seduces and devours an entire city, becoming wealthier and wealthier, parasitically draining the wealth and will of Paris's bourgeois male citizens. She accomplishes this destruction with her body, "the sovereign power of her flesh": "this shameful trifle, so powerful that it could move the world, and without the aid of machines invented by engineers" (1972: 44). With this power Nana shakes "Paris to its foundations," building a "fortune on the bodies of dead men" until she alone is "left standing, amid the accumulated riches of her mansion, while a host of men lay stricken at her feet. . . . The fly that had come from the dungheap of the slums, carrying the ferment of social decay, had poisoned all these men by simply alighting on them" (1972: 452–453).

At the novel's end Nana dies, the terrible death that her body—marked female, marked *classe dangereuse*—prefigured all along: the death that she deserves, a pox that corrupts her flesh as she had corrupted and infected so many. "What lay on the pillow was a charnel house, a heap of pus and blood, a shovelful of putrid flesh. . . . It was as if the poison she had picked up in the gutters, from the carcasses left there by a roadside, that ferment with which she had poisoned a whole people, had now risen to her face and rotted it" (1972: 469). Outside her window, as Nana dies, the crowd is shouting "To Berlin, To Berlin, To Berlin." The defeat and capture of Napoleon III at Sedan and the collapse of the Second Empire provide Zola with his denouement: Nana had destroyed a city, an empire. Like many other men of his time Zola chooses to suggest that the source of France's defeat is to be found in the female disorder figured by prostitution: "Who can say how much energy was destroyed, strength enervated, and spirit debilitated by that laxity . . .?" (1972: 7).

The novel then, performs Zola's "philosophical subject," a whole society hurling itself at the cunt and paying the price: not only its military defeat but the decadence and disorder, the "carnival," the "theater/brothel" (1972: 21, 37), that is this society's city, its body, its modernity; that is, in the end, the body of Nana.

Zola's story of Paris and its modernity is one that is written into planning texts of the period; a story of bodies, cities, and social order, and, more particularly, of female bodies and their production as a threat to male/social order. The female/body has a long history in Western thought and politics of figuring disorder against the male/order of the polis, the city, the state, the whole of civilization—which are conversely represented as the productions of reason, of male/mind. The authoring of Pandora, the first woman, as disorder in Greek myth; Eve's trangression in the garden; Aristotle's *Polis,* Plato's *Republic,* Hobbes's *Leviathan;* Bacon's vision of the human race mastering nature through science; Descartes's *res cogitans* and *res extensa;* Hegel's distinction between the "outer" world as the world of actuality associated with Civil Society and the shadowy, insubstantial, undifferentiated "inner" world associated with female and family; Freud's (male) civilization and its (female) discontents, his ego and id—all are exemplary authorings of the struggle between nature and culture that pit the order of male mind against the disorder of female body, a body that must be controlled if civilization, its knowledges and accomplishments, is to survive.

This tradition of female control has functioned in the West as a politics of male dominance based in the idea of "natural" differences between male and female bodies—a "union of the political and physiological" (Haraway 1991: 8) that founds and legitimizes determinations of who is and is not fit to rule. But as Joan Cocks suggest, "however male dominance happened historically or 'pre-historically' to arise, and however crucial to it various facets of bodily difference have been made to be, it rests at base not on differences in the brute sexed body, but on the harsh, systematic fashioning of brute bodies into masculine, feminine selves" (1989: 20)—a "fashioning" that has worked to support a constellation of male interests and desires.

It is my intention here to investigate what these desires and interests mean vis-à-vis planning history, theory, and practice. Modern planning at its inception was the idea of a plan, a scientific and rational plan, conquering the disorder of cities—the poverty and misery that were the effects of industrial capitalism and rapid urbanization. Good intentions, yes: by social utopianists like Charles Fourier and Robert Owens, by scientific socialists like Marx and Engels, by planner/regularizationists like Haussmann. But whose good intentions, and what baggage do these intentions carry? Focusing on planning's conceptual practices—its acknowledged *and* unacknowledged habits of thought—it is precisely these questions I ask. Specifically, I explore how planning, in the moment it was inventing itself as master, as knower, as producer of order, took on the baggage of the dominant cultural tradition and hence came to function not simply as the emancipatory practice it theorized but as a participant in new forms of social control directed at women—the modern discipline of bodies and cities that relied on new knowledges and technologies but was facilitated by the availability of ancient cultural traditions concerning the "nature" of male and female and dominant/subordinate heterosexist relations between them.

What I hope to suggest is that the Paris Baron Haussmann and later Le Corbusier planned to reorder in accord with their dreams of a transcendent rational geometry—a "fantasy of the straight line"—is a desire directed against the disorder of body, and more particularly against the dangerous curves and excesses of female body, a body "so powerful it could move the world without the aid of machines invented by engineers." My discussion includes consideration of the parallel discourses of urban pathology and public hygiene that produce body and city as social disorder; the representation of this disorder as female, as body, and more particularly as female prostitute body; and the relationship between doctors and planners, men of reason who purport to operate on, cure, transform, regularize, and reorder the diseased body and social body, men who, like Haussmann and Le Corbusier, author plans for "the modern city" as poems of male desire, fantasies of control, written against the fears and urban upheavals of the nineteenth century that the female body comes to represent.

I anchor my discussion in the context of the "new" critical urban theory, drawing on the works of Henri Lefebvre, Michel Foucault, and numerous feminist and postcolonial theorists (see Carter, Donald, and Squires 1993; Crow 1990; de Certeau 1988; *Differences* 1993; Hebdige 1991; Keith and Pile 1993; Soja 1989, 1996). At issue here is not the "physical" city alone but the entirety of its social space—the many layers of physical, social, historical, geographic, cultural, symbolic, and embodied/lived associations and relations that function to produce "Paris, capital of the nineteenth century" (Benjamin 1978: 146). Borrowing terminology from the sociology of literature, my analysis looks for lateral connections across "texts," for an "intertextuality" operating across the two domains of urban pathology and public hygiene and linking, both implicitly and explicitly, the policing of cities and female bodies in a language of order and regulation. My focus is on the production of order-in/as-difference: the project stated by planners, gynecologists, sanitation engineers, public hygienists, and other nineteenth-century disciplinary experts as the implementation of reason's "order" over and against the "disease" and "disorder" of the modern metropolis and its bodies.

The production of any autonomous order, any subject, involves the development of an exclusionary matrix, a domain of the abject that forms the constituting outside:

> The abject designates . . . those "unlivable" and "uninhabitable" zones of social life which are nonetheless densely populated by those who do not enjoy the status of subject, but whose living under the sign of the "unlivable" is required to circumscribe the domain of the subject. This zone of uninhabitability will constitute the defining limit of the subject's domain; it will constitute that site of dreaded identification against which, and by virtue of which—the domain of the subject will circumscribe its own claim to auton-

omy and life. In this sense, then, the subject is constituted through the force
of exclusion and abjection, one which produces a constitutive outside to
the subject, an abjected outside, which is afterall "inside" the subject as the
founding repudiation. (Butler 1993: 3)

Order and disorder are ideas, abstractions. Making them "real" necessi-
tates their embodiment, their concrete materialization. In the nineteenth-
century city this involves, in its most general formulation, the production
of order as the idea of a plan instituted by the authority of male science,
against the disorder that is concretized, enfleshed, made real in the bodies
and territories of the abjected, excluded other: the "filth" and "dirt" of the
slums, the colonized territories of Africa and Orient, the bodies of women,
the urban "masses," the insane, the sick, the criminal, and, most notori-
ously, the body of the prostitute. The production of this abjected, excluded
other as a mechanism of dominance, as a politics of difference, as fundamental in the production of social order, is the story I tell here. Although
this production is not restricted to women, to female, to female body—
and in fact the productions of sex, sexuality, and female body cannot be
separated from those of class and race—the former categories receive most
of my attention.

Let me quickly sketch my conceptual/theoretical *Guide Bleu*. In setting
out these relationships, my analytic is the social production of social space
(Lefebvre 1991)—the space of "bodies," "cities," and "texts." In Foucau-
dian terms, I am following the operation of knowledge and power organizing everyday practice into relations of domination and subordination. As
I center my analysis in the body, this can be restated as the ordering of
bodies in social space—discursive, physical, and lived. A body, a city, is not
its physical materiality alone; it is this and, inextricable from it, its materiality mediated and represented by culture-specific knowledges, sciences, arts,
everyday practices of being: a contingent production, then, produced in a
specific time and place, always volatile, always conflictual and politically
charged. As a socially produced space with no transhistorical or stable
definition, a body, a city, a social order, can be defined as the concretiza-
tion of mobile social relations. The spatiality of a body is not created by
"nature," or "biology"; likewise, that of a civilization, a city or a culture, is
not produced by "mind." Each is a social production existing only in its
performed reproductions and hence can be dis-ordered, re-ordered, re-
formed. A city, a body, a social order—each is a complex production, a
selective tradition, a socially produced regime of truth that may tumble
and fall.

In the West the production of order, the ordering of bodies in social
space, has proceeded according to a dominant logic of hierarchical binar-
ism—a logic based in the production of a valorized subject/entity/identity
and a repudiated, excluded other. While the specifics of this vary histori-

cally and geographically, the politics of order and difference are under-girded, at least in part, by a logic that developed in the classical Athenian polis and was never thereafter completely dislodged—that social order and good government are the product of the victory of mind over and against the thwarting, dangerous, and disorderly maneuvers of body. It is this idea, and the concomitant marking of the designation "mind" on the bodies of a select group of male citizens and the opposing designation "body" on the bodies of all others—women, slaves, metics, children, aliens, barbar-ians—that undergirds and legitimates the exclusion of these "abjected" bodies from positions of ruling and power while still allowing the publicly proclaimed ideals of freedom and equality to circulate. It is also in the polis, in accord with this logic, that the sexual division male/female and the heterosexist relation between them is set in place as a "natural" order of rulers and ruled (Aristotle 1988: 7). This lives on as one of the most powerful and fundamental mechanisms of domination in Western politics and culture.

This mechanism of domination functions as a binary order-in/as-differ-ence, a body politics that works to install masculinist order via the produc-tion and reproduction of abstract, artifactual differences marked on bod-ies that acquire, because of "the body's sheer material factualness" (Scary 1985: 14), the aura and authority of the "natural," the "real," and so cease to be seen as social productions. These controls operate discursively: in language itself (Kristeva 1984; Silverman 1983; Spender 1980; Trinh 1989); in the scientific and philosophical and cultural production of fe-male, female sexuality, female body as other, as deviant, as dangerous (Bordo 1993; Braidotti 1991; Butler 1993; Grosz 1994; Irigaray 1985; Jaco-bus, Keller, and Shuttleworth 1990; Jardine 1985; Le Doeuff 1990; Lloyd 1993; Sandercock and Forsyth 1992; Suleiman 1986); as blatantly spa-tialized enclosures and exclusions, such as purdah, veiling, the gynae-ceaum of classical Greece, taboos on contacts with menstruating women, marriage laws, "third world"/racist/colonial ghettoizations and restric-tions, prohibitions against the public life of governing, education, city streets, and professions (Colomina 1992; Frankenberg 1993; Hayden 1989; hooks 1990; Hurtado 1989; Katz and Monk 1993; Lugones 1994; Mazzoleni 1993; Spain 1992; Spelman 1988; Spivak 1988; Weisman 1992; Wilson 1991); and as technologies of self, the care of the body, gestures, behaviors that produce and perform the identity feminine/female (Bornstein 1994; Butler 1990, 1993; Cocks 1989; Garber 1992): in sum, an interlocking matrix of restrictions on movement, privilege, and oppor-tunity.

The order of male/female also functions, and this I ask you to remem-ber as it becomes important in my discussion of modern planning and its logic, as an economy of representation for other hierarchized social relations: order/disorder, culture/nature, mind/body, good/evil, spirit/flesh, form/matter, self/other, subject/object, transcendence/immanance, normal/pathological, healthy/diseased, and so forth. Without this matrix of control—this politics that seizes hold of the female body and makes it "different," makes it live as a fleshed signification of the abstraction "female"— "male" order would vanish into the fantasy that produces it.

This is the virulence motivating the politics of difference and its logic of borders: the unowned secret of dependency, the unacknowledged knowledge that the great divide separating male and female is not real, that it exists only in the incessant reiteration of the "narrow zone of the line" (Foucault, quoted in Gusevich 1987–1988: 95) that separates the produced categories. It is this inherent instability that explains the cultural importance of hegemonically produced borders: to eliminate differences as produced, to publicly proclaim "the threatening absence of boundaries between human bodies and among bodily acts" (Epstein and Straub 1991: 2), is to explode the entire order of the socius.

When the produced lines between different and same are threatened— when defining definitions of sexes, classes, and races are anarchic, demanding, and potentially revolutionary—hegemonic power reacts to reinforce them with all the resources in its arsenal. These resources include fusions of knowledge and power; economic, cultural, and military interventions; and, almost always, arguments for their "naturalness," their "givenness," their inherent "rightness," the transgression of which invites the end of order and civilization.

This is precisely the situation in nineteenth-century Paris when with the coming of industrial capitalism and new modern bourgeois forms of power—its laws and doctrines of liberty and equality, on the one hand, and its needs to legitimate relations of domination, on the other—a great deal of attention is paid to the "naturalness" of sexual difference and the dominant/subordinate relations between male and female. In this context all potential destabilizations of this difference as hegemonically produced—the militant agitations by feminists, suffragettes, and female socialists; the rise of the *nouvelle femme;* the mass participation of women in waged factory and clerical work—are coded unnatural, dangerous, disorderly threats to social order. This male anxiety and dread is inscribed in the language of urban pathology and public hygiene, in the language of urban planning. This language finds in the prostitute body the signification of almost the entirety of the century's anxieties and concerns, its cataclysmic upheavals and excesses. Although oppositions to dominant masculinist logic constitute a critical part of the totality of nineteenth-century French social and political reality, I will not deal with these oppositions here. My focus is hegemonic efforts of containment and the part modern planning played in them.

With the hope of suggesting the importance of enfleshing, embodying, the "subject" of planning, I offer a brief impressionistic sketch of one specific aspect of modernity: the relation between the planned city and the planned female body, a control of streets that I imagine and ask you to imagine with me (and perhaps with Freud) as the fantasy of the straight line. I leave the arcades and department stores, the *flânerie*, the phantasmagoria of commodities and sights, to Benjamin and Baudelaire and enter instead "pathological space" to explore the linked themes of order and disorder, mind and body, male and female, in nineteenth-century Paris where dangerous contagions and excesses are the obsessive concerns of city fathers, professional experts, and statesmen.

THE POEM OF MALE DESIRES, PART II, OR REGULARIZATION AND THE FANTASY OF THE STRAIGHT LINE

Paris Pathological: Dangerous Contagions and Excesses

To enter the nineteenth century from the time and space that preceded it is to enter a spectacular disorder. It is a century of volcanic upheaval— "all fixed fast-frozen relationships are swept away" (Marx and Engels 1978: 476)—a century of cataclysmic change and excess, of revolution and radical utopianism, of colonization and imperialism, the wild proliferation of people and things, the steady restructuring of order and tradition (Hobsbawm 1975, 1987; Price 1987). There is both the thrill and the fear of this, but in the end there is the desire to control it: to machine it, industrialize it, discipline it for use and exchange.

In this produced disorder, this condition of "everlasting uncertainty and agitation" (Marx and Engels 1978: 476), a feeling of the alien, the tenuous, the frightening, materializes. The world is no longer transparent but shot through with illusion and mystification and things false (Frisby 1986: 26). The mirror gives way to the mask; there is a sense of the fleeting, the transitory, the ephemeral (Baudelaire 1964; Benjamin 1978; Berman 1988; Buck-Morss 1990; Frisby 1986; Harvey 1989a). There develops in this time a fascination with light and openness: gas lamps, electricity, wide boulevards, parks, greenery, ventilation, circulation, sunlight; seeing, understanding, knowing, visibility, spectacle, surveillance, the bringing to light of dark, dirty secrets. At the same time there develops a corresponding distrust of dark and night, "the fear of darkened spaces, the pall of gloom" (Foucault 1977: 153), the slums and their denizens, the "dark continents" of Africa and female sexuality; a fear of pollution and contamination that disrupts the Enlightenment dream of a known, transparent society.

The urban spaces of the nineteenth century are disorder's text, modernity's heiroglyph. The wildly accelerated rates of urban growth and power urbanized consciousness and social relations even while the vast majority of people still lived outside cities: "In the nineteenth century the lure of the city emptied agrarian space of its substance (cultural, social)" (Virilio 1986: 20). The city *is* modernity, and invades imaginations and dreams as both the city of light and the city of dark (Williams 1973): as thrill, as excitement and possibility, as electricity and progress, a vast phantasmagoric display of glittering things and sights; but also something to be feared, that produces anxiety, that is eating up tradition, devouring the countryside, disordering and diseasing the entire social order. The whole of society seems threatened, on the brink of collapse. Knowledges, social relationships, and everyday habits of being are no longer "natural," certain, reflexive. Capital, proliferating and virulent, is doing its work. In contrast to the formality of the ancien regime, of the precise choreography of Versailles, its measured social distances, its well-defined borders and roles, Paris has become Zola's carnival with its confusions, its forced intimacies, its inversions: "Signs of social breakdown were everywhere. . . . Paris [was] a cauldron of social unrest, vulnerable to agitators of any stripe" (Harvey 1989a: 206).

In this situation of disorder, the body, with the city, comes to play a dominant role in discourse. The cultural tradition of seeing the individual body as both literal and metaphoric sign of the health or pathology of the social body develops insidiously in the nineteenth century (Douglas 1982, 1984; Gilman 1985; Mosse 1985; Stallybrass and White 1986). The body occupies the center of thought, becomes the object of a social discourse organized around the idea of dangerous contagions and their cures—a separating of the pure from the impure, the normal from the abnormal, the productive from the nonproductive, the healthy from the diseased.

Historically, in times of crisis and insecurity, when there is fear of social disintegration and regression, the accompanying desire to take control frequently becomes a hegemonic push for strict borders around those identities and social relations most fundamental to its constitution, that is, those borders around the "primordia" of sex, class, race, and territory (Appadurai 1990; Gilman 1985; Mosse 1985; Showalter 1990). It is not surprising, then, that these fears of contamination and disorder are expressed as the need to exert control over those bodies produced as particularly dangerous to the dominant body of the male bourgeois: women, prostitutes, criminals, slum dwellers, the insane, the sick, the hereditarily degenerate, homosexuals, the "dark races," beggars and street sellers, the dangerous classes. These are cast as foreign bodies, contagions, urban parasites who prey on the healthy social organism of the male bourgeois and contaminate it, siphoning off the lifeblood, the wealth and paternity, of industrious, productive society (Chevalier 1973; Gallagher 1987; Nord 1987).

These bodies, while marked dangerous, uncivilized, inferior, and perverse, are also marked as excitingly secret and degenerate. The reforming texts of hygienists and the texts of urban ethnographers, medical taxonomists, novelists, "painters of modern life" (Clark 1984), and the popular press of the time—all produce the bodies of stigmatized others as a locus not only of fear and disgust but also of an eroticized, sexualized fascination. Fantasies of bodies and forbidden places—the perversities and sexual excesses of prostitutes, the hypersexuality of Hottentots, slum fecundity and hereditary degeneration, syphilitic contagion, the clandestine plots of criminals and revolutionaries—intermingle with fantasies of the city's dark underworld of catacombs and sewers (Reid 1991; Stallybrass and White 1986). Paris is rife with illicit dealings and sexings and breedings. It is the age of sex and sexuality (Foucault 1990); "the golden age of venereal peril" (Corbin, quoted in Showalter 1990: 188); the age when masturbation becomes an antisocial act, a "lonely vice" that threatens family, nation, and humanity. It is an age in which each of the century's produced deviances and vices are feared to be flourishing in the dark secret recesses of the city. The city's scum, its filth—the slums, the sewers, the bodies of prostitutes and degenerates—all become central topoi in "the urban geography of the bourgeois Imaginary" (Stallybrass and White 1986: 126), dangerous bodies and places that menace society and hence must be controlled if the socius is to survive.

Public Hygiene: Bodies and Cities

It is in this situation that doctors, planners, and social scientists come together as public hygienists, "sanitation" experts who will make society healthy by the excision of dangerous and disorderly elements. Doctors *and* planners are "specialists of space" (Foucault 1977: 150), men of reason whose medical and medicalized attentions will restore the logic of borders—the logic of function and system—that is order and health. This is the practice of "surgery" and "physic" (Le Corbusier 1987: 253) that is the cure for capital's virulence and the militant agitation for revolution, for equal wages and rights, by women, the colonized, and the proletariat. The "cure" is based not in the idea of rechanneling flows of economic and political power but in the ideas of differentiation and control, the separation of the pure from the impure, healthy from diseased, and the regulation of flows in hegemonically prescribed directions: a plan of reason, a practice of enlightenment, that is authored as the eradication of darkness and disorder and the bringing in of a new regime of order and light.

These "practices of reason," of enlightenment (Rabinow 1989: 9), represent the coming together, beginning in the eighteenth century, of empiricism, new positivist social sciences, and architectural theory (Braham 1980; Lavin 1992, 1994; Vidler 1987)—a process Paul Rabinow, in his discussion of French modernity, describes as the "construction of norms and the search for forms adequate to understand and regulate modern society" (1989: 9). It is in the works of such architects as Claude-Nicholas Ledoux that there first develops the "idea of a plan" working in service of social, managerial, and technical needs. Ledoux's plans for factories anticipate future functionalist ideals of cities—"a play of geometries that reduced all movements to their simplest form" (Vidler 1987: 38), a reduction that facilitated surveillance, the disciplinary apparatus whose epitome is Jeremy Bentham's Panopticon. In his design of the factory village of Chaux, Ledoux produces the prototype of the nineteenth-century city plan: "a model of an Enlightenment ideal city, one constructed according to the laws of a geometric system that united powers of sight with those of spatial order, . . . [an] idea and a project of a space of social order, classified and divided into units that were geometrically identified and architecturally reified" (Vidler 1987: 41, 51).

Foucault develops these practices as "disciplinary strategies," the complicitous operation of knowledge and power that is the ordering of social space in accord with hegemonic interests. Discipline is a new kind of power that develops in modernity along with the state and the state's interest in controlling its population via the introduction of economy and order through all aspects of social life. With it rise the ideas of "the social," "the social body," and "the city" as objects of study and social engineering. This involves a combination of efforts: (1) the medical/scientific production of norms and their abjected/excluded others—the binaries normal/abnormal, healthy/pathological, productive/nonproductive—by the "corrective sociology" (Choay 1969: 108) of positivist social and natural sciences such as Darwinian biology, medicine, psychiatry, geography, statistics, criminology, and urban ethnography; (2) the attempt to provide these norms with architectural and urban forms; and (3) the rise of the power of professional experts who, with governments, produce and operate the normalizing disciplines. Discipline is, in its most general formulation, *the orderly arrangement of bodies in space,* physical, discursive, and lived; a hierarchical separation of bodies in lived/material space that corresponds to their "scientific" separation in discursive space, for example, the location of the poor in slums, the insane in mental institutions, the criminal in prisons, and the sick in hospitals and the assignment of women to private/domestic spaces and the colonized to colonies. It is *the geometry of difference lived,* a reified arrangement of bodies in space—the separation of reason from reason's others—that is *the performed, enfleshed version of Ledoux's ideal Enlightenment city.*

In the nineteenth century these disciplinary strategies emerge forcefully as a "politics of health" (Rabinow 1989: 9); as the "fundamental spatialization and verbalization of the pathological, . . . a generalized medical consciousness, . . . linked to each individual existence as well as to the collective life of the nation" (Foucault 1994: xi, 30). This is an idea associated with the French Revolution, seen as the initiator of a new order: "The Revolution is a 'sublime vaccine' that destroys the 'virus' of servitude and superstition. 'What is the French Revolution!' Hugo asks, and then replies: 'A vast cleansing. There had been a plague, the past. The fiery furnace burned this miasma' " (Victor Hugo in *Paris Guide,* quoted in Ferguson 1988: 64). By this logic, the death of civilizations, the degeneration of races, the health of populations and individuals, and the order of cities are all imagined in terms of normal and pathological. The production of the new order becomes a vast cleansing, the creation of new modern space, clean space, rational space, over and against the dark, diseased, dirty space of the unenlightened past.

The politics of health and pathology are given scientific and philosophic support by a new idea of order that develops with the Enlightenment: the replacement of the preordained and fixed order of God with the idea of History, a manipulable man-made order whose telos is the steady enlightened progress of rational man. In this idea discipline finds both its instrumental and its self-legitimating logic: the idea of the differentiation and hierarchization of the globe's population according to those who impede and those who further the goals of history/progress/modernity; the orderly arrangement of bodies in space as the "great chain of being" on which humanity is calibrated from "the lowliest Hottentot" to "glorious Milton and Newton" (Gates 1985: 8). The same Enlightenment logic that is the source of the Revolution's idea of a government of free humans arranged equally in the public sphere, a dissolution of the borders between higher and lower orders, is also the source of the idea of equality by geometry, the repression of difference and particularity that is disciplinary society, disciplinary strategy.

As practioners of reason, of physic and surgery, nineteenth-century planners join with other disciplinary experts—sanitary engineers, doctors, gynecologists, urban ethnographers, colonial overseers, heads of nation-states—engaged in the production of modern order as enlightenment, as cleansing, as the elimination of the pathological spaces of the city. These efforts take the form of sanitation and beautification movements (Goubert 1986; Hall 1988; Peterson 1983a, 1983b; Sutcliffe 1981), of regularization and rationalization (Choay 1969; Pinkey 1958; Sutcliffe 1970), of "modern management" (Benevolo 1993): the imposition of a city of straight lines and right angles that asserts the enlightened authority of science over the diseased body of the city and orders it in productive, efficient directions. This is the work of "modern" planning: the "march towards order"

(Le Corbusier 1987: 17) whose geometry, its applied reason, will gain control of disorderly flows and contagions and hence rid the city of crime, squalor, congestion, poverty, disease, and pollution.

It is in Paris, with the efforts of Louis Napoleon and Baron Haussmann that "the crucial experiment takes place" (Benevolo 1993: 171): the first attempt to reorder an entire old city, to implement on a massive scale the model of an ideal Enlightenment city. Haussmannization is described by traditional planning historians as varieties of rationalization, functionalism, and modern management, as regularization: "that form of critical planning whose explicit purpose is to regularize the disordered city, to disclose its new order by means of a pure, schematic layout which will disentangle it from its dross" (Choay 1969: 15).

With Haussmann enlightenment is literal: "Air, light, greenery . . . become symbols of progress. . . . The right angle acquires an almost mystical value. . . . [T]he straight line symbolizes the break with the past and the advent of reason" (Choay 1969: 32, 98). The idea of regularization reproduces not only the Enlightenment valorization of reason but its idea of the body as Reason's enemy. It is the diseased body of the city that is the "dross" that is to be subjected to surgery, operated on by reason, by mind. The city is conceived in the body language of organs, tissues, arteries, veins, lungs, and heart: a body language of functionalism imported from natural science. In its diseased state the city is leprous, cancerous, a chancre (Choay 1969: 10; Le Corbusier 1987: 255), while the cure is conceived in the language of geometry, the straight line, an order of abstraction and rationalization that is the straightening of curves, the elimination of excesses and wastes.

Haussmann's "method of attack" (Choay 1969: 17) is to conquer the body of the city with statistical and empirical analysis, a detailed planimetric and topographical mapping followed by the development and imposition of a comprehensive plan. This "urban surgery" is the removal of diseased organs, the opening of clogged arteries and lungs, the demolition of slums—changes that were the most massive Paris would undergo between the Revolution and World War II. Keywords for the "Haussmann pattern" are circulation, ventilation, functions, nodes, flows, hygiene, geometry, traffic, classification, system. Haussmannization is a disciplinary strategy of differentiation and control; the separation of functions, the disassociation of contaminating parts, the production of discretely bordered and hierarchically ordered "spatial cells" (Benevolo 1993: 172): public space separated from private space, moving vehicles separated from pedestrians, recreation and housing separated from work, underground from aboveground, poor from rich, respectable from dangerous, sick from well, dead from living (Gille 1986); women from men (Davidoff and Hall 1983; Hayden 1981; Pollack 1988; Wolff 1990). It is a scheme of streets, straight lines, a grid to achieve regulated flows in the interest of achieving the "efficient unity" of the city; and elimination of frictions, tensions, and congestions and the making of Paris into "a single organism quickened with life" (Choay 1969: 17).

Haussmann's demolition of the Old Paris and his reassertion of the modern, the new; his clearing away of darkness and bringing in of light, straight lines, wide vistas, clean air, and staged theatricality of monumental sights; his building into the architecture of the city a clear demarcation between privilege and squalor; his attempted eradication of the dark and disorderly spaces in which plots thicken, revolutionaries hide, prostitutes and criminals escape policing; his keeping the slums contained, enclosed, bounded so that the neighborhoods of the bourgeoisie might continue clean, well lighted, unpolluted—all this enacts the cure for social and economic inequality that is the practice of enlightened reason.

This rationalization and regularization of the city is repeated in the nineteenth-century struggle to control the female body. Ridding the city of pathological spaces by controlling the streets comes to mean, in language that is frequently stunning in its explicitness, a ridding of the city of the disorderly, pathological, sexually dangerous female—paradigmatically the prostitute but potentially any body marked female—and her replacement with a planned or controlled body that functions in accord with hegemonic needs. As Paris is conceptualized as a diseased body, a "she" (Le Corbusier 1987; Nesbit 1992), so the female body is conceptualized as a medicalized, pathologized city, a geography to be conquered and operated on by the authority and science of male mind.

Thomas Laqueur and Carole Pateman locate the beginnings of this process in the eighteenth century when there is a "radical . . . reconstitution of female, and more generally human, sexuality in relation to the equally radical Enlightenment political reconstitution of 'Man'—the universalistic claim, stated by Condorcet, that 'the rights of men result simply from the fact that they are sentient beings, capable of acquiring moral ideas and of reasoning concerning these ideas. [And that] women, having these same qualities, must necessarily possess equal rights' " (Laqueur 1987: 1). It is at this time that the "disorder of women" becomes notorious and is vigorously asserted as having a negative effect on all social and political life (Pateman 1989: 18).

To deal with this dilemma of asserted equality and enacted subordination, a complete revamping of sexual difference takes place in the direction of producing female sexuality as a category of the dangerous, the irrational, the potentially pathological: as reason's Other, as body, as inherently disorderly and hence threatening to "enlightened" clean, modern society. This "doctoring" involves the medical/biological/scientific production of two types of difference, an imposition of straight lines rigidly dividing the categories male and female and, within the category female, the strict division between orderly and disorderly.

The first difference, that between male and female, defines all women as biologically different from and inferior to all men. In this medical/biological model women are authored as naturally passive, irrational, weak, emotional, and prone to illness and madness, to sexual maladies and anarchies. That is, they are beings who exhibit all the characteristics of a body not under the control of mind. As scientific validation of this fact, women are anatomically and sexually reformulated. Their bodies are rematerialized as an asymmetry of large pelvis, small brain; a biological, anatomical destiny of function and place that removes them from the public space of ruling and power—the reasoning place—and locates them in the private house—the body/pelvis place—in accord with their "natural" reproductive function. A revival and revamping, then, of the old polis-logic, an Aristotelian, Platonic order of body and mind.

The second type of difference concerns the problem of the excessive pelvis, the site of "natural" reproductive energies but also of "unnatural" and potentially dangerous sexual energies that the small female brain is incapable of controlling. Within the category female, further straightening is required, another enclosure demanded to contain these dangerous excesses. Borders are produced to establish and regularize the difference between orderly and disorderly women, that is, those whose productive/reproductive/sexual capacities are under male control and those who are not. While all women are potentially dangerous, those who have been domesticated by men, who live within the confines of men's houses and names as libidinal and economic dependents, have their sexual/mental dangers mitigated, straightened, brought in line with social ends—the sublimating of the sexual body to the reproductive body, the canalizing of female erotics into the male-controlled logic of the heterosexist reproductive couple.

Just as nineteenth-century discourse refigures the city as two conflictual opposites—the orderly planned city, the disorderly unplanned city—so it refigures female, female body, as dichotomous. On the one hand, there is the controlled, regularized, domesticated body, the planned body of the good, respectable bourgeois wife, the "virtuous" woman living under a patriarchal roof who is the upholder of social and moral order and whose body is devoid of excesses, irregularities, surprises, appetitites, and desires. On the other hand, there is the prostitute body, the obscene, unclean, unplanned body that with its contagions, excesses, and syphilitic fluids infects city and empire, subverts social order, and brings sickness and racial degeneration to an entire people. Significantly, this list of disorderly bodies includes not only prostitutes, lesbians, excessive masturbators, nymphomaniacs, and hysterics (Ehrenreich and English 1978; Foucault 1990; Groneman 1994; Sheehan 1985) but also suffragettes, female socialists, feminists, and independent wage earners. The prostitute, the lesbian, the nymphomaniac, the hysteric—women whose sexuality was not in service of the "heterosexual imperative" (Butler 1990, 1993), the "law of male sex right" (Pateman 1989)—is pathologized as a form of *sexual/mental* deviance.

But it is the prostitute body, the century's paradigmatic disorderly body, toward which the nineteenth century directs its most strenuous revilings, its most obsessive concerns, its most persistent attempts at female control (Bernheimer 1989; Corbin 1990; Harsin 1985). In Paris in the nineteenth century there is a fascination with the prostitute: "it was above all around the figure of the prostitute that the gaze and touch, the desires and contaminations, of the bourgeois male were articulated" (Stallybrass and White 1986: 137). Prostitutes become the social evil of the century, incarnations of disorder who, like Nana, are represented as the cause of social regression and decay, the spreaders of a moral and syphilitic contagion that would infect the bourgeoisie and destroy city, nation, and empire— the entirety of civilization. The prostitute body is, like the disorderly city, produced as the antithesis of enlightenment—a dark and dirty place, a putrid hole, a sewer, a destructive regressive potential that is racialized in its connections with the hypersexuality of African Hottentots (Gilman 1985), classed in connections to the hereditary degenerations of criminals and the denizens of slums (Chevalier 1973), pathologized, like the lesbian and nymphomaniac, in relation to sexual excesses and perversities (Buci-Glucksmann 1987; Groneman 1994). The prostitute body is produced as a criminal body, a working-class body, a slum-dwelling hereditarily degenerate body, a physically diseased and morally decadent body, a contagious body: that is, as the terrifying outlaw woman who is in every woman, the dangerously desublimated sexual woman whose libidinal economy no longer flows in reproductive, heterosexist, male-oriented directions.

There is an obsessive need to control these "loose" women, and it is in France that the regularization of prostitution, like that of the city, first develops. The "regulatory system" advocated for control of prostitutes is similar to that for cities, a "Haussmann pattern" for controlling sexuality based in the same principles of empirical/statistical analysis and the development and implementation of a comprehensive plan based in differentiation, circulation, and control. The surveillance of prostitutes, the control of flows, is a disciplinary strategy of clearance and containment (Harsin 1985: 51): keep them spatially separate and regulate their movement throughout the city. What Haussmann names control of "traffic flow," *police de mouers* (morals police) name control of the streets—a severe restriction of liberty that included forced registration of prostitutes with police, the issuing of cards, regular medical exams, raids, sweeps, mass arrests, and the attempted containment of prostitutes in state-regulated houses.

Like the body of the city, the individual prostitute body is well researched, well imagined. It is a geography that is surveyed and mapped, subjected to analysis and quantification, examinations and probings. In a linked analogical process of imagining the city as a diseased body, city/ sewer metaphors are used to describe the prostitute body. Like sewers, like the putrefaction of slums, like cancerous, leprous flesh, the prostitute body is known to smell bad: it is putrid (from *putain*, Latin for whore); it excretes an excess of seminal fluid and waste and hence, like the diseased body of the city, is in need of draining, circulation, and flux of air (Corbin 1987: 217). Disorderly women, like the diseased and disorderly body of Paris, were similarly subjected to physic and surgery. Haussmann's urban surgery has disturbing resonance with the gynecologist's surgeries on disorderly women whose diseased organs, clitoris and ovaries, were removed in effecting a psychogynecological cure (Ehrenrich and English 1978; Groneman 1994; Sheehan 1985).

As regularization tightened there was a corresponding fear of public women who escaped policing, who vanished into the dark recesses of the city. Fears of clandestinity were wed to fears that syphilis—"the new leprosy," "the new plague" (Harsin 1985: 251)—carried and spread by prostitutes, permeated society, endangering the patrimony of the male bourgeois, the health and wealth of nations. A virtual mania developed for tracking down and inscribing prostitutes, women who, having escaped surveillance, were secretly contaminating the socius. A fear gripped the city, the bourgeois: if the prostitute was not controlled, analyzed, counted, and contained, she would *circulate* in the social body and randomly spread disease and disorder: They "come back into the world. . . . [T]hey surround us. . . . They penetrate our houses, our interiors" (Parent-Duchatelet, quoted in Clark 1984: 105).

This regularization, this fear, is not directed toward prostitutes alone. Its significance lies in its "vast cleansing," the separation of the pure from the impure—the virtuous wife from all women who are her other—in the interests of disciplining female libidinal and economic flows in hegemonic directions. In the same way that the city is subjected to the discipline of straight lines, the female body's dangerous curves and excesses are "straightened" by the regularization that most overtly targets the prostitute body but that works on all female bodies. It is in this move, as well as in those more explicit moves—the sexed/gendered/heterosexist ordering of urban space that produced the design of male cities and female suburbs, the ideas of function and place that worked to divide the private life of the house from the public life of the street and polis (Davidoff and Hall 1983;

Hayden 1981; Pollack 1988; Wilson 1991; Wolff 1990)—that planners, as disciplinary experts, became participants in the control of female/female-body/female sexuality.

In Paris, "capital of the nineteenth century," in the texts of planners, public hygienists, sanitation engineers, city fathers, and heads of family and church and state, female/female body becomes synonymous with that which disorders, threatens, undoes the work of Man, the idea of the plan. Female factory workers and department store clerks, housewives and matrons, female utopianists, socialists, and revolutionaries, bourgeois women whose first "respectable" unescorted excursions into public space were into department stores—all these women, in addition to prostitutes, had their movements throughout the city restricted, controlled, and monitored by what masculinist power produced. Wherever they moved, inside or outside the borders of bourgeois respectability, women performed, concretized in their flesh, their very being, the abjected, excluded other of hegemonic masculinist order.

Le Corbusier: The Climax

The ideas of Haussmann, Zola, and public hygienists like Parent-Duchatelet did not die with the Second Empire. In *The City of Tomorrow and Its Planning,* Le Corbusier continues the tradition, reinscribing in his plan for Paris the idea of planning as a discipline founded in mind at war with the thwartings of body. This repetition can be read in his conceptualizations of the city as a diseased body in need of the attentions of "physic" and "surgery"; in his setting out the idea of a plan as reason's creation, a creation that is enabled only by the overcoming of body, animality, and emotions; in his perpetuation of an unnamed relation of ruling that occurs in his specific embodying/concretizing of mind as male planner/architect, as culture, as order and policing, in opposition to the embodying/concretizing of body as female, as savage, as animal, as disorder, as chaos, as an undergrowth that must be hacked away. In what follows I present, in Le Corbusier's own words (worth presenting verbatim for the full unguarded force of their imagery), his ardent authoring of the manifesto of the straight line.

For Le Corbusier (1987), the order of the straight line is Male:

> The straight line is deeply impressive in the confusion of nature; it is
> the *work of men.* (271)

It is not-animal, not-nature, but the mastery of these:

> The winding road is the Pack-Donkey's Way, the straight line is man's
> way. (12)

Man walks in a straight line because he has a goal and knows where he is going. (5)

[T]he winding road is the result . . . of looseness, lack of concentration and animality [while] the straight road is . . . an action, a positive deed, the result of self-mastery. (12)

It is not-body, not feeling:

Man governs his feelings by reason; he keeps his feelings and his instincts in check, subordinating them to the aim he has in view. (5)

The things [man] makes for himself are a creation which contrasts all the more with his natural surroundings because its aim is closer to mind, and further away and more detached from body. . . . When man is free, his tendency is toward pure geometry. It is then that he achieves what we call order. (21)

It is man, it is culture, it is policing:

The town is being policed, culture is manifesting itself and Man is able to create. (9)

It is geometry, divinity, perfection:

Geometry is the means. . . . Geometry is the foundation, . . . the material basis on which we build those symbols which represent to us perfection and the divine. (xxi)

It is a calling:

A time has now come when modern town planning can be conceived of as a possibility. . . . It is directed by a lofty desire for truth. The awakening spirit of man is already rearranging our social forms. (xxi–xxii)

It is the health of nations:

A heedless people, or society, or town, in which effort is relaxed and not concentrated, quickly becomes dissipated, overcome, and absorbed by a nation or a society that goes to work in a positive way and controls itself. It is in this way that cities sink to nothing and ruling classes are overthrown. (12)

It is modernity:

The modern sentiment is a spirit of geometry. . . . [W]e see, emerging from the chaos, ordered and logical aspirations. (38–39)

A modern city lives by the straight line. (10)

It is progress on the great chain of being:

All the works that man has achieved are an ordering. . . . As we move higher in the scale of creation, so we move towards a more perfect order. . . . What an immense difference between the hut of a savage and the Parthenon! (23)

It is the mastering of Paris as something diseased: "Paris was sick, deadly sick" (253); as something dangerous: "Paris is a dangerous magma, . . . a menacing disaster" (25); as something female (23)—and man must "for his own security" (22) protect himself against this, or it will thwart him:

> The house, the street, the town . . . should be ordered. . . . [I]f they are not ordered, they oppose themselves to us, they thwart us, as nature all around us thwarts us. (15)

The order of the straight line is a struggle:

> Man undermines and hacks at Nature. He opposes himself to her, he fights with her, he digs himself in. (24)

> . . . digs and hacks through her undergrowth, and out of these evils is tending toward an ordered system of straight lines and right angles. . . . [T]his clearing process is indispensable to the expression of her spirit. (23)

It is the *climax*—reached when man is bold enough, potent enough, *straight* enough:

> Straight lines . . . are arrived at when man is strong enough, determined enough, sufficiently equipped and sufficiently enlightened to desire and be able to trace straight lines. In the history of forms, the moment in which he sees the straight line is a climax. (37)

For Le Corbusier the ordered city, the planned city, is "the grip of man upon nature." The disordered city is a body that, like a wanton female, has slipped that grip and is in need of "straightening up"; a dangerous "miasma" of matter that if mastered, rationalized, ennobled, and enlightened by the "right" angles and straight lines, will be, like the virtuous wife, transformed into something more worthy of Man.

MASCULINIST ORDER: *RES COGITANS* VS. *RES EXTENSA*

The writing of planning and planning history has depended on a view of both planning and history that is particularist, masculinist—that is, "work which, while claiming to be exhaustive, forgets about women's existence and concerns itself only with the position of men" (Le Doeuff 1990: 42). It has been particularist not only in taking the male as the pivotal center of analysis—"The Copernican revolution has yet to have its final effects in the male imaginary" (Irigaray 1985: 133)—and in its assumptions of a particular kind of male—white, heterosexual, Western, elite—but also in its productions of what must be eliminated (abjected, excluded) for its order to be sustained. In the dominant binary tradition of the West, in which planning is located, it is female/body that is produced as that which must be eliminated in the interests of public order. This is the "genealogical violence at the origin" (de Certeau 1986: 6), a miming of the separation of the male from the body world of mother in exchange for entry into the symbolic world of mind/father. It is this mimesis that establishes the paradigmatic male relation to space: male *res cogitans* versus female *res extensa*, which is to be mastered, conquered, tamed by the persistent reassertion of the difference that upholds the identity and order of male.

In the modern West order has been authored as Reason's order, with Reason set forth as something real, something that proceeds from mind, something different from and superior to the chaotic sensings and respondings of body, the realm of female and female's analogical correlates: the lower orders, savages and primitives, desires, animals, irrationality, dreams, magics, confusions, and, most dangerously, uncontrolled sexuality. Nonetheless, as Frances Jaffer's imagery suggests, it has not been male mind from which the social order of the West proceeds.

> . . . all that fear, almost terror, of the women . . . of being caught in the old stereotype—woman/body . . . an inferior kind of mind. . . . But that male body, how IT dominates the culture, the language, the environment. Since 3000 B.C. in Sumeria, Tiamet's monsters again and again, and every myth an effort to keep the sun rising. Save the sun everybody, from the watery deeps, from the dark underneath it must go—Into—Every night into such dangers, such soft inchoate darkness, what will become of it, will it rise again will it will it rise again? The language of criticism: "lean, dry, terse, powerful, strong, spare, linear, focused, explosive"—god forbid it should be "limp"!!! But "soft, moist, blurred, padded, irregular, going around in circles, and other descriptions of our bodies—the very abyss. . . . That limp dick—an entire civilization based on it, help the sun rise, watch out for the dark underground, focus focus focus, keep it high, let it soar, let it transcend, let it aspire to the godhead—." (Frances Jaffer, quoted in DuPlessis 1988: 136)

It has been body, then, male body, all along: the anxious distancing from female that means the possession of the autonomous identity male; the separation that must be endlessly repeated—the Oedipal fort/da game, the heterosexist paradigm, the fantasy of permanent potency and "straightness"—if the identity is to be sustained. It is this "originary" embodied relation to space, a relation based not in mind but in the production and incessant reproduction of bodily difference, which founds and sustains the masculinist order.

The nineteenth century provides modern planning with its ruling metaphor, a rephrasing of Le Corbusier that reads: The plan! it is the grip of man upon the city! The produced set of cultural representations regarding male mind and female body and the heterosexist dominant/subordinate relations between them is a hegemonic economy of representation to which modern planning had recourse as it developed as a discipline and profession. To the notion of the plowed field, the conquered territory, the penetration of darkness that is named mastery, enlightenment, and knowledge, we must add the notion of the planned city—a masculinist notion that is still operative today. In its conceptualizations of the intercourse between planner and planning object—the disorderly city, the underdeveloped country, the region in chaos—that is to be tamed, planning reproduces a relation of ruling expressed in the nineteenth-century plan, a practice of domination that mimes the masculinist relation to space—male *res cogitans* conquering female *res extensa*, the killing of the body to usher in the reign of mind.

This conceptualization of installing order must be understood, at least in part, as a masculinist fantasy of control, a fantasy that reverberates from planning's inception into the present. Not with the explicitness of Le Corbusier or Haussmann and not only in the ways that are most overt—the elimination of body that has worked in service of planning's idea of pure objective knowledge, the ideas of a singular "human" subject/actor/agent, of a disembodied "public" domain that exists as somehow separate from the embodied "private" domain. But also, and perhaps more daunting, in the presence of unannounced fantasies and desires that work themselves unconsciously and unexplicitly into the good, even the best, intentions of planning's knowledges, histories, and plans. The work of deconstructing planning's positivist knowledges and epistemologies has begun, as has a feminist analysis of its excluded others (see Sandercock, Kenney, Holston, and Woods, this volume). But it is here, in this other domain of the less explicit, I think, that the most recalcitrant obstacles to making the invisible visible still lie.

I have not entered the body into a discussion of planning as a consideration of the marginal. As planners, we assume the importance of theorizing cities; what I hope to have suggested here is the equal importance of theorizing bodies. The ordering of body space is absolutely central to the organization of city space, to all social order and control. An understanding of how body and city, body and body politic, are implicitly and explicitly linked, of how these are conceptualized and used in producing the global social space in which we live—and in which we, as planners, attempt to plan and intervene—will help us to remain aware that it is not nature, or disorder, or disease that produces "healthy" or "unhealthy" cities and environments, but cities, like bodies, are produced and in their production exist as concretizations of multiple sets of social relations of domination and subordination.

REFERENCES

Appadurai, Arjun. 1990. "Disjuncture and Difference in the Global Cultural Economy." *Public Culture* 2, no. 2 (Spring): 1–24.

Aristotle, 1988. *The Politics.* Ed. Stephen Everson. Cambridge: Cambridge University Press.

Baudelaire, Charles. 1964. *The Painter of Modern Life and Other Essays.* London: Phaidon Press.

Benevolo, Leonardo. 1993. *The European City.* London: Blackwell.

Benjamin, Walter. 1978. "Paris, Capital of the Nineteenth Century." In *Reflections: Walter Benjamin, Essays, Aphorisms, Autobiographical Writings,* ed. Peter Demetz, 146–162. New York: Schocken Books.

Berman, Marshall. 1988. *All that Is Solid Melts into Air.* London: Penguin.

Bernheimer, Charles. 1989. *Figures of Ill Repute: Representing Prostitution in Nineteenth-Century France.* Cambridge, Mass.: Harvard University Press.

Bordo, Susan. 1993. *Unbearable Weight: Feminism, Western Culture, and the Body.* Berkeley: University of California Press.

Bornstein, Kate. 1994. *Gender Outlaw: Men, Women, and the Rest of Us.* London: Routledge.

Braham, Allan. 1980. *The Architecture of the French Enlightenment.* Berkeley: University of California Press.

Braidotti, Rosi. 1991. *Patterns of Dissonance: A Study of Women in Contemporary Philosophy.* New York: Routledge.

Buci-Glucksmann, Christine. 1987. "Catastrophic Utopia: The Feminine as Allegory of the Modern." In *The Making of the Modern Body: Sexuality and Society in the Nineteenth Century,* ed. Catherine Gallagher and Thomas Laqueur, 220–230. Berkeley: University of California Press.

Buck-Morss, Susan. 1990. *The Dialectics of Seeing: Walter Benjamin and the Arcades Project.* Cambridge, Mass.: MIT Press.

Butler, Judith. 1990. *Gender Trouble, Feminism and the Subversion of Identity.* New York: Routledge.

———. 1993. *Bodies that Matter: On the Discursive Limits of "Sex."* New York: Routledge.

Carter, Erica, James Donald, and Judith Squires, eds. 1993. *Space and Place: Theories of Identity and Location.* London: Lawrence and Wishart.

Chevalier, Louis. 1973. *Laboring Classes and Dangerous Classes in Paris during the First Half of the Nineteenth Century.* New York: Fertig.

Choay, Françoise. 1969. *The Modern City: Planning in the Nineteenth Century.* New York: Braziller.

Clark, T. J. 1984. *The Painting of Modern Life: Paris in the Art of Manet and His Followers.* Princeton, N.J.: Princeton University Press.

Cocks, Joan. 1989. *The Oppositional Imagination: Feminism, Critique and Political Theory.* London: Routledge.

Colomina, Beatriz. 1992. *Sexuality and Space.* Princeton Papers on Architecture. New York: Princeton Architectural Press.

Corbin, Alain. 1986. *The Foul and the Fragrant: Odor and the French Social Imagination.* Cambridge, Mass.: Harvard University Press.

———. 1987. "Commercial Sexuality in Nineteenth-Century France: A System of Images and Regulations." In *The Making of the Modern Body: Sexuality and Society in the Nineteenth Century,* ed. Catherine Gallagher and Thomas Laqueur, 209–219. Berkeley: University of California Press.

———. 1990. *Women for Hire: Prostitution and Sexuality in France after 1850.* Cambridge, Mass.: Harvard University Press.

Crow, Dennis, ed. 1990. *Philosophical Streets: New Approaches to Urbanism.* Washington, D.C.: Maisonneuve Press.

Davidoff, Leonore, and Catherine Hall. 1983. "The Architecture of Public and Private Life: English Middle-Class Society in a Provincial Town, 1780–1850." In *The Pursuit of Urban History,* ed. Derek Fraser and Anthony Sutcliffe. London: Arnold.

de Certeau, Michel. 1986. *Heterologies: Discourse on the Other.* Minneapolis: University of Minnesota Press.

———. 1988. "Walking in the City." In *The Practice of Everyday Life.* Berkeley: University of California Press.

Differences: a Journal of Feminist Cultural Studies. 1993. Special Issue: "The City." Vol. 5, no. 5 (Fall).

Douglas, Mary. 1982. *Natural Symbols: Explorations in Cosmology.* New York: Pantheon Books.

———. 1984. *Purity and Danger: An Analysis of the Concepts of Pollution and Taboo.* London: Ark Paperbacks.

DuPlessis, Rachel Blau, and Members of Workshop 9. 1988. "For the Etruscans: Sexual Difference and Artistic Production—The Debate over a Female Aesthetic." In *The Future of Difference,* ed. Hester Eisenstein and Alice Jardine, 128–156. New Brunswick, N.J.: Rutgers University Press.

Ehrenreich, Barbara, and Deidre English. 1978. *For Her Own Good: 150 Years of the Experts' Advice to Women.* New York: Doubleday.

Epstein, Julia, and Kristina Straub. 1991. *Body Guards: The Cultural Politics of Gender Ambiguity.* New York: Routledge.

Ferguson, Priscilla Parkhurst. 1988. "Reading Revolutionary Paris." In *Literature and Social Practice,* ed. Philippe Desan, Priscilla Parkhurst Ferguson, and Wendy Griswold, 46–68. Chicago: University of Chicago Press.

Foucault, Michel. 1977. *Power/Knowledge: Selected Interviews and Other Writings, 1972–1977.* Ed. Colin Gordon. New York: Pantheon Books.

———. 1979. *Discipline and Punish: The Birth of the Prison.* New York: Vintage Books.

———. 1984. *The Birth of the Clinic: An Archaeology of Medical Perception.* New York: Vintage Books.

———. 1990. *The History of Sexuality.* Vol.1. New York: Vintage Books.

Frankenberg, Ruth. 1993. *White Women, Race Matters: The Social Construction of Whiteness.* Minneapolis: University of Minnesota Press.

Frisby, David. 1986. *Fragments of Modernity.* Cambridge, Mass.: MIT Press.

Gallagher, Catherine. 1987. "The Body versus the Social Body in the Works of Thomas Malthus and Henry Mayhew." In *The Making of the Modern Body: Sexuality and Society in the Nineteenth Century,* ed. Catherine Gallagher and Thomas Laqueur, 83–106. Berkeley: University of California Press.

Gallagher, Catherine, and Thomas Laqueur, eds. 1987. *The Making of the Modern Body: Sexuality and Society in the Nineteenth Century.* Berkeley: University of California Press.

Garber, Marjorie. 1992. *Vested Interests: Cross-Dressing and Cultural Anxiety.* New York: Harper Perennial.

Gates, Henry Louis, Jr. 1985. *"Race," Writing, and Difference.* Chicago: University of Chicago Press.

Gille, Didier. 1986. "Maceration and Purification." In *City, Zone 1/2,* ed. Michel Feher and Sanford Kwinter, 227–281. New York: Urzone.

Gilman, Sander L. 1985. *Difference and Pathology: Stereotypes of Sexuality, Race, and Madness.* Ithaca, N.Y.: Cornell University Press.

Goubert, Jean-Pierre. 1986. *The Conquest of Water: The Advent of Health in the Industrial Age.* Oxford: Polity Press.

Groneman, Carol. 1994. "Nymphomania: The Historical Construction of Female Sexuality." *Signs* 19, no. 2 (Winter): 337–367.

Grosz, Elizabeth. 1994. *Volatile Bodies: Toward A Corporeal Feminism.* Bloomington: Indiana University Press.

Guillaumin, Colette. 1988. "Race and Nature: The System of Marks." *Feminist Issues* 8, no. 2 (Fall): 25–43.

———— 1993. "The Constructed Body." In *Reading the Social Body,* ed. Catherine B. Burroughs and Jeffrey David Ehrenrich, 40–60. Iowa City: University of Iowa Press.

Gusevich, Miriam. 1987–1988. "Purity and Transgression: Reflections on the Architectural Avantgarde's Rejection of Kitsch." *Discourse* 10, no. 1 (Fall-Winter): 90–115.

Hall, Peter. 1988. *Cities of Tomorrow: An Intellectual History of City Planning and Design in the Twentieth Century.* Oxford: Blackwell.

Haraway, Donna. 1991. *Simians, Cyborgs, and Women: The Reinvention of Nature.* New York: Routledge.

Harsin, Jill. 1985. *Policing Prostitution in Nineteenth-Century Paris.* Princeton, N.J.: Princeton University Press.

Harvey, David. 1989a. *The Condition of Postmodernity.* Oxford: Blackwell.

————. 1989b. *The Urban Experience.* Baltimore: Johns Hopkins University Press.

Hayden, Dolores. 1986. *Redesigning the American Dream: The Future of Housing, Work, and Family Life.* New York: Norton.

————.1989. *The Grand Domestic Revolution.* Cambridge, Mass.: MIT Press.

Hebdige, Dick. 1991. "Subjects in Space." Special issue. *New Formations* 11 (Summer): v–x.

Hobsbawn, Eric. 1975. *The Age of Capital, 1848–1875.* New York: New American Library, Scribner's.

————. 1987. *The Age of Empire, 1875–1914.* New York: Vintage Books.

hooks, bell. 1990. *Yearning: Race, Gender, and Cultural Politics.* Boston: South End Press.

Hurtado, Aida. 1989. "Relating to Privilege: Seduction and Rejection in the Subordination of White Women and Women of Color." *Signs* 14, no. 4 (Summer): 833–855.

Irigaray, Luce. 1985. *Speculum of the Other Woman.* Ithaca, N.Y.: Cornell University Press.

Jacobus, Mary, Evelyn Fox Keller, and Sally Shuttleworth, eds. 1990. *Body/Politics: Women and the Discourses of Science.* New York: Routledge.

Jardine, Alice A. 1985. *Gynesis: Configurations of Woman and Modernity.* Ithaca, N.Y.: Cornell University Press.

Katz, Cindi, and Janice Monk, eds. 1993. *Full Circles: Geographies of Women over the Life Course.* London: Routledge.

Keith, Michael, and Steve Pile, eds. 1993. *Place and the Politics of Identity.* London: Routledge.

Kristeva, Julia. 1984. *Revolution in Poetic Language.* New York: Columbia University Press.

Laqueur, Thomas. 1987. "Orgasm, Generation and the Politics of Reproductive Biology." In *The Making of the Modern Body: Sexuality and Society in the Nineteenth Century,* ed. Catherine Gallagher and Thomas Laqueur, 1–41. Berkeley: University of California Press.

———. 1990. *Making Sex: Body and Gender from the Greeks to Freud.* Cambridge, Mass.: Harvard University Press.

Lavin, Sylvia. 1992. *Quatremere De Quincy and the Invention of a Modern Language of Architecture.* Cambridge, Mass.: MIT Press.

———. 1994. "Re-Reading the Encyclopedia: Architectural Theory and the Formation of the Public in Late-Eighteenth-Century France." *Journal of the Society of Architectural Historians* (June): 184–192.

Le Corbusier. 1987. *The City of Tomorrow and Its Planning.* New York: Dover.

Le Doeuff, Michele. 1990. *Hipparchias's Choice: An Essay Concerning Women, Philosophy, Etc.* Oxford: Blackwell.

Lefebvre, Henri. 1991. *The Production of Space.* Oxford: Blackwell.

Lloyd, Genevieve. 1993. *The Man of Reason: "Male" and "Female" in Western Philosophy.* Minneapolis: University of Minnesota Press.

Lugones, Maria. 1994. "Purity, Impurity, and Separation." *Signs* 19, no. 2 (Winter): 458–479.

Marx, Karl, and Friedrich Engels. 1978. "Manifesto of the Communist Party." In *The Marx-Engels Reader,* 2d ed., ed. Robert C. Tucker, 469–500. New York: Norton.

Mazzoleni, Donatella. 1993. "The City and the Imaginary," trans. John Koumantarakis. In *Space and Place: Theories of Identity and Location,* ed. Erica Carter, James Donald, and Judith Squires, 285–301. London: Lawrence and Wishart.

Mosse, George L. 1985. *Nationalism and Sexuality: Respectability and Abnormal Sexuality in Modern Europe.* New York: Fertig.

Nesbit, Molly. 1992. " 'In The Absence of the Parisienne.' " In *Sexuality and Space,* ed. Beatriz Colomina, 307–326. Princeton Papers on Architecture. New York: Princeton Architectural Press.

Nord, Deborah Epstein. 1987. "The Social Explorer as Anthropologist: Victorian Travelers among the Urban Poor." In *Visions of the Modern City,* ed. William Sharpe and Leonard Wallock, 122–134. Baltimore: Johns Hopkins University Press.

Pateman, Carole. 1989. *The Disorder of Women: Democracy, Feminism, and Political Theory.* Stanford, Calif.: Stanford University Press.

Peterson, Jon A. 1983a. "The City Beautiful Movement." In *Introduction to Planning History in the United States,* ed. Donald A. Krueckeberg, 40–57. New Brunswick, N.J.: Center for Urban Policy Research, Rutgers University.

———. 1983b. "The Impact of Sanitary Reform upon American Urban Planning, 1840–1890." In *Introduction to Planning History in the United States,* ed. Donald A. Krueckeberg, 13–39. New Brunswick, N.J.: Rutgers University Press.

Pinkney, David H. 1958. *Napoleon III and the Rebuilding of Paris.* Princeton, N.J.: Princeton University Press.

Pollack, Griselda. 1988. *Vision and Difference: Femininity, Feminism and the History of Art.* London: Routledge.

Price, Roger. 1987. *A Social History of Nineteenth-Century France.* London: Hutchinson.

Rabinow, Paul. 1989. *French Modern: Norms and Forms of the Social Environment.* Cambridge, Mass.: MIT Press.

Reid, Donald. 1991. *Paris Sewers and Sewermen: Realities and Representations.* Cambridge, Mass.: Harvard University Press.

Sandercock, Leonie, and Ann Forsyth. 1992. "A Gender Agenda: New Directions for Planning Theory." *Journal of the American Planning Association* 58(1): 49–59.

Sheehan, Elizabeth. 1985. "Victorian Clitoredectomy: Issac Baker Brown and His Harmless Procedure." *Feminist Issues* 5, no. 1 (Spring): 39–53.

Showalter, Elaine. 1990. *Sexual Anarchy: Gender and Culture at the Fin de Siècle.* London: Penguin Books.

Silverman, Kaja. 1983. *The Subject of Semiotics.* New York: Oxford University Press.

Soja, Edward W. 1989. *Postmodern Geographies: The Reassertion of Space in Critical Social Theory.* London: Verso.

———. 1996. *Thirdspace: Journeys to Los Angeles and Other Real-and-Imagined Places.* Oxford: Blackwell.

Spain, Daphne. 1992. *Gendered Spaces.* Chapel Hill: University of North Carolina Press.

Spelman, Elizabeth V. 1988. *Inessential Woman: Problems of Exclusion in Feminist Thought.* Boston: Beacon Press.

Spender, Dale. 1980. *Man-Made Language.* London: Pandora Press.

Spivak, Gayatri Chakravorty. 1988. *In Other Worlds: Essays in Cultural Politics.* London: Routledge.

Stallybrass, Peter, and Allon White. 1986. *The Politics and Poetics of Transgression.* Ithaca, N.Y.: Cornell University Press.

Suleiman, Susan Rubin, ed. 1986. *The Female Body in Western Culture: Contemporary Perspectives.* Cambridge, Mass.: Harvard University Press.

Sutcliffe, Anthony. 1970. *The Autumn of Central Paris: The Defeat of Town Planning, 1850–1970.* London: Arnold.

———. 1981. *Towards the Planned City: Germany, Britain, the United States and France, 1780–1914.* Oxford: Blackwell.

Trinh, T. Minh-ha. 1989. *Woman, Native, Other: Writing Postcoloniality and Feminism.* Bloomington: Indiana University Press.

Vidler, Anthony. 1987. *The Writing of the Walls: Architectural Theory in the Late Enlightenment*. Princeton, N.J.: Princeton University Press.

Virilio, Paul. 1986. "The Overexposed City." In *City, Zone 1/2*, ed. Michel Feher and Sanford Kwinter, 15–31. New York: Urzone.

Weisman, Leslie Kanes. 1992. *Discrimination by Design: A Feminist Critique of the Man-Made Environment*. Urbana: University of Illinois Press.

Williams, Raymond. 1973. *The Country and the City*. New York: Oxford University Press.

Wilson, Elizabeth. 1991. *The Sphinx in the City: Urban Life, the Control of Disorder, and Women*. London: Virago Press.

Wolff, Janet. 1990. *Feminine Sentences: Essays on Women and Culture*. Berkeley: University of California Press.

Zola, Emile. 1970. *L'assommoir*. London: Penguin Books.

———. 1972. *Nana*. London: Penguin Books.

CONTRIBUTORS

Robert A. Beauregard is Professor of Planning at the New School for Social Research in New York. He is editor of *Atop the Urban Hierarchy* (1989) and author of *Voices of Decline: The Postwar Fate of U.S. Cities* (1993) as well as numerous articles on urban development and social theory.

Iain Borden is Sub-Dean of the Faculty of the Built Environment and Lecturer in Architectural History at The Bartlett, University College London. He is a founding member of Strangely Familiar and coeditor of *Architecture and the Sites of History: Interpretations of Buildings and Cities* (1995), *Strangely Familiar: Narratives of Architecture in the City* (1996), and *The Unknown City* (1998). His current research concerns the history of urban spatiality.

Gail Lee Dubrow is Associate Professor of Urban Design and Planning and Director of the Preservation Planning and Design Program at the University of Washington. She is the author of *Planning for the Preservation of American Women's History* (forthcoming) and numerous articles on preservation planning.

Dora Epstein is a doctoral student in the Department of Architecture at the University of California, Los Angeles, working on the co-construction of sexualities and space. She has published a number of articles on critical urban studies in journals and books.

James Holston is Associate Professor of Anthropology at the University of California, San Diego. His research focuses on citizenship, law, and democratic change in the Americas, especially Brazil, and transformations in the social and spatial organization of cities. He is author of *The Modernist*

City, editor of *Cities and Citizenship,* and currently working on a book about the disjunctions of democratic citizenship in São Paulo.

Barbara Hooper is a doctoral student in the Department of Urban Planning at the University of California, Los Angeles, working on the body, the city, and social order, a comparative study of ancient Athens, nineteenth-century Paris, and contemporary Los Angeles. She has published a number of articles on critical urban studies in journals and edited collections.

Theodore S. Jojola is Associate Professor of Planning in the School of Architecture and Planning and former Director of Native American Studies (1980–1996) at the University of New Mexico. He is also a monthly columnist for the *Albuquerque Journal,* a consultant on Native American issues, a community activist, and a prolific academic researcher.

Moira Rachel Kenney is a project associate at the Getty Research Institute for the History of Art and the Humanities in Los Angeles. She is the author of "Strategic Visibility: Gay and Lesbian Place Claiming in Los Angeles, 1970–1994" (Ph.D. dissertation, University of California, Los Angeles).

Olivier Kramsch is a doctoral student in the Department of Urban Planning within the School of Public Policy and Social Research at the University of California, Los Angeles. In 1995–1996 he was a Fulbright Scholar in residence at the Autonomous University of Barcelona. He is currently writing his dissertation on the economic restructuring of Spanish-language literary book publishing in Catalonia, Spain.

Jane Rendell trained as an architect at the Universities of Sheffield and Edinburgh. She is conducting her Ph.D. research at Birkbeck College in constructions of space and gender in London, 1810–1830. She teaches architectural design, feminist theory, and urban history at University College London and Winchester School of Art. She is coeditor of *Strangely Familiar: Narratives of Architecture in the City* (1996) and *The Unknown City* (1998).

Leonie Sandercock is Professor of Human Settlements and Head of the Department of Landscape, Environment, and Planning at Royal Melbourne Institute of Technology. She is author of *Cities for Sale* (1975), *The Land Racket* (1979), *Property, Politics and Urban Planning: A History of Australian City Planning, 1890–1990* (1990), and, with M. Berry, *Urban Political Economy: The Australian Case* (1983). She is also a produced screenwriter. Her next book is *Dreaming Cosmopolis: Planning for Multicultural Cities* (1998).

Helen Thomas trained as an architect at Liverpool University and graduated in architectural history from The Bartlett, University College London. She has practiced in Seville and London. She now combines both practice and the teaching of design and history in various London schools. She is the author of numerous articles on spatial theory and Latin American architecture.

June Manning Thomas is Professor at Michigan State University, with a joint appointment in the Urban and Regional Planning and Urban Affairs programs. She has written extensively on planning history and race, with a focus on Detroit. She is author of *Redevelopment and Race: Planning a Finer City in Postwar Detroit* (1997) and coeditor of *Urban Planning and the African American Community* (1997).

Susan Marie Wirka is a doctoral student in history at the University of Wisconsin, Madison, and contributor to a number of publications on planning history, including *Planning the Twentieth-Century American City* (1996) and *The American Planner: Biographies and Recollections* (1994).

Clyde Woods is Assistant Professor in the Department of African and African American Studies at the Pennsylvania State University. His Ph.D. dissertation, "Development Arrested: The Delta Blues, the Delta Council, and the Lower Mississippi Delta Development Commission" (Urban Planning Program, University of California, Los Angeles, 1993), is in press. He is currently researching the history of African Americans in Los Angeles.

INDEX

abortions, 154
Achtenberg, Roberta, 124
ACLU (American Civil Liberties Union), 10
Act to Quiet Title Lands Within Pueblo Indian Lands, 113
ACT UP, 131
Addams, Jane, 8, 72
Additon, Henrietta, 24, 150–60
Adelaide, 171
Adler, Sy, 126–27
adoption, 154
Adorno, Theodor, 42
Africa, 231, 234
African Americans, 9–11, 14, 25; Green Revolution and, 86–91; historic preservation and, 58; LMDDC and, 92–96; in Lower Mississippi Delta, 22, 78–97; in Seattle, 60; women, 9, 81, 91
African National Congress (ANC), 188–89
agency, 176, 210; human, 20; individual, 5; planners', 4; of poor people, 6; structure and, 186–87
Aglietta, Michel, 138
Agrest, Drone, 143
Agricultural Adjustment Administration, 87–88
agriculture, 79–82, 86, 88–89, 91–92, 95. See also Green Revolution
AIDS, 124, 131
AIPC (All Indian Pueblo Council), 100–118
AIPRC (American Indian Policy Review Commission), 114

Alaska, 100
Alcatraz, 114
Alexander, Avery, 91
Alice Paul Centennial Foundation, 66n
All Indian Pueblo Council (AIPC), 100–118
All Indian Pueblo Cultural Center, 115
Alvarado, Captain, 108
American City Planning Since 1890 (Scott), 3–5, 10, 168–70, 180
American Indian Movement, 114
American Indian Policy Review Commission (AIPRC), 114
American Indians. *See* Native Americans
American Institute of Planners, 3,168
American Red Cross, 152n.3
ANC (African National Congress), 188–89
Apaches, 111–12
apartheid, 185, 188–89, 193, 199
architecture, 21, 37–43, 53, 55, 145, 237; history of, 135, 143–44; Pueblo, 109; Seattle, 60; sexuality and, 144
Aristotle, 229, 241
Arizona, 71, 107
Arizona State University, 67
Arkansas, 78, 93
Arkansas Industrial Development Commission, 94
art history, 135, 143
Ashworth, G. J., 136
Asia: immigrants from, 59, 61
Asian Americans, 9–10, 61

Index: Laurie Reith Winship
Composition: Maple-Vail Manufacturing Group
Text: 10/12 Baskerville
Display: Baskerville